GEZER IV:
The 1969–71 Seasons in Field VI, the "Acropolis"

Editor and Principal Author
WILLIAM G. DEVER

with the assistance of
H. Darrell Lance

Contributions by
Reuben G. Bullard, Dan P. Cole, Seymour Gitin,
John S.Holladay, Jr., Joe D. Seger, Anita M. Walker, Robert B. Wright

Appendices by
Baruch Brandl, Michael J. Hughes,
Steven A. Rosen, R. J. Smith

PART 2, PLATES, PLANS
VOLUME IV

Annual of the
NELSON GLUECK SCHOOL OF BIBLICAL ARCHAEOLOGY

Jerusalem
13 King David Street

International Standard
Book Number ISBN 0–87820–304–4

Jerusalem 1986
Printed in Israel
Set, printed and bound by Keter Press Enterprises, Jerusalem

TABLE OF CONTENTS

POTTERY AND OBJECTS

The conventions for pottery description used in this volume are somewhat revised from those used in *Gezer* I. Details of this revised system are outlined more fully in the volume in Gezer field methods; cf. W. G. Dever and H. D. Lance, eds., *A Manual of Field Excavation: Handbook for Field Archaeologists* (New York, 1978).

Pottery descriptions are all presented in the following pattern:

(1) *Technique:*
(Handmade, Wheelmade, etc.)

(2)*Ware Paste:*

a. Color (of sherd section, using the *Munsell Soil Color Charts*, Baltimore, Md.)

b. Inclusions (according to five standard type groups as observed by the naked eye)

"sand" - appearing as sand particles: a subgroup of this category, involving larger particles, is noted as "wadi gravel"

"lime" - appearing as white chalky particles

"ceramic" - appearing as angular red or black particles

"crystal" - appearing as angular translucent or 'sparkling' particles

"organic" - appearing as straw, or as remnant patterns of straw in the fabric, or as black carbon deposits

Indications as to the size (small, medium, large0 and to the frequency of appearance (few, some, many) or inclusions are provided according to established standards.

c. Firing (described according to the observable degree of oxidation of carbon in the core of the paste, as either "no core," "light gray core," "gray core," or "dark gray core.")

d. hardness (on a threefold scale as 'soft," "hard" or "metallic.")

(3) *Ware Surface:*

(Interior)

a. Color (Munsell)

b. Treatment ("wash," "slip," "burnish" [including type and decoration[, "paint [including type], either "oxide" or "organic," and color (using Munsell), etc.

(Exterior)
Color and treatment as for Interior.

Thus, e.g.,

Whelmade: *Paste:* 5 Yr "light reddish brown" 6/4; some medium to large lime; grey core;hard. *Surface:* (Interior): as paste; (Exterior): 2.5 YR "red" 5/6 slip, burnished on rim.

Note:
All object drawings are to the scale of 1:2 unless otherwise indicated.

Plate Number	Pottery Type	Number and locus (see LOCUS INDEX)	Description (p. 277)
1.	Jar	G71, VI.NE4,237, No. 3 L. 4121	*Technique:* Wheelmade. *Paste:* 1OYR "light yellow brown" 6/4; some small to large lime, few wadi gravel; no core; hard. *Surface (Interior):5 10YR "very pale brown" 8/4. (Exterior):* as interior and 1OR "light red" 6/8.
2.	Juglet	G71, VI.NE4.237, No. 5 L. 4121	*Technique:* Wheelmade. *Paste:* 5YR "reddish yello 7/6; many very small and small and few medium wadi gravel and crystal, few small and medium lime and ceramic; no core; hard. *Surface (Interior):* as paste. *(Exterior):* 2.5YR "reddish brown" 4/4 to 2.5YR "red" 4/6 slip and vertical and horizontal burnish.
3.	Juglet	G71, VI.NE4.295, No. 1 L. 4121	*Technique:* Wheelmade. *Paste:* 7.5YR "reddish yellow" 8/6; many very small and small crystal, few small and medium wadi gravel and ceramic, few medium lime, few small organic; light grey core; hard. *Surface (Interior):* as paste. *(Exterior):* 1OR "red" 4/6; slip and vertical burnish.
4.	Bowl	G71, VI.NE4.295, L. 4121	*Technique:* Wheelmade. *Paste:* 7.5YR "pink" 8/4; few small ceramic, many small wadi gravel, no core; hard. *Surface (Interior):* as paste; slip 1OR "red" 4/6; wheel burnish on rim. *(Exterior):* slip as interior; hand burnish, horizontal and vertical.
5.	Juglet	G71, VI.NE23.310, No. 1 L. 23110	*Technique:* Wheelmade. *Paste:* 5YR "pink" 7/4; many small crystal and ceramic; no core; hard. *Surface (Interior):* as paste. *(Exterior):* 2.5HR "red" 4/6; vertical hand burnish.
7.	Jar	G71, VI.NE23.304, No. 2 L. 23110	*Technique:* Wheelmade. *Paste:* 5YR "pink" 7/4; some small to medium ceramic and crystal; grey core; hard. *Surface (Interior):* as paste. *(Exterior):* as paste.

PLATE 1

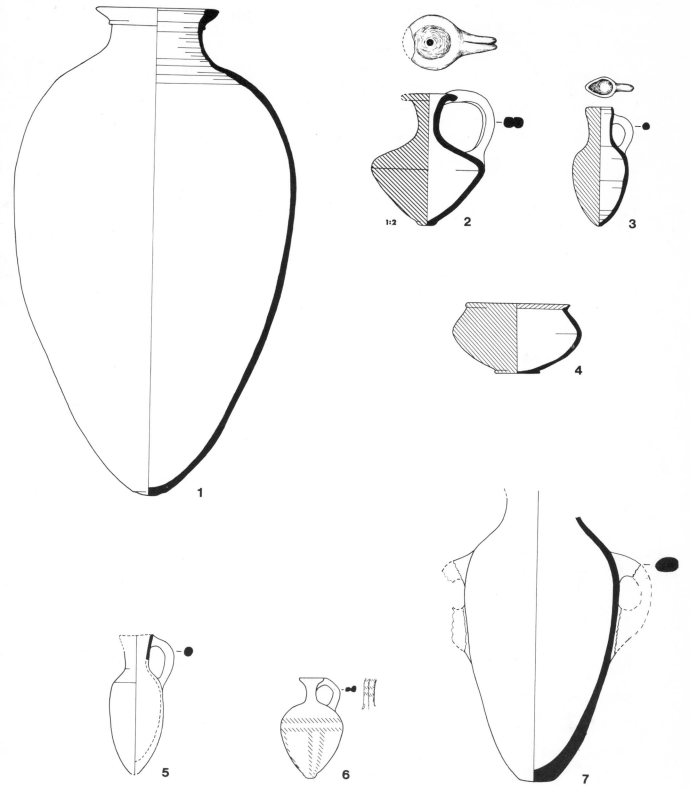

Plate Number	Pottery Type	Number and locus (see LOCUS INDEX)	Description (p. 277)
1.	Bowl	G71, VI.NE4.295, No. 3 L. 4121	*Technique:* Wheelmade. *Paste:* 5YR "reddish yellow" 6/6; few very small lime, no core; hard. *Surface (Interior):* 5YR "reddish yellow" 7/6; 1OR "weak red" 5/4 slip on and below rim. *(Exterior):* slip as interior; wheel burnish.
2.	Bowl	G71, VI.NE4.295, No. 2 L. 4121	*Technique:* Wheelmade. *Paste:* 7.5YR "pink" 7/4' many very small to small organic, few small lime; no core; hard. *Surface (Interior):* as paste; 2.5YR "red" 5/6 slip on rim. *(Exterior):* slip as interior; horizontal burnish.
3.	Jar	G71, VI.NE4.320, No. 1 L. 4146.1	*Technique:* Wheelmade. *Paste:* 5YR "reddish yellow" 6/6; some small and few medium to large lime and small crystal, few medium to large organic and medium ceramic; light grey core; hard. *Surface (Interior):* as paste. *(Exterior):* as paste.
4.	Jar	G71, VI.NE4.320, No. 9 L. 4146.1	*Technique:* Wheelmade. *Paste:* 5YR "reddish yellow" 6/6; many very small and few large lime, few medium wadi gravel and organic and very small crystal; grey core; hard. *Surface (Interior):* as paste. *(Exterior):* as paste.
5.	Jar	G71, VI.NE4.320, No. 4 L. 4146.1	*Technique:* Wheelmade. *Paste:* 7.5YR "light brown" 6/4; some very small to large lime, few medium ceramic and very small crystal; no core; hard. *Surface (Interior):* as paste. *(Exterior):* as paste.
6.	Bowl	G71, VI.NE4.320, No. 3 L. 4146.1	*Technique:* Wheelmade. *Paste:* 5YR "yellowish red" 5/6; few very small crystal, small to large lime, small organic and medium ceramic; grey core; hard. *Surface (Interior):* 2.5YR "red" 4/6; slip and radial burnish. *(Exterior):* slip and hand burnish on rim as interior.
7.	Juglet base	G71, VI.NE4.320, No. 5 L. 4146.1	*Technique:* Wheelmade. *Paste:* 5YR "reddish yellow" 6/6; few small and some medium to large lime, few medium and large organic and small ceramic; grey core; hard. *Surface (Interior):* 7.5YR "pink" 7/4. *(Exterior):* as paste.
8.	Bowl	G71, VI.NE14.376, No. 11 L. 13100.1	*Technique:* Wheelmade. *Paste:* 5YR "reddish yellow" 7/6; some small and few medium to large lime, few small ceramic; grey core; hard. *Surface (Interior):* as paste. *(Exterior):* as paste.
9.	Baking tray	G71, VI.NE13.367, No. 1 L. 13116.1	*Technique:* Wheelmade. *Paste:* 5YR "reddish brown" 5/4; many small to large lime, few very small crystal, medium wadi gravel and large organic; dark grey core; hard. *Surface (Interior):* as paste. *(Exterior):* as paste.
10.	Bowl	G71, VI.NE13.367, No. 12 L. 133116.1	*Technique:* Wheelmade. *Paste:* 2.5YR "reddish brown" 5/4; some medium to large lime, few medium gravel and very small crystal; dark grey core; hard. *Surface (Interior):* as paste. *(Exterior):* as paste.
11.	Jar	G71, VI.NE13.366, No. 3 L. 13116.1	*Technique:* Wheelmade. *Paste:* 5YR "reddish brown" 5/4; few small to large lime, medium ceramic and very small crystal; grey core; hard. *Surface (Interior):* as paste. *(Exterior):* as paste.
12.	Jar	G71, VI.NE13.363, No. 1 L. 13125	*Technique:* Wheelmade. *Paste:* 7.5YR "pink" 8/4; some medium to few large lime, some small organic and few small ceramic and very small crystal; grey core; hard. *Surface (Interior):* as paste. *(Exterior):* as paste.
13.	Jar	G71, VI.NE13.363, No. 3 L. 13125	*Technique:* Wheelmade. *Paste:* 7.5YR "pink" 8/4; some small to large lime, few medium to large ceramic and medium organic; grey core; hard. *Surface (Interior):* as paste. *(Exterior):* as paste.
14.	Jar	G71, VI.NE13.363, No. 7 L. 13125	*Technique:* Wheelmade. *Paste:* inner: 7.5YR "light brown" 6/4; outer: 2.5YR "light red" 6/6; many small and some medium to large lime, few medium ceramic; no core; hard. *Surface (Interior):* 5YR "pink" 7/4.
15.	Cooking pot	G71, VI.NE13.363, No. 10 L. 13125	*Technique:* Wheelmade. *Paste:* 2.5YR "reddish brown" 4/4; some very small to large lime, few small organic; no core; hard. *Surface (Interior):* as paste. *(Exterior):* as paste.
16.	Cooking pot	G71, VI.NE13.363, No. 5 L. 13125	*Technique:* Wheelmade. *Paste:* 2.5YR "red" 4/6; many very small to small crystal; no core; hard. *Surface (Interior):* as paste. *(Exterior):* as paste.
17.	Jar	G71. VI.NE14.351, No. 6 L. 14141	*Technique:* Wheelmade. *Paste:* 10YR "very pale brown" 8/4; many medium to large organic, few medium wadi gravel, small ceramic and very small crystal; core (5YR "reddish yellow" 7/6); hard. *Surface (Interior):* as paste. *(Exterior):* as paste.
18.	Base	G71, VI.NE14.351, No. 16 L. 14141	*Technique:* Wheelmade. *Paste:* 5YR "reddish yellow" 6/6; some very small and few small to large lime, few small wadi gravel and ceramic; grey core; hard. *Surface (Interior):* as paste. *(Exterior):* 1OR "red" 4/6 slip; vertical burnish.
19.	Jar	G71, VI.NE14.351, No. 6	*Technique:* Wheelmade. *Paste:* 2.5YR "red" 4/6; few very small to large lime and very small crystal; grey core; hard. *Surface (Interior):* as paste to 5YR "grey" 5/1. *(Exterior):* as paste.
20.	Jar	G71, VI.NE13.371, No. 6 L. 13122	*Technique:* Wheelmade. *Paste:* 5YR "reddish yellow" 6/6; few small and large and some medium lime, few small and medium organic; no core; hard. *Surface (Interior):* as paste. *(Exterior):* as paste.
21.	Juglet	G71, VI.NE14.353, No. 2 L. 14141	*Technique:* Wheelmade. *Paste:* 7.5YR "grey" 6/1; outer: 7.5YR "pinkish grey"; 7/2 few very small and small lime, very small ceramic and crystal; no core; hard. *Surface (Interior):* 10YR "very pale brown" 7/3; traces of vertical burnish.
22.	Juglet	G71, VI.NE14.354, No. 5 L. 14141	*Technique:* Wheelmade. *Paste:* inner: 7.5 "grey" N6/1; outer, 7.5YR "pink" 7/4; some very small crystal, few small organic and very small and small lime; no core; hard. *Surface (Interior):* as inner paste. *(Exterior):* as outer paste; vertical burnish.
23.	Bowl	G71, VI.NE14.351, No. 14 L. 14141	*Technique:* Wheelmade. *Paste:* 7.5YR "pink" 8/4; some very small wadi gravel; no core; hard. *Surface (Interior):* as paste. *(Exterior):* as paste; band of 2.5YR "red" 4/6 slip; wheel burnish.
24.	Bowl	G71, VI.NE14.351, No. 11 L. 14141	*Technique:* Wheelmade. *Paste:* 5YR "reddish yellow" 7/6; few very small to small lime and wadi gravel and very small crystal; core: 7.5YR "pink" 7/4; hard. *Surface (Interior):* as paste; burnish on rim as exterior. *(Exterior):* as paste; wheel burnish.
25.	Bowl	G71, VI.NE14.351, No. 3 L. 14141	*Technique:* Wheelmade. *Paste:* 7.5YR "pink" 7/4; very many medium to large wadi gravel, some medium to large lime, some very small crystal; light grey core; hard. *Surface (Interior):* as paste. *(Exterior):* as paste.

PLATE 2

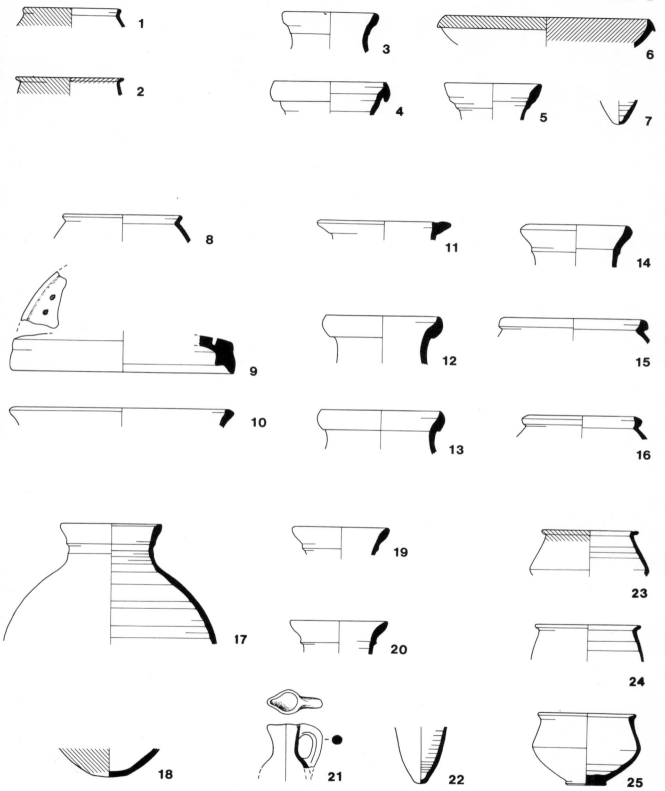

Plate Number	Pottery Type	Number and locus (see LOCUS INDEX)	Description (p. 277)
1.	Jar	G71, VI.NE24.414, No. 1 L. 24148	*Technique:* Wheelmade. *Paste:* 7.5YR "light brown" 6/4; some large wadi gravel, few small to medium lime, and small ceramic; no core; hard. *Surface (Interior):* as paste. *(Exterior):* as paste.
2.	Jar	G71, VI.NE24.452, No. 6 L. 24148	*Technique:* Wheelmade. *Paste:* 5YR "reddish yellow" 7/6; few small to medium and some large lime, few very small sand; no core; hard. *Surface (Interior):* as paste. *(Exterior):* as paste.
3.	Base	G71, VI.NE24.414, No. 5 L. 24148	*Technique:* Wheelmade. *Paste:* 5YR "yellowish red" 5/6; few small to large lime, medium organic, and small crystal; no core; hard. *Surface (Interior):* as paste. *(Exterior):* as paste. hand burnish.
4.	Bowl	G71, VI.NE24.436, No. 3 L. 24148	*Technique:* Wheelmade. *Paste:* 2.5YR "light red" 6/8; few very small to medium crystal, small to medium lime, and small wadi gravel and ceramic; dark grey core; hard. *Surface (Interior):* as paste; traces of 1OR "weak red" 5/4 slip. *(Exterior):* as paste; slip as interior.
5.	Jar	G71, VI.NE24.419, No. 1 L. 24167	*Technique:* Wheelmade. *Paste:* 7.5YR "pink" 7/4; many very small lime, few small ceramic; no core; hard. *Surface (Interior):* as paste. *(Exterior):* as paste.
6.	Base	G71, VI.NE24.419, No 3 L. 24167	*Technique:* Wheelmade. *Paste:* 5YR "reddishyellow" 6/6; some very small to small wadi gravel, few medium lime, some very small to small crystal; core: 7.5YR "pink" 7/4; hard. *Surface (Interior):* as paste. *(Exterior):* as paste.
7.	Cooking pot	G71, VI.NE24.411, No. 15 L. 24167	*Technique:* Handmade. *Paste:* 2.5YR "reddish brown" 4/4; some medium and large organic, few very small and large lime, and large wadi gravel; dark grey core; hard. *Surface (Interior):* as paste. *(Exterior):* as paste.
8.	Cooking pot	G71, VI.NE24.417, No. 14 L. 24167	*Technique:* Wheelmade. *Paste:* 2.5YR "red" 4/6; few small to large lime; no core; hard. *Surface (Interior):* as paste. *(Exterior):* as paste.
9.	Bowl	G71, VI.NE24.417, No. 5 L. 24167	*Technique:* Wheelmade. *Paste:* 5YR "reddish yellow" 7/6; some very small to small lime, crystal and wadi gravel; core: 7.5YR "pink" 7/4; hard. *Surface (Interior):* 7.5YR "pink" 8/4 slip on rim as exterior. *(Exterior):* 1OR "red" 5/6 slip; wheel burnish.
10.	Bowl	G71, VI.NE24.419, No. 2 L. 24167	*Technique:* Wheelmade. *Paste:* 10YR "very pale brown" 7/3; some to many very small to small lime, few small ceramic; no core; hard. *Surface (Interior):*as paste; slip on rim as exterior. *(Exterior):* 10R "weak red" 5/4 slip; wheel burnsih.
11.	Base	G71, VI.NE24.417, No. 6 L. 24107	*Technique:* Wheelmade. *Paste:* 10YR "very pale brown" 7/4; very many small crytal; no core; hard. *Surface (Interior):* as paste. *(Exterior):* as paste.
12.	Bowl	G71, VI.NE24.410. No. 2 L. 24187	*Technique:* Wheelmade. *Paste:* 5YR "reddish yellow" 7/6; very many small crystal, few small to medium lime and medium to large organic; core: 7.5YR "pink" 7/4; hard. *Surface (Interior):* as paste. *(Exterior):* as paste to 7.5YR "pink" 7/4.
13.	Juglet	G71, VI.NE24.349, No. 16 L. 24198	*Technique:* Wheelmade. *Paste:* 7.5YR "pink" 7/4; few large lime and ceramic, few medium wadi gravel, many small crystal, few medium wadi gravel, many small crystal; no core; hard. *Surface (Interior):* 7.5YR "pinkish white" 8/2. *(Exterior):* as interior.
14.	Jar	G71, VI.NE24.369, No. 1 L. 24174	*Technique:* Wheelmade. *Paste:* 5YR "reddish brown" 5/3; few small and some large lime, few medium ceramic; grey core; hard. *Surface (Interior):* as paste. *(Exterior):* as paste.
15.	Juglet	G71, VI.NE24.360. No. 1 L. 24167	*Technique:* Wheelmade. *Paste:* 5YR "reddish brown" 7/6; very many small crystal, few small to large lime; no core; hard. *Surface (Interior):* as paste. *(Exterior):* 10R "red" 4/6 slip; hand burnsih.
16.	Bowl	G71, VI.NE24.437, No. 2 L. 24198	*Technique:* Wheelmade. *Paste:* 2.5YR "light red" 6/6; many small crystal, few small lime; core: 10YR " "very pale brown" 7/3; hard. *Surface (Interior):* 7.5YR "pinkish white" 8/2. *(Exterior):* as interior.
17.	Jar	G71, VI.NE24.349, No. 2 L. 24198	*Technique:* Wheelmade. *Paste:* 7.5YR "light brown" 6/4; few small and some medium to large lime, few large wadi gravel and small ceramic; light grey core; hard. *Surface (Interior):* as paste. *(Exterior):* as paste.
18.	Cooking pot	G71, VI.NE24.451, No. 5 L. 24215	*Technique:* Wheelmade. *Paste:* 2.5YR "reddish brown" 4/4; few small and some medium to large lime, few very small sand; dark grey core; hard. *Surface (Interior):* as paste. *(Exterior):* as paste.
19.	Juglet	G71, VI.NE24.451, No. 3 L. 24215	*Technique:* Wheelmade. *Paste:* inner: 5YR "dark grey" 4/1; outer; 7.5YR "light brown" 6/4; some very small and few small lime, few medium ceramic and medium to large organic; no paste. *(Exterior):* as outer paste.
20.	Bowl	G71, VI.NE24.451, No. 9 L. 24215	*Technique:* Wheelmade. *Paste:* 5YR "reddish yellow" 7/6; many very small and small crystal, few medium lime and organic, medium to large ceramic and large wadi gravel; light grey core; hard. *Surface (Interior):* as paste. *(Exterior):* as paste to 7.5YR "pink" 8/4.
21.	Bowl	G71, VI.NE24.451, No. 2 L. 24215	*Technique:* Wheelmade. *Paste:* 7.5YR "pink" 7/4; some very small and few small lime, few small ceramic and organic; no core; hard. *Surface (Interior):* 10YR "very pale brown" 7/3; wheel burnish on rim *(Exterior):* as interior.
22.	Bowl	G71, VI.NE24.443, No. 1 L. 24206	*Technique:* Wheelmade. *Paste:* 5YR "reddish yellow" 6/6; few small ceramic, many small and few large crystal; no core; hard. *Surface (Interior):* as paste; 10R "red" 5/8 slip on rim. *(Exterior):* as paste; slip on rim as interior; horizontal burnish on rim.
23.	Bowl	G71, VI.NE24.451, No. 1 L. 24215	*Technique:* Wheelmade. *Paste:* 10YR "very pale brown" 7/4; many very small and few medium to large lime, few medium and large wadi gravel and medium ceramic; light grey core; hard. *Surface (Interior):* as paste. *(Exterior):* as paste.
24.	Bowl	G71, VI.NE34.327, No. 1 L. 34107	*Technique:* Wheelmade. *Paste:* 7.5YR "reddish yellow" 7/6; few medium to large lime, few small organic and very small crystal; no core; hard. *Surface (Interior):* 10YR "very pale brown" 8/3; band of 2.5YR "red" 5/8 organic paint on rim and decoration. *(Exterior):* 7.5YR "pink" 7/4 paint on rim as interior.

PLATE 3

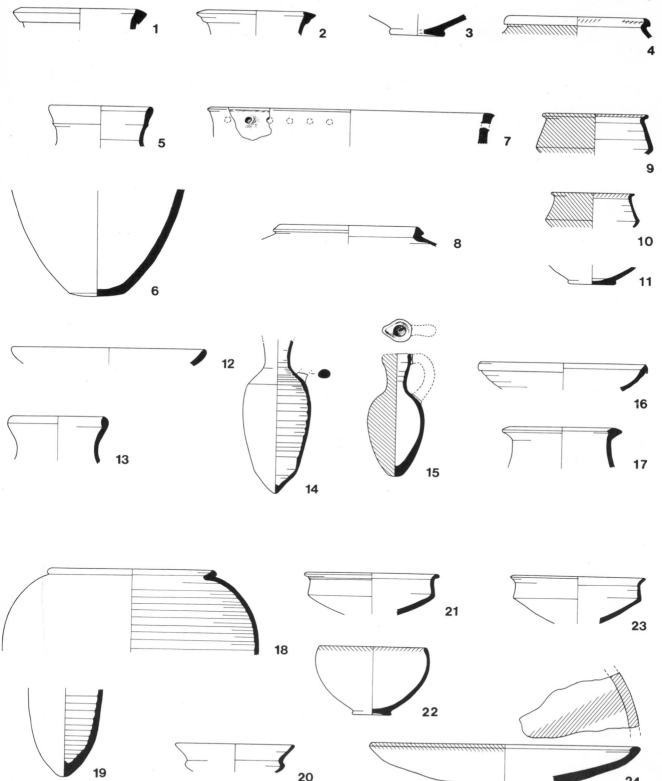

Plate Number	Pottery Type	Number and locus (see LOCUS INDEX)	Description (p. 277)
1.	Jar	G71, VI.NE13.356, No. 6 L. 13116.1	*Technique:* Wheelmade. *Paste:* 7.5YR "pinkish grey" 6/2; some small to medium wadi gravel, few medium lime, small organic and very small crystal; no core; hard. *Surface (Interior):* 10YR "very pale brown 7/4. (Exterior):* 5YR "pink" 7/3 to 7.5YR "pink" 7/4.
2.	Cooking pot	G71, VI.NE13.356, No. 16 L. 13116.1	*Technique:* Wheelmade. *Paste:* 2.5YR "reddish brown" 4/4; some very small to few large lime few very small crystal; nor core; hard. *Surface (Interior):* as paste. *(Exterior):* as paste.
3.	Jar	G71, VI.NE13.336, No. 15 L. 13116.1	*Technique:* Wheelmade. *Paste:* 5YR "reddish yellow" 6/6; few very small crystal, small ceramic, small to medium lime and organic and large wadi gravel; grey core; hard. *Surface (Interior):* as paste. *(Exterior):* as paste.
4.	Bowl	G71, VI.NE13.367, No. 4 L. 13116.1	*Technique:* Wheelmade. *Paste:* 5YR "light reddish brown" 6/4; some small lime, few very small crystal; grey core; hard. *Surface (Interior):* 5YR "reddish yellow" 6/6; wheel burnish; traces of 2.5YR "red" 5/8 slip on rim. *(Exterior):* 7.5YR "pink" 7/4; slip and burnish on rim as interior.
5.	Cooking pot	G71, VI.NE13.370, No. 9 L. 13122	*Technique:* Wheelmade. *Paste:* 2.5YR "red" 4/6; few small and some medium to large lime, few small ceramic and very small sand; dark grey core; hard. *Surface (Interior):* as paste. *(Exterior):* as paste.
6.	Jar	G71, VI.NE13.361, No. 7 L. 13122	*Technique:* Wheelmade. *Paste:* 2.5YR "light red" 6/8; many small crystal, few small organic and lime; grey core; hard. *Surface (Interior):* as paste; as exterior on rim. *(Exterior):* 2.5YR "red" 4/6 slip on rim; circular burnish.
7.	Jar	G71, VI.NE13.370, No. 17 L. 13122	*Technique:* Wheelmade. *Paste:* 5YR "yellowish red" 5/6; many very small to small crystal, some large lime; grey core; hard. *Surface (Interior):* 5YR "reddish brown" 5/3. *(Exterior):* as paste.
8.	Base	G71, VI.NE13.361, No. 1 L. 13122	*Technique:* Wheelmade. *Paste:* 5YR "light reddish brown" 6/4; some very small crystal and small to few large lime, few medium organic and ceramic; light grey core; hard. *Surface (Interior):* as paste. *(Exterior):* 10YR "red" 5/6 slip.
9.	Jar	G71, VI.NE13.361, No. 3 L. 13122	*Technique:* Wheelmade. *Paste:* 5YR "reddish brown" 5/4; some small to large lime, few small organic and very small sand; grey core; hard. *Surface (Interior):* as paste. *(Exterior):* as paste.
10.	Jar	G71, VI.NE23.239, No. 9 L. 23112	*Technique:* Wheelmade. *Paste:* 2.5YR "red" 5/6; few small to medium crystal and lime, small organic and ceramic; dark grey core; hard. *Surface (Interior):* as paste. *(Exterior):* as paste.
11.	Base	G71, VI.NE23.337, No. 4 L. 23129	*Technique:* Wheelmade. *Paste:* inner: 5YR "light reddish brown" 6/4; outer: 5YR "reddish yellow" 6/6; many very small to medium crystal, few small to medium lime; light grey core; hard. *Surface (Interior):* as inner paste. *(Exteerior):* as outer paste.
12.	Jar	G71, VI.NE23.335, No. 10 L.23129	*Technique:* Wheelmade. *Paste:* 5YR "reddish yellow" 6/6; some very small to small crystal and few small wadi gravel; no core; hard. *Surface (Interior):* as paste. *(Exterior):* as paste.
13.	Bowl	G71, VI.NE23.337, No. 10 L. 23129	*Technique:* Wheelmade. *Paste:* 5YR "yellowish red" 5/6; some very small and few medium to large lime, few very small and medium crystal, few small organic; grey core; hard. *Surface (Interior):* as paste. *(Exterior):* 5YR "dark grey" 4/1 slip.
14.	Krater	G71, VI.NE23.345, No. 1 L. 23129	*Technique:* Wheelmade. *Paste:* inner: 7.5YR "pink" 8/4; outer: 5YR "pink" 7/4; many very small crystal, few small to medium lime; light grey core; hard. *Surface (Interior):* as inner paste. *(Exterior):* as outer paste.
15.	Cooking pot	G71, VI.NE23.341, No. 4 L. 23129	*Technique:* Handmade. *Paste:* 2.5YR "reddish brown" 4/4; many very small crystal and some large wadi gravel and lime; grey core; hard. *Surface (Interior);* as paste. *(Exterior):* as paste applique.
16.	Cooking pot	G71, VI.NE13.341, No. 10 L. 13114	*Technique:* Wheelmade. *Paste:* 5YR "reddish brown" 5/4; some very small to large lime; no core; hard. *Surface (Interior):* as paste. *(Exterior):* as paste.
17.	Jar	G71, VI.NE13.357, No. 15 L. 13121	*Technique:* Wheelmade. *Paste:* 2.5YR "red" 5/8; some very small lime, few very small crystal and wadi gravel; 7.5YR "strong brown" 5/8 core; hard. *Surface (Interior):* 5YR "reddish yellow" 7/6. *(Exterior):* as interior.
18.	Jar	G71, VI.NE14.345, No. 9 L. 14132	*Technique:* Wheelmade. *Paste:* 5YR "light reddish brown" 6/4; some very small and few large lime, some very small crystal, few large ceramic; no core; hard. *Surface (Interior):* as paste. *(Exterior):* as paste.
19.	Jar	G71, VI.NE14.338, No. 4 L. 14132	*Technique:* Wheelmade. *Paste:* 2.5YR "red" 5/6; few small to medium wadi gravel, lime and ceramic; no core; hard. *Surface (Interior):* as paste. *(Exterior):* as paste.
20.	Jar	G71, VI.NE14.347, No. 1 L. 14136.1	*Technique:* Wheelmade. *Paste:* 10R "red" 5/8; some small lime, few very small crystal; grey core; hard. *Surface (Interior):* as paste. *(Exterior):* as paste.
21.	Bowl	G71, VI.NE23.324, No. 7 L. 23117	*Technique:* Wheelmade. *Paste:* 5YR "reddish yellow" 7/6; some very small wadi gravel, few very small organic; no core; hard. *Surface (Interior):* 7.5YR "pink" 8/4. *(Exterior):* as interior.
22.	Cooking pot	G71, VI.NE33.158, No. 2 L. 33067	*Technique:* Handmade. *Paste:* 7.5YR "light brown" 6/4; few small wadi, very small snd and crystal; dark grey core; hard. *Surface (Interior):* as paste. *(Exterior):* as paste.

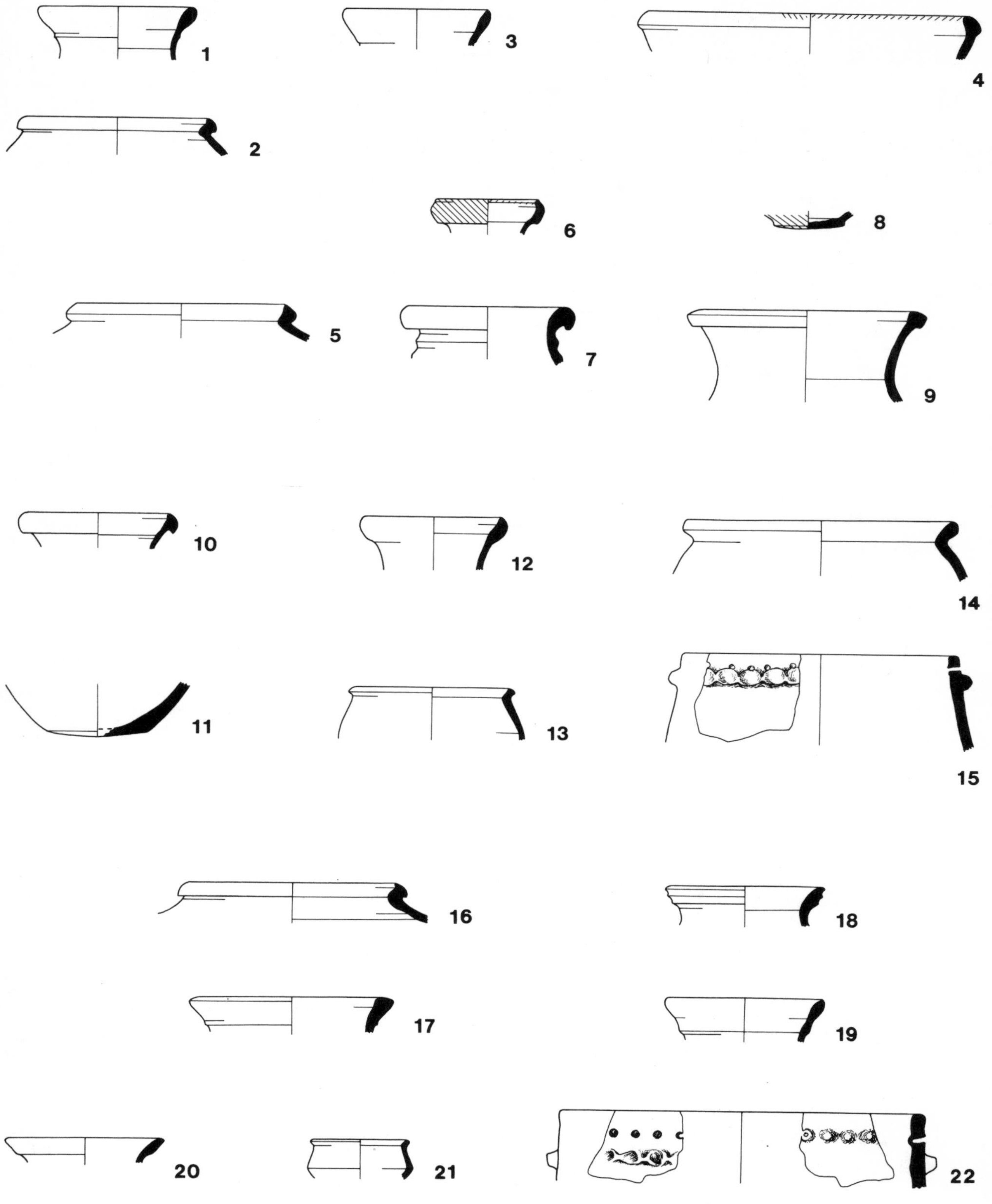
1
3
4
2
6
8
5
7
9
10
12
14
11
13
15
16
18
17
19
20
21
22

Plate Number	Pottery Type	Number and locus (see LOCUS INDEX)	Description (p. 277)
1.	Jar?	G71, VI.NE13.332, No. 12 L. 13102	*Technique:* Wheelmade. *Paste:* 5YR "reddish yellow" 6/6; few very small to medium lime, very small ceramic, wadi gravel and crystal; no core; hard. *Surface (Interior):* as paste; hand burnish. *(Exterior):* as paste.
2.	Jar	G71, VI.NE13.334, No. 5 L. 13102	*Technique:* Wheelmade. *Paste:* 2.5YR "grey" 5/0; very many very small to few large, few small wadi gravel and very small crystal; no core; hard. *Surface (Interior):* as paste. *(Exterior):* as paste.
3.	Jar	G71, VI.NE13.334, No. 2 L. 13102	*Technique:* Wheelmade. *Paste:* 5YR "reddish yellow" 6/6; some very small to small crystal and small to few large lime, few small to medium wadi gravel, ceramic and organic; grey core; hard. *Surface (Interior):* as paste. *(Exterior):* as paste.
4.	Jar	G71, VI.NE13.348, No. 2 L. 13102	*Technique:* Wheelmade. *Paste:* 2.4YR "light red" 6/8; many small to large lime, few very small ceramic and crystal; dark grey core; hard. *Surface (Interior):* as paste. *(Exterior):* as paste.
5.	Jar	G71, VI.NE13.340, No. 13 L. 13102	*Technique:* Wheelmade. *Paste:* 5YR "reddish yellow" 6/6; some very small and wadi gravel, few small to medium lime, small sand and very small crystal; no core; hard. *Surfce (Interior):* 5YR "pink" 7/4 to 7.5YR "pink 8/4. *(Exterior):* 5YR "pink" 7/4.
6.	Jar	G71, VI.NE13.332, No. 10 L. 1312	*Technique:* Wheelmade. *Paste:* 2.5YR "red" 5/6; some very small to few large lime, few medium ceramic, wadi gravel and medium to large organic; grey core; hard. *Surface (Interior):* as paste. *(Exterior):* as paste.
7.	Jar	G71, VI.NE13.344, No. 8 L. 13102	*Technique:* Wheelmade. *Paste:* 5YR "reddish yellow" 6/6; many very small to few large lime, few very small ceramic, crystal, and organic; grey core; hard. *Surface (Interior):* 5YR "pink" 7/5. *(Exterior):* as interior.
8.	Jar	G71, VI.NE13.332, No. 8 L. 13102	*Technique:* Wheelmade. *Paste:* 2.5YR "light red" 6/8; some small to medium lime, few very small to small wadi gravel, very small crystal; 10YR "brown" 5/3; hard. *Surface (Interior):* 5YR "pink" 7/4. *(Exterior):* as interior.
9.	Jar	G71, VI.NE13.350, No. 6 L. 13102	*Technique:* Wheelmade. *Paste:* 5YR "light brown" 6/4; many very small to small crystal, few medium ceramic, wadi gravel and medium to large lime; light grey core; hard. *Surface (Interior):* as paste. *(Exterior):* as paste.
10.	Base	G71, VI.NE13.349, No. 1 L. 13102	*Technique:* Wheelmade. *Paste:* 5YR "reddish yellow" 6/6; few small wadi gravel and organic, very small crystal; light grey core; hard. *Surface (Interior):* as paste. *(Exterior):* 10YR "red" 4/6 slip; vertical and horizontal burnish on side; random burnish on bottom.
11.	Cooking pot	G71, VI.NE13.348, No. 5 L. 13102	*Technique:* Wheelmade. *Paste:* 2.5YR "reddish brown" 4/4; many medium to some large lime, few medium to large wadi gravel; no core; hard. *Surface (Interior):* as paste. *(Exterior):* as paste.
12.	Cooking pot	G71, VI.NE13.336, No. 18 L. 13102	*Technique:* Wheelmade. *Paste:* 2.5YR "red" 4/4; some very small to small crystal, few small to large lime; dark grey core; hard. *Surface (Interior):* as paste. *(Exterior):* as paste.
13.	Cooking pot	G71, VI.NE13.332, No. 1 L. 13102	*Technique:* Wheelmade. *Paste:* 5YR "reddish brown" 5/4; many very small and few medium to large lime; dark grey core; hard. *Surface (Interior):* as paste. *(Exterior):* as paste.
14.	Cooking pot	G71, VI.NE13.348, No. 9 L. 13102	*Technique:* Wheelmade. *Paste:* 5YR "reddish brown" 4/3; some very small to small and few medium to large lime; no core; hard. *Surface (Interior):* as paste. *(Exterior):* as paste.
15.	Cooking pot	G71, VI.NE13.332, No. 3 L. 13102	*Technique:* Wheelmade. *Paste:* inner: 5YR "reddish yellow" 6/6; outer: 5YR "light reddish brown" 6/4; some very small and few medium to large lime, few small ceramic and very small crystal; dark grey core; hard. *Surface (Interior):* as paste. *(Exterior):* 10YR "very pale brown" 7/3 slip; hand burnish.
16.	Bowl	G71, VI.NE13.339, No. 17 L. 13102	*Technique:* Wheelmade. *Paste:* inner: 7.5YR "brown" 5/4; outer: 7.5YR "light brown" 6/4; many very small to small crystal, few medium wadi gravel; no core; hard. *Surface (Interior):* 10YR "very pale brown" 7/3 horizontal burnish on interior of rim. *(Exterior):* 10YR "weak red" 4/4 slip on rim; horizontal burnish.
17.	Bowl	G71, VI.NE13.332, No. 21 L. 13102	*Technique:* Wheelmade. *Paste:* 5YR "light reddish brown" 6/4; some very small and few medium to large lime, some medium organic, few small to medium organic; dark grey core; hard. *Surface (Interior):* as paste. *(Exterior):* as paste.
18.	Bowl	G71, VI.NE13.350, No. 4 L. 13102	*Technique:* Wheelmade. *Paste:* 2.5YR "red" 4/8; some small to medium lime, few very small crystal; 5YR "reddish brown" 5/4 core; hard. *Surface (Interior):* 7.5YR "pink" 8/4. *(Exterior):* as interior; traces of 10YR "red" 5/6 slip.
19.	Bowl	G71, VI.NE13.349, No. 3 L. 13102	*Technique:* Wheelmade. *Paste:* 2.5YR "red" 4/8; some small to medium lime, few very small crystal; 5YR "reddish brown" 5/4 core; Hard. *Surface (Interior):* 7.5YR "pink" 8/4. *(Exterior):* as interior.
20.	Bowl	G71, VI.NE13.332, No. 17 L. 13102	*Technique:* Wheelmade. *Paste:* 5YR "yellowish red" 4/6; few small to medium wadi gravel, very small to small lime, small organic; no core; hard. *Surface (Interior):* 5YR "light reddish brown" 6/3. *(Exterior):* as interior; hard.
21.	Bowl	G71, VI.NE13.339, No. 1 L. 13102	*Technique:* Wheelmade. *Paste:* 2.5YR "light red" 6/6; many very small and few large crystal, few large wadi gravel and organic; grey core; hard. *Surface (Interior):* as paste; 10YR "red 4/6 slip. *(Exterior):* as paste; slip on rim as interior.
22.	Bowl	G71, VI.NE13.344, No. 4 L. 13102	*Technique:* Wheelmade. *Paste:* 5YR "light reddish brown" 6/4; very many very small crystal, few small organic; no core; hard. *Surface (Interior):* 10£weak red" 5/4 slip. *(Exterior):* as interior; traces of slip as interior.
23.	Bowl	G71, VI.NE13.332, No. 13 L. 13102	*Technique:* Wheelmade. *Paste:* 7.5YR "light brown" 6/4; many very small wadi gravel, few large lime, small organic and very small crystal; light grey core; hard. *Surface (Interior):* 2.5YR "light red" 6/8 slip; wheel burnish. *(Exterior):* 5YR "pink" 7/4; slip and burnish on rim as interior.
24.	Bowl	G71, VI.NE13.334, No. 6 L. 13102	*Technique:* Wheelmade. *Paste:* 5YR "light reddish brown" 6/4; many very small to few large lime, some very small to small crystal, few medium to large organic; no core; hard. *Surface (Interior):* 2.5YR "light red" 6/6 slip. *(Exterior):* as paste; trace of burnish on rim.
25. B	aking tray	G71, VI.NE13.349, No. 9 L. 13102	*Technique:* Wheelmade. *Paste:* 5YR "reddish yellow" 6/6; many very small crystal, few very small to large lime and wadi gravel, few very small ceramic; no core; hard. *Surface (Interior):* as paste to 5YR "dark grey" 4/1. *(Exterior):* as paste.
26.	Juglet	G71, VI.NE13.336, No. 16 L. 13102	*Technique:* Wheelmade. *Paste:* 5YR "reddish yellow" 6/6; few small to medium wadi gravel and very small to small crystal; no core; hard. *Surface (Interior):* as paste. *(Exterior):* 10R "red" 5/8 slip and hand burnish.
27.	Bowl	G71, VI.NE13.336, No. 8 L. 13102	*Technique:* Wheelmade. *Paste:* 5YR "reddish yellow" 7/6; many very small to small and few medium crystal, few medium lime, organic and ceramic; no core; hard. *Surface (Interior):* as paste; slip on rim as exterior. *(Exterior):* 1OR "red" 5/6 slip.
28.	Bowl	G71, VI.NE13.344, No. 6 L. 13102	*Technique:* Wheelmade. *Paste:* 5YR "reddish yellow" 6/6; some small wadi gravel, few large organic and very small crystal; 7.5YR "light brown 6/4 core; hard. *Surface (Interior):* 7.5YR "pink" 8/4; 1OR "red" 4/8 slip on rim. *(Exterior):* slip on rim as interior; vertical burnish.

PLATE 5

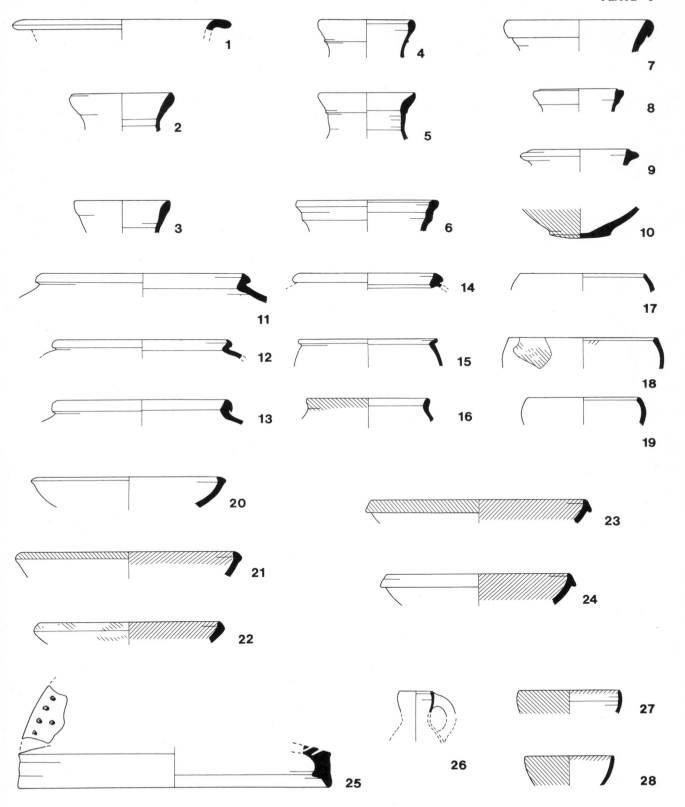

Plate Number	Pottery Type	Number and locus (see LOCUS INDEX)	Description (p. 277)
1.	Bowl	G71, VI.NE13.299, No. 8 L. 13087	*Technique:* Wheelmade. *Paste:* 5YR "reddish yellow" 6/6; few small to medium wadi gravel, small organic, small lime and very small crystal; no core; hard. *Surface (Interior):* as paste; 10R "red" 5/8 slip on rim. *(Exterior):* as paste; slip on rim as interior.
2.	Jar	G71, VII.NE13.347, No. 2 L. 13095.1	*Technique:* Wheelmade. *Paste:* 5YR "light reddish brown" 6/4; some small wadi gravel, few small lime and very small crystal; no core; hard. *Surface (Interior):* 7.5YR "pink" 8/4. *(Exterior):* as interior.
3.	Jar	G71, VI.NE13.343, No. 5 L. 13095.1	*Technique:* Wheelmade. *Paste:* 2.5YR "light red" 6/6; very many small and few medium lime, few large wadi gravel; core: 5YR "reddish brown" 5/3; hard. *Surface (Interior):* as paste. *(Exterior):* as paste.
4.	Jar	G71, VI.NE13.347, No. 5 L. 13095.1	*Technique:* Wheelmade. *Paste:* 5YR "reddish yellow" 6/6; some medium and few small and large lime, few medium wadi gravel and organic and very small crystal; grey core; hard. *Surface (Interior):* as paste. *(Exterior):* as paste.
5.	Jar	G71, VI.NE13.337, No. 13 L. 13095.1	*Technique:* Wheelmade. *Paste:* 7.5YR "light brown" 6/4; some very small to small and few medium to large lime and medium to large wadi gravel, few medium ceramic and very small crystal; grey core; hard. *Surface (Interior):* as paste. *(Exterior):* as paste.
6.	Bowl	G71, VI.NE13.347, o. 8 L. 13117.1	*Technique:* Wheelmade. *Paste:* 5YR "reddish yellow" 6/6; many very small to small crystal; light grey core; hard. *Surface (Interior):* 10R "red" 4/6 slip and horizontal burnish. *(Exterior):* as paste; slip and burnish on rim as interior.
7.	Jar	G71, VI.NE13.355, No. 8 L. 13104.1	*Technique:* Wheelmade. *Paste:* 7.5YR "light brown" 6/4; many small to medium and few large lime, few large wadi gravel and very small crystal; light grey core; hard. *Surface (Interior):* as paste. *(Exterior):* as paste.
8.	Bowl	G71, VI.NE13.317, No. 12 L. 13104.1	*Technique:* Wheelmade. *Paste:* 7.5YR "pink" 7/4; some very small wadi gravel, few small organic and very small crystal; no core; hard. *Surface (Interior):* 1OR "red" 5/6 slip; radial and circular hand burnish. *(Exterior):* as paste; slip as interior and hand burnish on rim.
9.	Bowl	G71, VI.NE13.317, No. 5 L. 13104.1	*Technique:* Wheelmade. *Paste:* 5YR "reddish yellow" 6/6; few medium to large lime, small wadi gravel and very small crystal; no core; hard. *Surface (Interior):* as paste. *(Exterior):* as paste.
10.	Base	G71, VI.NE14.335, No. 11 L. 14116.1	*Technique:* Wheelmade. *Paste:* 2.5YR "light red" 6.6; some very small to medium lime, few medium organic and very small crystal; core: 5YR "reddish brown" 5/3; hard. *Surface (Interior):* as paste. *(Exterior):* as paste; hand burnish.
11.	Cooking pot	G71, VI.NE14.337, No, 4 L. 14116.1	*Technique:* Handmade. *Paste:* 5YR "reddish brown" 5/3; few large organic, very small to large crystal, small and medium lime, small wadi gravel and small ceramic; dark grey core; hard. *Surface (Interior):* as paste. *(Exterior):* as paste to 7.5YR "dark grey' N4/0.
12.	Bowl	G71, VI.NE14.335, No. 3 L. 14116.1	*Technique:* Wheelmade. *Paste:* 5YR "yellowish red" 5/6; few small to large lime and small to medium wadi gravel, ceramic and organic; dark grey core; hard. *Surface (Interior):* 2.5YR "red" 4/8 slip and wheel burnish. *(Exterior):* as paste; as interior on rim.
13.	Krater	G71, VI.NE24.368, No. 1 L. 24160	*Technique:* Wheelmade. *Paste:* 5YR "yellowish red" 5/6; some very small to medium and few very large wadi gravel, few medium lime and very small crystal; no core; hard. *Surface (Interior):* as paste. *(Exterior):* as paste; raised band with incised decoration.
14.	Jar	G71, VI.NE35.354, No. 3 L. 34085	*Technique:* Wheelmade. *Paste:* 7.5YR "light brown" 6/4; some small to large wadi gravel, some medium and few small lime, few small and medium organic; no core; hard. *Surface (Interior):* 10YR "very pale brown" 8/3. *(Exterior):* as interior.
15.	Jar?	G71, VI.NE35.452, No. 2 L. 34085	*Technique:* Wheelmade. *Paste:* 2.5YR "light red" 6/6; few very small to medium lime, small organic and ceramic and very small crystal; grey core; hard. *Surface (Interior):* as paste. *(Exterior):* as paste.
16.	Jar	G71, VI.NE35.337, No. 11 L. 13095.1	*Technique:* Wheelmade. *Paste:* 5YR "reddish yellow" 6/6; few medium to large lime, few medium ceramic, some very small sand; light grey core; hard. *Surface (Interior):* as paste. *(Exterior):* as paste.
17.	Bowl	G71, VI.NE13.347, No. 10 L. 13095.1	*Technique:* Wheelmade. *Paste:* 2.5YR "reddish brown" 4/4; some very small crystal, few medium to large wadi gravel, lime and organic; no core; hard. *Surface (Interior):* as paste; hand burnish. *(Exterior):* as paste; wheel burnish on rim.
18.	Jar	G71, VI.NE13.343, No. 4, L. 13095.1	*Technique:* Wheelmade. *Paste:* 2.5YR "red" 5/6; some small to large lime, few medium wadi gravel and organic and very small crystal; core: 7.5YR "light brown" 6/4; hard. *Surface (Interior):* as paste. *(Exterior):* as paste.
19.	Juglet handle	G71, VI.NE13.366, No. 3 L. 13095.1	*Technique:* Handmade. *Paste:* inner: 5YR "reddish brown" 5/3; outer: 2.5YR "red" 5/6; some small to medium and few large lime, few small organic; no core; hard. *Surface (Interior):* as exterior. *(Exterior):* 2.5YR "reddish brown" 4/4 slip and hand burnish.
20.	Jar	G71, VI.NE34.351, No. 2 L. 34103.1	*Technique:* Wheelmade. *Paste:* 7.5YR "brown" 5/4; some small and large wadi gravel, some small organic, few small and medium lime and small crystal; no core; hard. *Surface (Interior):* 7.5YR "light brown" 6/4. *(Exterior):* as interior.
21.	Jar	G71, VI.NE34.343, No. 1 L. 34103.1	*Technique:* Wheelmade. *Paste:* 5YR "reddish yellow" 6/6; many small to medium and few large lime, some very small wadi gravel and very small crystal, few small to large lime; dark grey core; hard. *Surface (Interior):* as paste. *(Exterior):* 10YR "very pale brown" 8/3.
22.	Cooking pot	G71, VI.NE34.329, No. 4 L. 34106	*Technique:* Wheelmade. *Paste:* 5YR "yellowish red" 5/6; some small to medium, few large and very large wadi gravel, few small lime, crystal organic; dark grey core; hard. *Surface (Interior):* 5YR "reddish brown" 5/4; *(Exterior):* as interior.
23.	Bowl	G71, VI.NE34.335, No. 1 L. 34103.1	*Technique:* Wheelmade. *Paste:* 5YR "reddish yellow" 7/6l some very small crystal and wadi gravel, few small and large lime and small organic; grey core; hard. *Surface (Interior):* as paste to 7.5YR "pinkish white" 8/2 burnish. *(Exterior):* as paste.
24.	Jar	G71, VI.NE34.355, No. 1 L. 34119	*Technique:* Wheelmade. *Paste:* 7.5YR "light brown" 6/4; many medium and large wadi gravel, few small to large lime, some small to medium organic; light grey core; hard. *Surface (Interior):* as paste. *(Exterior):* as paste.
25.	Jar	G71, VI.NE34.348, L. 34119	*Technique:* Wheelmade. *Paste:* 5YR "yellowish red" 5/6; some very small and large lime, some large wadi gravel, few medium organic; light grey core; hard. *Surface (Interior):* as paste. *(Exterior):* as paste.
26.	Bowl	G71, VI.NE34.347, No. 1 L. 34119	*Technique:* Wheelmade. *Paste:* 7.5YR "pink" 7/4; some very small, few small and medium wadi gravel, some small organic; grey core; hard. *Surface (Interior):* as paste. *(Exterior):* as paste.

PLATE 6

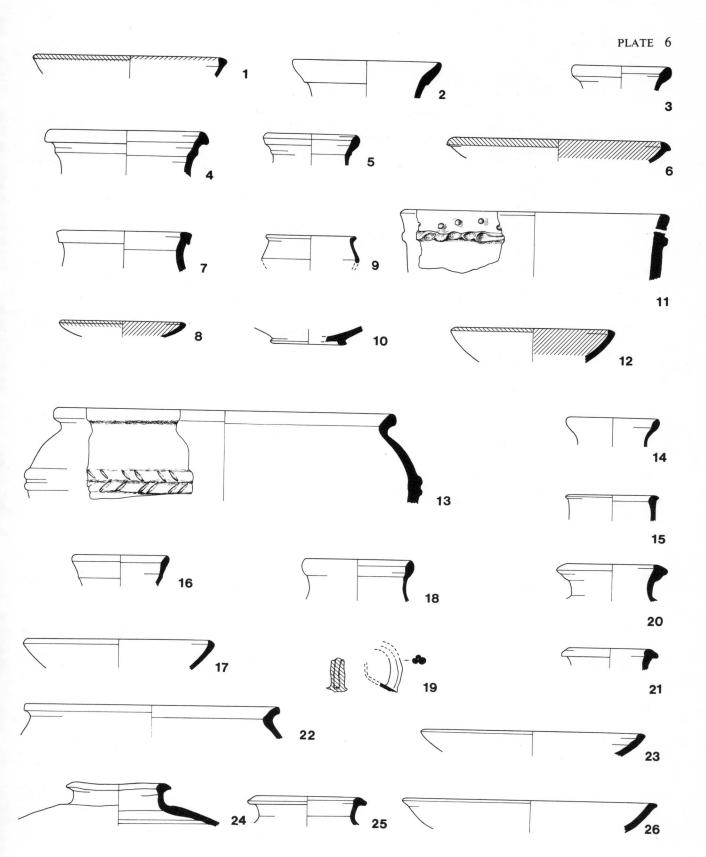

Plate Number	Pottery Type	Number and locus (see LOCUS INDEX)	Description (p. 277)
1.	Bowl	G71, VI.NE23.257, No. 3 · L. 23092	*Technique:* Wheelmade. *Paste:* 5YR "reddish yellow" 6/6; few very small and small lime, very small wadi gravel and crystal; core: 7.5YR "light brown" 6/4; hard. *Surface (Interior):* as paste. *(Exterior):* as paste.
2.	Bowl	G71, VI.NE23.264, No. 4 L. 24150	*Technique:* Wheelmade. *Paste:* 2.5YR "light red" 6/8; few small to medium lime, few medium organic, many very small crystal; 10YR "light yellowish brown" 6/4; hard. *Surface (Interior):* 10YR "very pale brown" 8/4; paint as exterior on rim. *(Exterior):* as paste; band of 2.5YR "red" 4/6 organic paint decoration; wheel burnish over decoration below rim.
3.	Base	G70, VI.NE33.126B, No. 7 L. 33056	*Technique:* Wheelmade. *Paste:* 5YR "pinkish grey" 7/2 to "pink" 7/3; many small crystal and ceramic; no core; hard. *Surface (Interior):* same as exterior. *(Exterior):* 2.5YR "dusky red" 3/2.
4.	Base	G70, VI.NE33.126B, No. 5 L. 33056	*Technique:* Wheelmade. *Paste:* 5YR "reddish yellow" 7/6; many small crystal, (quartz); no core; hard. *Surface (Interior):* as paste. *(Exterior):* as paste.
5.	Jar	G71, VI.NE35.414, No. 15 L. 35083	*Technique:* Wheelmade. *Paste:* 2.5YR "light red" 6.6; few very small to large lime, large wadi gravel and very small crystal; core: 7.5YR "light brown" 6.4; hard. *Surface (Interior):* as paste. *(Exterior):* as paste.
6.	Jar	G71, VI.NE35.405, No. 8 L. 35083	*Technique:* Wheelmade. *Paste:* 5YR "reddish yellow" 6/6; few small to large lime; dark grey core; hard. *Surface (Interior):* as paste. *(Exterior):* as paste.
7.	Jar	G71, VI.NE35.420, No. 3 L. 35083	*Technique:* Wheelmade. *Paste:* 5YR "reddish yellow" 6/6; few small to large wadi gravel, small to medium lime, small organic and very small crystal; core; 5YR "reddish brown" 5/3; *Surface (Interior):* as paste. *(Exterior):* as paste.
8.	Jar	G71, VI.NE35.407, No. 21 L. 35083	*Technique:* Wheelmade. *Paste:* 5YR "reddish brown" 5/4; some small crystal, few small to large lime and wadi gravel, small to medium organic; grey core; hard. *Surface (Interior):* as paste. *(Exterior):* as paste.
9.	Jar	G71, VI.NE35.407, No. 9 L. 35083	*Technique:* Wheelmade. *Paste:* 7.5YR "light brown" 6/4; many very small and few small lime, few small and medium ceramic, and very small sand; light grey core; hard. *Surface (Interior):* as paste. *(Exterior):* 10YR "white" 8/2.
10.	Base	G71, VI.NE35.405, No. 16 L. 35083	*Technique:* Wheelmade. *Paste:* 5YR "reddish brown" 5/4; many small to large lime and some medium to large wadi gravel; no core; hard. *Surface (Interior):* as paste. *(Exterior):* as paste.
11.	Bowl	G71, VI.NE35.425, No. 1 L. 35083	*Technique:* Wheelmade. *Paste:* 5YR "yellowish red" 5/6; some very small and few large wadi gravel, few very small and large lime, small organic and very small crystal; no core hard. *Surface (Interior):* as paste. *(Exterior):* as paste.
12.	Bowl	G71, VI.NE35.414, No. 9 L. 35083	*Technique:* Wheelmade. *Paste:* 5YR "yellowish red" 4/6; some medium to large wadi gravel and small to large lime; dark grey core; hard. *Surface (Interior):* as paste to 7.5YR "very dark grey" N3/0. *(Exterior):* as paste.
13.	Bowl	G71, VI.NE35.420, No. 2 L. 35083	*Technique:* Wheelmade. *Paste:* 5YR "reddish yellow" 7/6; some small and few very small and large wadi gravel, few small and medium lime, small organic and very small crystal; grey core; hard. *Surface (Interior):* 7.5YR "pink" 7/4. *(Exterior):* as interior.
14.	Bowl	G71, VI.NE35.425, No. 5 L. 35083	*Technique:* Wheelmade. *Paste:* 5YR "reddish yellow" 7/8; many small to large wadi gravel, few small to large lime, very small and medium crystal and small organic; 7.5YR "light brown" 6/4; hard. *Surface (Interior):* 5YR "pink" 7/4. *(Exterior):* as interior.
15.	Base	G71, VI.NE35.425, No. 9 L. 35083	*Technique:* Wheelmade. *Paste:* 5YR "light reddish brown" 6/4; some very small to small crystal, few small wadi gravel and medium lime no core; hard. *Surface (Interior):* 10YR "white" 8/2. *(Exterior):* as interior.
16.	Base	G71, VI.NE35.414, No. 33 L. 35083	*Technique:* Wheelmade. *Paste:* 5YR "light reddish brown" 6/4; some very small to small crystal, few small wadi gravel and medium lime; no core; hard. *Surface (Interior):* 10YR "white" 8/2. *(Exterior):* as interior.
17.	Cooking pot	G71, VI.NE35.408, No. 1 L. 35083	*Technique:* Wheelmade. *Paste:* 5YR "reddish brown" 5/4; some small and medium lime, few small and medium wadi gravel, small organic and very small crystal; dark grey core; hard. *Surface (Interior):* as paste. *(Exterior):* as paste.
18.	Cooking pot	G71, VI.NE35.420, No. 1 L. 35083	*Technique:* Wheelmade. *Paste:* 5YR "reddish brown" 5/4; some small to large lime, few small organic and very small crystal; dark grey core; hard. *Surface (Interior):* as paste. *(Exterior):* as paste.
19.	Bowl		G71, VI.NE35.423, No. 1 L. 35083 *Technique:* Wheelmade. *Paste:* 5YR "reddish yellow" 7/6; many small and medium to few large lime, some very small and few large and very large wadi gravel, few very small organic; grey core; hard. *Surface (Interior):* as paste. *(Exterior):* as paste to 5YR "light grey" 7/1.
20.	Bowl	G71, VI.NE35.405, No. 19 L. 35083	*Technique:* Wheelmade. *Paste:* 5YR "reddish yellow" 6/6; few small and large and some medium lime, few large wadi gravel, small ceramic and very small crystal; light grey core; hard. *Surface (Interior):* as paste. *(Exterior):* as paste.
21.	Bowl	G71, VI.NE35.425, No. 4 L. 35083	*Technique:* Wheelmade. *Paste:* 5YR "reddish yellow" 6/6; few very small to large lime, very small wadi gravel and crystal; no core; hard. *Surface (Interior):* as paste. *(Exterior):* as paste.
22.	Bowl	G71, VI.NE35.424, No. 15 L. 35083	*Technique:* Wheelmade. *Paste:* 5YR "reddish yellow" 7/76; many very small wadi gravel, few small and some medium and large lime, few very small and medium organic; few very small and small crystal; core; 7.5YR "brown" 5/2; hard. *Surface (Interior):* as paste. *(Exterior):* as paste.
23.	Krater	G71, VI.NE35.413, No. 9 L. 35083	*Technique:* Wheelmade. *Paste:* 5YR "light reddish brown" 6/4; very many small lime, few medium organic and ceeramic and very small crystal; dark grey core; hard. *Surface (Interior):* as paste; band of slip as exterior below rim. *(Exterior):* 2.5YR "white" 8/2; slip, wheel burnish; band of floral decoration on body, rope decoration on rim.
24.	Cooking pot	G71, VI.NE35.407, No. 3 L. 35083	*Technique:* Wheelmade. *Paste:* 5YR "reddish brown" 4/4; some very small and large lime; dark grey core; hard. *Surface (Interior):* as paste. *(Exterior):* as paste.

PLATE 7

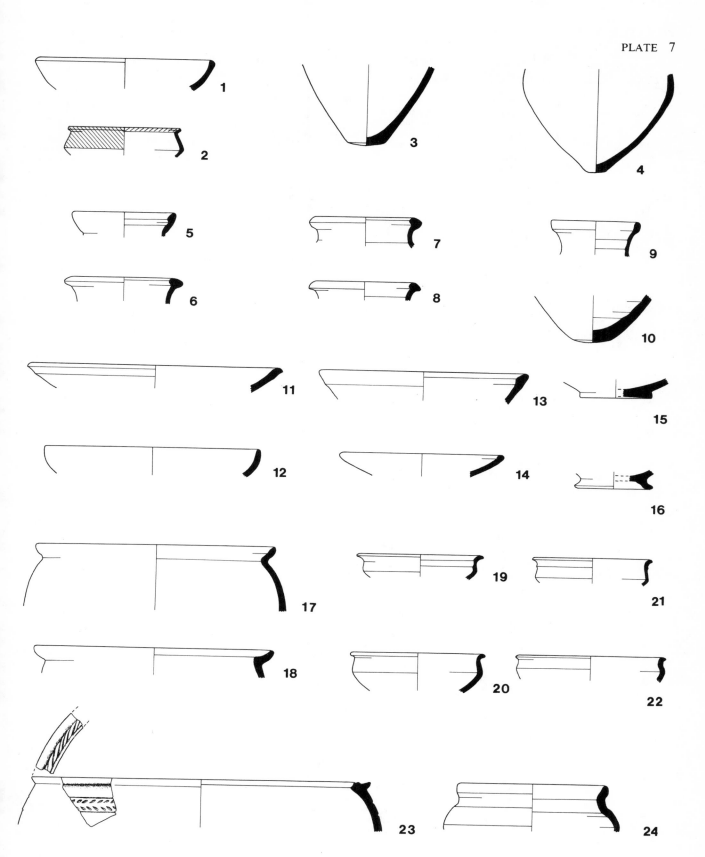

Plate Number	Pottery Type	Number and locus (see LOCUS INDEX)	Description (p. 277)
1.	Jar	G71, VI.NE4.303, No. 3 L. 4143.1	*Technique:* Wheelmade. *Paste:* 5YR "reddish yellow" 7/6; many very small wadi gravel, few small to medium lime and very small crystal; no core; hard. *Surface (Interior):* 5YR "pink" 7/4. *(Exterior): (Interior):* as interior.
2.	Jar	G71, VI.NE4.303, No. 2 L. 4143.1	*Technique:* Wheelmade. *Paste:* 2.5YR "light red" 6/8; few small lime, medium wadi gravel, very small crystal; 5YR "reddish yellow" 6/6; hard. *Surface (Interior):* as paste. *(Exterior):* as core.
3.	Jar	G71, VI.NE4.300, No. 3 L. 4143.1	*Technique:* Wheelmade. *Paste:* 5YR "yellowish red" 5/8; some small to medium lime, few small ceramic, small organic, very small crystal; 7.5YR "brown" 5/4; hard. *Surface (Interior):* 5YR "pink" 7/3. *(Exterior):* as interior.
4.	Jar	G71, VI.NE4.299, No. 9 L. 4143.1	*Technique:* Wheelmade. *Paste:* 5YR "light reddish brown" 6/4; some very small crystal, few very small and medium lime, small wadi gravel and very small ceramic; dark grey core; hard. *Surface (Interior):* 10YR "red" 5/6 slip; wheel burnish. *(Exterior):* 10YR "pale red" 6/2 slip, vertical burnish, slip and burnish on rim as interior.
5.	Base	G71, VI.NE13.363, No. 6 L. 13095	*Technique:* Wheelmade. *Paste:* 2.5YR "red" 5/6; some small to medium and few large lime, few small ceramic and very small crystal; grey core; hard. *Surface (Interior):* 7.5YR "pinkish grey" 7/2. *(Exterior):* as paste.
6.	Bowl	G71, VI.NE4.299, No. 8 L. 4143.1	*Technique:* Wheelmade. *Paste:* 5YR "light reddish brown" 6/4; few medium organic, small wadi gravel and lime, and very small crystal; dark grey core; hard. *Surface (Interior):* as paste. *(Exterior):* 10YR "red" 5/6 slip with horizontal and vertical burnish.
7.	Bowl	G71, VI.NE4.499, No. 1 L. 4143.1	*Technique:* Wheelmade. *Paste:* 7.5YR "pink 7/4; no core; hard. *Surface (Interior):* as paste; band of 10YR "red" 5/8 slip, hard burnish. *(Exterior):* as paste; hand burnish on rim.
8.	Jar	G71, VI.NE13.316, No. 8 L. 13099	*Technique:* Wheelmade. *Paste:* 5YR "reddish yellow" 7/6; some very small to large lime and small organic, few medium wadi gravel; light grey core; hard. *Surface (Interior):* as paste. *(Exterior):* as paste.
9.	Base	G71, VI.NE13.315, No. 3 L. 13089	*Technique:* Wheelmade. *Paste:* inner: 7.5YR "pinkish grey" 6/2; outer: 5YR "reddish yellow" 6/6; some small to medium lime, few small wadi gravel and very small crystal; no core; hard. *Surface (Interior):* as inner paste. *(Exterior):* 2.5YR "red" 5/6 slip; vertical and horizontal burnish on side and bottom.
10.	Base	G71, VI.NE13.302, No. 3 L. 13084	*Technique:* Wheelmade. *Paste:* 5YR "reddish yellow" 6/6; some small ceramic, few small wadi gravel and lime and very small crystal; no core; hard. *Surface (Interior):* 5YR "pink" 7/4. *(Exterior):* as interior.
11.	Base	G71, VI.NE13.313, No. 2, L. 13089	*Technique:* Wheelmade. *Paste:* 7.5YR "pink" 7/4; very any very small wadi gravel, few medium organic and very small crystal; no core; hard. *Surface (Interior):* as paste. *(Exterior):* as paste. *(Exterior):* 2.5YR "red" 4/6 slip; vertical burnish on body, circular burnish on bottom of base.
12.	Bowl	G71, VI.NE13.300, No. 2 L. 13089	*Technique:* Wheelmade. *Paste:* 5YR "reddish yellow" 7/6; many very small wadi gravel, few small lime and crystal; light grey core; hard. *Surface (Interior):* as paste; diagonal burnish. *(Exterior):* as paste.
13.	Bowl	G71, VI.NE13.305, No. 2 L. 13089	*Technique:* Wheelmade. *Paste:* 2.5YR "light red" 6/6; many very small wadi gravel and crystal, few small to medium lime, ceramic, and organic; core: 715YR "pink" 7/4; hard. *Surface (Interior):* as paste; 10YR "red" 4/6 slip on rim. *(Exterior): (Interior):* as paste; slip on rim as interor.
14.	Bowl	G71, VI.NE4.290, No. 1 L. 4124.1	*Technique:* Wheelmade. *Paste:* 5YR "yellowish red" 6/6; some medium organic, few to some small lime, few very small crystal; light grey core; hard. *Surface (Interior):* 2.5YR "red" 5/6; radial burnish. *(Exterior):* as paste; band of 10YR "light red" 6/6 slip.
15.	Bowl	G71, VI.NE13.308, No. 4 L. 13089	*Technique:* Wheelmade. *Paste:* 5YR "reddish yellow" 6/6; some medium organic; few very small to medium lime, few very small crystal; light grey core; hard. *Surface (Interior):* 10YR "weak red" 4/4; slip and radial and circular burnish. *(Exterior): (Interior):* as paste.
16.	Bowl	G71, VI.NE4.286, No. 1	*Technique:* Wheelmade. *Paste:* 5YR "yellowish red" 5/8; some very small crystal, few small wadi gravel and very small crystal; grey core; hard. *Surface (Interior):* 10YR "weak red" 4/4 slip; radial burnish. *(Exterior): (Interior):* slip and burnish on interior; circular hand burnish on rim.
17.	Jar	G71, VI.NE13.319, No. 1 L. 13101	*Technique:* Wheelmade. *Paste:* 5YR "grey" 6/1; many small to some medium and large wadi gravel, few small and medium lime and small organic; no core; hard. *Surface (Interior):* as exterior to 5YR "reddish yellow" 7/6. *(Exterior):* 7.5YR "pink" 7/4.
18.	Jar	G71, VI.NE13.319, No. 5 L. 13101	*Technique:* Wheelmade. *Paste:* 2.5YR "red" 5/6; few small and some medium lime, few small wadi gravel; no core; hard. *Surface (Interior):* as paste. *(Exterior):* as paste.
19.	Jar	G71, VI.NE13.324, No. 1 L. 13107	*Technique:* Wheelmade. *Paste:* 5YR "reddish yellow" 7/6; many small to some medium and large wadi gravel, few small and medium lime and small organic; grey core; hard. *Surface (Interior):* as paste. *(Exterior):* as paste.
20.	Jar	G71, VI.NE13.324, No. 23 L. 13107	*Technique:* Wheelmade. *Paste:* 5YR "reddish yellow" 7/6; some small and medium and few very small wadi gravel, few small and medium ceramic; small lime and very small crystal; *Surface (Interior):* 7.5YR "pink" 8/4. *(Exterior): (Interior):* 7.5YR "pink" 7/4.
21.	Bowl	G71, VI.NE12.325, No. 1 L. 14129	*Technique:* Wheelmade. *Paste:* 5YR "reddishyellow" 6/6; some small organic, few small and large lime, small iron and ceramic and very small crystal; dark grey core; hard. *Surface (Interior):* 7.5YR "pink" 7/4. *(Exterior): (Interior):* as interior.
22.	Jar	G71, VI.NE14.362, No. 1 L. 14129	*Technique:* Wheelmade. *Paste:* 5YR "yellowish red" 5/6; some medium to large wadi gravel, few small organic and very small crystal; no core;hard. *Surface (Interior):* 7.5YR "pink" 7/4. *(Exterior): (Interior):* as interior.
23.	Bowl	G71, VI.NE14.362, No. 4 L. 14131	*Technique:* Wheelmade. *Paste:* 5YR "reddish yellow" 6/6; some very small to small wadi gravel and crystal, few small and medium lime; core: 7.5YR "light brown" 6/4; hard. *Surface (Interior):* as paste; 10YR "red" 5/8 slip under rim. *(Exterior): (Interior):* as paste; slip as interior and burnish on rim.

PLATE 8

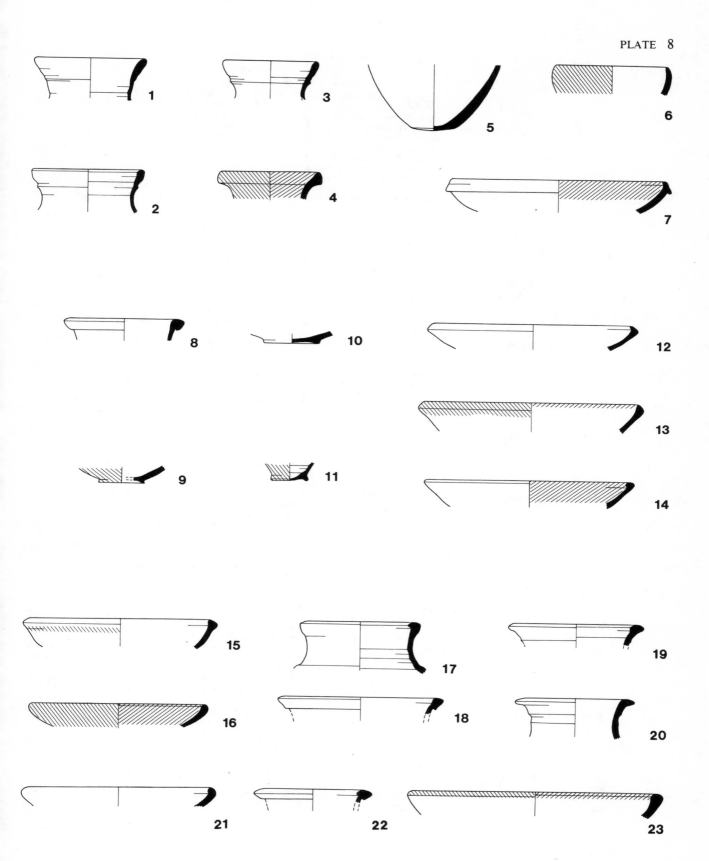

Plate Number	Pottery Type	Number and locus (see LOCUS INDEX)	Description (p. 277)
1.	Bowl	G71, VI.NE4.279, No. 8 L. 4132.1	*Technique:* Wheelmade. *Paste:* 7.5YR "pink" 7/4; few small wadi gravel and lime, very small ceramic and crystal; light grey core; hard. *Surface (Interior):* 7.5YR "pink" 8/4; 10YR "red" 5/8 slip and hand burnish on rim. *(Exterior):* slip and burnish as interior.
2.	Jar	G71, VI.NE13.316, No. 5 L. 13089	*Technique:* Wheelmade. *Paste:* 5YR "reddish yellow" 6/6; few medium lime and wadi gravel, very small and small crystal and organic; light grey core; hard. *Surface (Interior):* 54R "pink" 7/4. *(Exterior):* as interior.
3.	Jar	G71, VI.NE13.317, No. 1 L. 13089	*Technique:* Wheelmade. *Paste:* 5YR "reddish yellow" 7/6; some medium and large and few small wadi gravel, few small to medium lime, some organic very small crystal; grey core; hard. *Surface (Interior):* as paste. *(Exterior):* as paste.
4.	Jar	G71, VI.NE13.313, No. 3 L. 13089	*Technique:* Wheelmade. *Paste:* 5YR "yellowish red" 5/6; some small, few medium and large lime, few small organic, very small to large wadi grvel, very small crystal; no core; hard. *Surface (Interior):* 5YR "pink" 7/4. *(Exterior):* as interior.
5.	Jar	G71, VI.NE13.313, No. 4 L. 13089	*Technique:* Wheelmade. *Paste:* 5YR "reddish yellow" 7/6; few large organic, small to large wadi gravel and very small to medium lime; light grey core; hard. *Surface (Interior):* as paste. *(Exterior):* as paste.
6.	Krater	G71, VI.NE13.313, No. 9 L. 13089	*Technique:* Wheelmade. *Paste:* 2.5YR "reddish brown" 4/4; few very small to large lime, medium wadi gravel and very small crystal and organic grey core: 2.5YR "dusky red" 3/2; hard. *Surface (Interior):* as paste. *(Exterior):* as paste.
7.	Krater	G71, VI.NE13.302, No. 7 L. 13089	*Technique:* Wheelmade. *Paste:* 5YR "reddish yellow" 6/6' few small to large lime, wadi gravel, small ceramic and very small crystal; light grey core; hard. *Surface (Interior):* as paste. *(Exterior):* as paste.
8.	Jar	G71, VI.NE14,.331, No. 4 L. 14125.1	*Technique:* Wheelmade. *Paste:* 75YR "light brown" 6/4; many small and medium wadi gravel, few small to some large lime, few small organic and very small crystal; no core; hard. *Surface (Interior):* 2.5YR "light red" 6/6. *(Exterior):* 5YR "pink" 8/4.
9.	Base	G71, VI.NE14.331, No. 1 L. 14125.1	*Technique:* Wheelmade. *Paste:* 7.5YR "pink" 7/4; some small and medium wadi gravel and small organic, few small to large lime, medium ceramic and very small crystal; grey core; hard. *Surface (Interior):* as paste. *(Exterior):* as paste.
10.	Jar	G71, VI.NE23.229, No. 12 L. 23075	*Technique:* Wheelmade. *Paste:* 2/5YR "light red" 6/6; some very small to medium wadi gravel, few small to medium lime, very small organic and crystal; core: 10YR "light yellowish brown" 6/4; hard. *Surface (Interior):* 5YR "reddish yellow" 7/6. *(Exterior):* as interior.
11.	Bowl	G71, VI.NE23.229, No. 11 L. 23075	*Technique:* Wheelmade. *Paste:* 5YR "yellowish red" 5/6; some small lime, few small to large wadi gravel, medium ceramic, small organic and very small crystal; grey core; hard. *Surface (Interior):* as paste; slip and burnish on rim as exterior. *(Exterior):* 10YR "red" 5/6 slip, wheel burnished.
12.	Handle (Cypriot)	G71, VI.NE23.333, No. 11 L. 23075	*Technique:* Handmade. *Paste:* 10YR "light grey" 7/2; some very small wadi gravel, few very small organic and crystal; no core; metallic. *Surface (Interior):* as paste; hand burnish, 10YR "very dark greyish brown" 3/2 organic paint decoration.
13.	Jar base	G71, VI.NE23.268, No. 9	*Technique:* Wheelmade. *Paste:* inner: 5YR "light reddish brown" 6/4. Outer: 2.5YR "reddish brown" 5/4; few small to large lime, very small wadi gravel and crystal; grey core; hard. *Surface (Interior):* as inner paste. *(Exterior):* as outer paste.
14.	Jug handle	G71, VI.NE23.288, No. 1 L. 23075	*Technique:* Handmade. *Paste:* 5YR "reddish yellow" 6/4; many very small wadi gravel, few very small and medium crystal, very small to small lime and very small ceramic; no core; hard. *Surface (Interior):* as paste. *(Exterior):* as paste, hand burnish.
15.	Bowl	G71, VI.NE24.339, No. 1 L. 24159	*Technique:* Wheelmade. *Paste:* 7.5YR "pink" 7/4; many very small wadi gravel, few very small crystal; light grey core; hard. *Surface (Interior):* 7.5YR "pinkish white" 8/2. *(Exterior):* as paste and interior.
16.	Jar	G71, VI.NE34.322, No. 15 L. 34098	*Technique:* Wheelmade. *Paste:* 5YR "light reddish brown" 6/4; some small to medium and few large lime, few medium wadi gravel, small organic and very small crystal; dark grey core; hard. *Surface (Interior):* as paste. *(Exterior):* as paste.
17.	Jar	G71, VI.NE23.311, No. 6 L. 34098	*Technique:* Wheelmade. *Paste:* inner: 7.5YR "pink" 7/4. Outer: 2.5YR "light red" 6/6; many very small wadi gravel, some small organic and very small crystal, few small and large lime; grey core; hard. *Surface (Interior):* as inner paste. *(Exterior):* as outer paste.
18.	Krater	G71, VI.NE34.311, No. 18 L. 34098	*Technique:* Wheelmade. *Paste:* 7.5YR "reddish yellow" 8/6; many very small, few medium wadi gravel, few small organic and lime, very small crystal; grey core; hard. *Surface (Interior):* as paste; 2.5YR "reddish brown" 5/4 organic paint decoration. *(Exterior):* as paste.
19.	Bowl	G71. VI.NE34.322, No. 1 L. 34098	*Technique:* Wheelmade. *Paste:* 10YR "very pale brown" 8/4; many very small wadi gravel, some medium to large organic, few medium to large lime and very small crystal; no core; hard. *Surface (Interior):* 2.5YR "white" 8/2, burnish. *(Exterior):* as interior.
20.	Bowl	G71. VI.NE34.305, No. 7 L. 34098	*Technique:* Wheelmade. *Paste:* 5YR "light reddish brown" 6/4; many very small and few large wadi gravel, some very small crystal, few small to medium lime and small organic; grey core; hard. *Surface (Interior):* as paste. *(Exterior):* as paste.
21.	Bowl	G21, VI.NE34.311, No. 3 L. 34098	*Technique:* Wheelmade. *Paste:* 5YR "reddish yellow" 7/7; some very small wadi gravel, few very small, small and large lime and ceramic, medium organic and very small crystal; grey core; hard. *Surface (Interior):* as paste. *(Exterior):* as paste.
22.	Cooking pot	G71, VI.NE34.311, No. 11 L. 34098	*Technique:* Wheelmade. *Paste:* 5YR "reddish yellow" 6/6; few small and some medium lime, few very small to small wadi gravel, small organic and very small crystal; dark grey core; hard. *Surface (Interior):* as paste. *(Exterior):* as paste.
23.	Bilbil (Base Ring I)	G71, VI.NE34.311, No. 9 L. 34098	*Technique:* Handmade. *Paste:* 5YR "light reddish brown" 6/4; few very small lime and crystal; no core; metallic. *Surface (Interior):* as paste. *(Exterior):* 7.5YR "dark brown" 3/2; slip.
24.	Bowl (White Slip II)	G71, VI.NE34.311, No. 37 L. 34098	*Technique:* Handmade. *Paste:* 5YR "reddish brown" 5/4; many small and small lime, some small organic, few very small crystal; core: 7.5YR "grey" 6/0; metallic. *Surface (Interior):* 10YR "dark greyish brown", 4/2 slip; hand burnish. *(Exterior):* 10YR "pale brown" 6/3 slip; hand burnish. 5YR "dark reddish brown" 3/3 slip; organic paint decoration.

PLATE 9

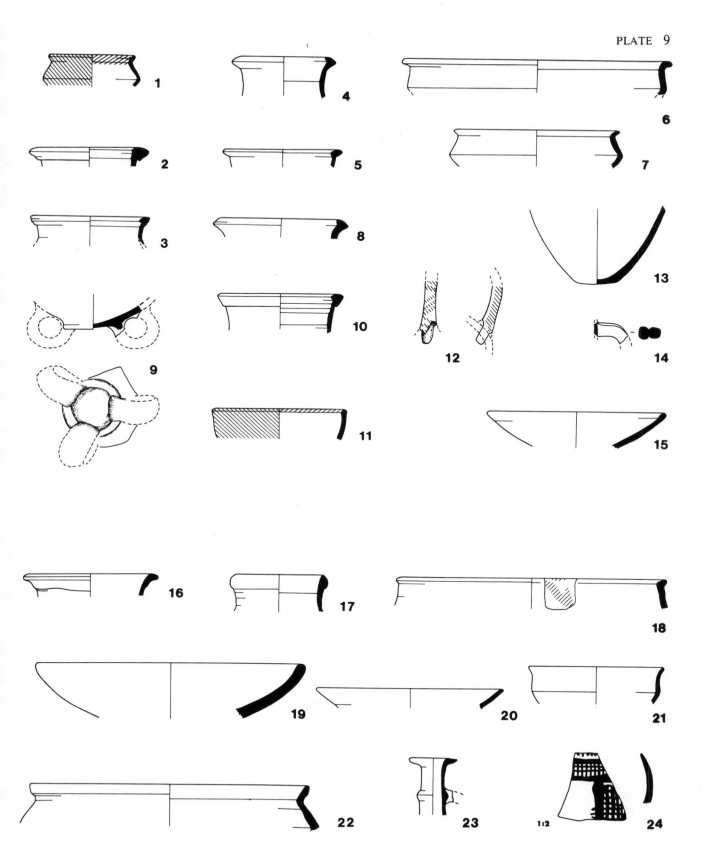

Plate Number	Pottery Type	Number and locus (see LOCUS INDEX)	Description (p. 277)
1.	Bowl	G71, VI.NE24.303, No. 1 L. 24144	*Technique:* Wheelmade. *Paste:* 2.5YR "light red" 6/6; some small to large lime, few small to large ceramic, few small wadi gravel; light grey core; hard. *Surface (Interior):* as paste. *(Exterior):* as paste.
2.	Bowl	G71, VI.NE24.319, No. 2 L. 24150	*Technique:* Wheelmade. *Paste:* 5YR "light reddish brown" 6/4; some large and small and medium organic, some very small and few small to large lime, few large iron and very small and medium crystal; grey core; hard. *Surface (Interior):* as paste. *(Exterior):* as paste.
3.	Bowl	G71, VI.NE24.301, No. 21 L. 24144	*Technique:* Wheelmade. *Paste:* 7.5YR "pink" 7/4; many small to medium lime and calcite; grey core; hard. *Surface (Interior):* as paste. *(Exterior):* as paste.
4.	Bowl	G71, VI.NE24.301, No. 1 L. 24144	*Technique:* Wheelmade. *Paste:* 7.5YR "pink" 7/4; many small to medium lime and calcite; grey core; hard. *Surface (Interior):* as paste. *(Exterior):* as paste.
5.	Base	G71, VI.NE24.319, No. 3 L. 24144	*Technique:* Wheelmade. *Paste:* 5YR "reddish yellow" 7/6; very many small to very large organic, few small to large lime, very small and medium wadi gravel, very small crystal; dark grey core; hard. *Surface (Interior):* as paste. *(Exterior):* as paste.
6.	Jar or flask	G71, VI.NE24.301, No. 6 L. 24144	*Technique:* Wheelmade. *Paste:* 10YR "very pale brown" 8/3; many small to medium lime slight grey core, hard. *Surface (Interior):* as paste. *(Exterior):* as paste.
7.	Jar	G71, VI.NE24.301, No. 14 L. 24144	*Technique:* Wheelmade. *Paste:* 2.5YR "light red" 6/6; some very small wadi gravel, few small to large iron, very small to medium lime and very small crystal; grey core; hard. *Surface (Interior):* as paste to 7.5YR "pinkish white" 8/2.
8.	Chalice	G71, VI.NE24.301, No. 1 L. 24144	*Technique:* Wheelmade. *Paste:* 10YR "red" 5/6; many small to medium lime and calcite; grey core; hard. *Surface (Interior):* as paste. *(Exterior):* as paste.
9.	Lamp	G71, VI.NE24.320, No. 1 L. 24144	*Technique:* Wheelmade. *Paste:* 5YR "light reddish brown" 6/4; some very small and few large wadi gravel, few large organic and ceramic, very small to large iron and lime and very small crystal; grey core; hard. *Surface (Interior):* as paste. *(Exterior):* as paste.
10.	Chalice	G71, VI.NE24.301. No. 17 L. 24144	*Technique:* Wheelmade. *Paste:* 7.5YR "pink" 7/4; many small to medium lime and calcite; grey core; hard. *Surface (Interior):* as paste. *(Exterior):* as paste.
11.	Goblet	G71, VI.NE24.289, No. 1 L. 24144	*Technique:* Wheelmade. *Paste:* 5YR "reddish yellow" 7/6; few small iron, organic and wadi gravel and very small crystal; grey core; hard. *Surface (Interior):* as paste; band of 2.5YR "red" 5/6 organic paint on rim. *(Exterior):* as paste; organic paint as interior on rim and decoration.
12.	Bowl	G71, VI.NE24.328, No. 4 L. 24144	*Technique:* Wheelmade. *Paste:* 7.5YR "light brown" 6/4; many very small and few large wadi gravel, few medium and large organic, few very small and small iron and crystal and small lime; grey core; hard. *Surface (Interior):* as paste; wheel burnish. *(Exterior):* as paste.
13.	Bowl	G71, VI.NE24.332, No. 10 L. 24150	*Technique:* Wheelmade. *Paste:* 2.5YR "light red" 6/6; some very small wadi gravel, few small to large iron, very small to medium lime and very small crytal; grey core; hard. *Surface (Interior):* as paste. *(Exterior):* as paste to 7,5YR "pinkish white" 8/2.
14.	Bowl	G71, VI.NE24.332, No. 126 L. 24150	*Technique:* Wheelmade. *Paste:* 7.5YR "light brown" 6/4; many small to medium lime; grey core; hard. *Surface (Interior):* as paste. *(Exterior):* as paste.
15.	Bowl	G71, VI.NE24.328, No. 6 L. 24150	*Technique:* Wheelmade. *Paste:* 7.5YR "reddish yellow" 7/6; few small wadi gravel, lime and organic, very small crystal; grey core; hard. *Surface (Interior):* as paste; hand burnish; band of 7.5YR "dark brown" 4/2 organic paint. *(Exterior):* as paste; hand burnish on rim.
16.	Base	G71, VI.NE24.328, No. 8 L. 24150	*Technique:* Wheelmade. *Paste:* 5YR "pink" 7/4; some small to medium organic, very small to small lime, very small wadi gravel, few very small crystal; grey core; hard. *Surface (Interior):* 7YR "white" 8/1. *(Exterior):* as paste to interior.
17.	Lamp	G71, VI.NE24.332, No. 1 L. 24150	*Technique:* Wheelmade. *Paste:* 5YR "reddish yellow" 7/6; many very small and few large wadi gravel, few very small to large lime, small to large iron and very small crystal; no core; hard. *Surface (Interior):* as paste. *(Exterior):* as paste.
18.	Lamp	G71 VI.NE24.332, No. 2 L. 24150	*Technique:* Wheelmade. *Paste:* 7.5YR "pink" 7/4; few small wadi gravel, few very small to medium lime, few very small crystal, few very small and large organic and ceramic; grey core; hard. *Surface (Interior):* as paste. *(Exterior):* as paste.
19.	Lamp	G71, VI.NE24.324, No. 2 L. 24150	*Technique:* Wheelmade. *Paste:* 7.5YR "light brown" 6/4; some small to medium organic, few small to medium lime, small iron, very small crystal; grey core; hard. *Surface (Interior):* as paste. *(Exterior):* as paste.
20.	Bowl	G71, VI.NE24.332, No. 24 L. 24150	*Technique:* Wheelmade. *Paste:* 5YR "light reddish brown" 6/4; some very small and few medium wadi gravel, few small ceramic, very small and small lime and very small crystal; grey core; hard. *Surface (Interior):* as paste. *(Exterior):* as paste.
21.	Bowl	G71, VI.NE34.305, No. 6 L. 34098	*Technique:* Wheelmade. *Paste:* 7.5YR "pink" 7/4; many small to medium lime and calcite; grey core; hard. *Surface (Interior):* as paste. *(Exterior):* as paste.
22.	Bowl (Cypriot Monochrome)	G71, VI.NE24.324, No. 3 L. 24150	*Technique:* Handmade. *Paste:* 2.5YR "red" 5/6; some very small organic, few very small lime no core; metallic. *Surface (Interior):* as paste; slip on rim as exterior. *(Exterior):* 2.5YR "reddish brown" 4/4 to 7.5YR "dark brown 3/2 slip.
23.	Cooking pot	G71, VI.NE34.322, No. 17 L. 34098	*Technique:* Wheelmade. *Paste:* 7.5YR "brown" 5/4; many medium to large calcite and wadi gravel; no core; hard. *Surface (Interior):* as paste. *(Exterior):* as paste.
24.	Base	G71, VI.NE24.324, No. 14 L. 24150	*Technique:* Wheelmade. *Paste:* 7.5YR "pink;; 8/4; some very small wadi gravel, few large iron, very small to medium lime, very small and small ceramic and very small crystal; no core; hard. *Surface (Interior):* as paste. *(Exterior):* as paste.

PLATE 10

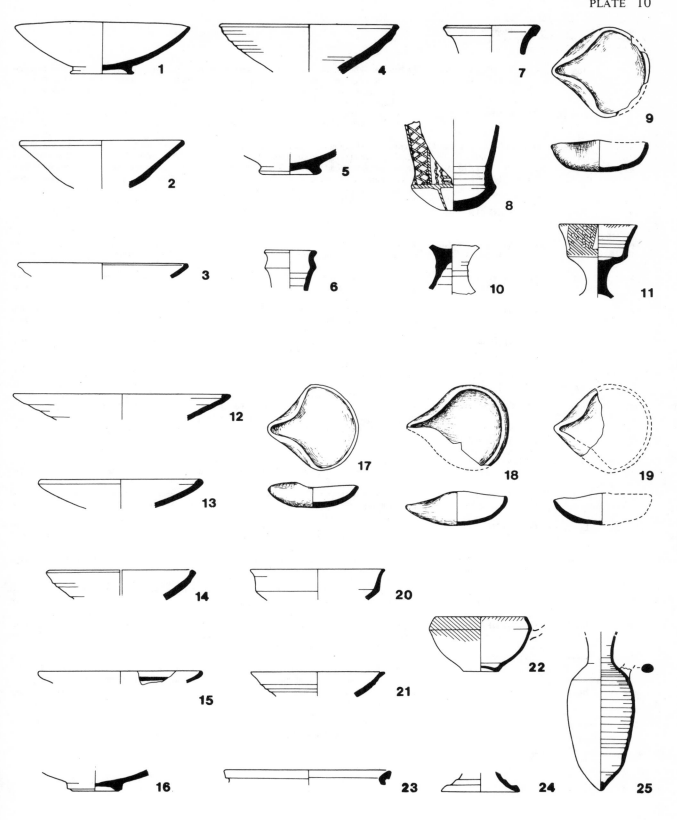

Plate Number	Pottery Type	Number and locus (see LOCUS INDEX)	Description (p. 277)
1.	Jug	G71, VI.NE23.171. No. 1 L. 23046	*Technique:* Wheelmade. *Paste:* 5YR "reddish yellow" 7/6; many very small to small and few medium to large lime, few medium to large wadi gravel, few large organic, few medium ceramic, few very small crystal; dark grey core; hard. *Surface (Interior):* as paste to 1.5YR "pinkish grey" 6/2. *(Exterior):* as paste, 10YR "red" 5/6 organic painted decoration.
2.	Cooking pot	G71, VI.NE34.275, No. 19 L. 34082	*Technique:* Wheelmade. *Paste:* 5YR "light reddish brown" 6/4; some small organic and wadi gravel, few small to large lime and very small crystal; grey core; hard. *Surface (Interior):* as paste. *(Exterior):* as paste.
3.	Bowl	G71, VI.NE34.278, No. 11 L. 34088	*Technique:* Wheelmade. *Paste:* 7.5YR "light brown" 6/4; very many very small wadi gravel and many very small crytal; no core; hard. *Surface (Interior):* 10YR "white" 8/2. *(Exterior):* as interior.
4.	Jar	G71, VI.NE34.270, No. 6 L. 34086	*Technique:* Wheelmade. *Paste:* 5YR "reddish yellow" 7/6; many very small and few medium wadi gravel, some small and large organic, few medium iron, small lime and very large organic, few medium iron, small lime and very small crystal; grey core; hard. *Surface (Interior):* as paste to 7.5YR "pink" 8/4. *(Exterior):* as paste.
5.	Jar	G71, VI.NE34.275, No. 7 L. 34088	*Technique:* Wheelmade. *Paste:* 5YR "pik" 7/4. many very small, few small and medium wadi gravel, few medium lime, small organic and iron; core: 7.5YR "pink" 8/4; hard. *Surface (Interior):* as paste. *(Exterior):* as paste.
6.	Jar	G71, VI.NE34.275, No. 4 L. 34088	*Technique:* Wheelmade. *Paste:* 5YR "pink" 8/4; some small to medium organic, few small and medium lime, very small and small crystal; grey core; hard. *Surface (Interior):* as paste. *(Exterior):* as paste.
7.	Jar	G71, VI.NE34.281, No. 5 L. 34088	*Technique:* Wheelmade. *Paste:* 5YR "reddish yellow" 7/6; very many very small wadi gravel, some medium organic, few medium iron and very small crystal; grey core; hard. *Surface (Interior):* as paste. *(Exterior):* as paste.
8.	Base	G71, VI.NE34.278, No. 9 L. 34088	*Technique:* Wheelmade. *Paste:* 5YR "pink" 7/4; many small to large organic, some very small wadi gravel, few small to large lime, medium iron, very small crystal; grey core; hard. *Surface (Interior):* as paste. *(Exterior):* as paste.
9.	Bowl	G71 VI.NE34.277, No. 2 L. 34088	*Technique:* Wheelmade. *Paste:* 5YR "reddish yellow" 7/6; some very small wadi gravel, few small iron and ceramic, very small and small lime and very small crystal; light grey core; hard. *Surface (Interior):* as paste. *(Exterior):* as paste.
10.	Bowl (Cypriot Monochrome)	G71, VI.NE34.275, No. 14 L. 34088	*Technique:* Handmade? *Paste:* inner: 7.5YR "reddish brown" 4/4; few very small organic, crystal, lime and wadi gravel;no core; metallic. *Surface (Interior):* 7.5YR "brown" 5/4 slip, hand burnish. *(Exterior):* 5YR "very dark grey" 3/1 to 5YR "reddish brown" 5/3 slip, hand burnish.
11.	Base	G71, VI.NE34.270, No. 11 L. 34088	*Technique:* Wheelmade. *Paste:* inner: 7.5YR "pink" 7/4; outer: 2.5YR "light red" 6/6; some very small wadi gravel, very small and large lime, few large iron and very small crystal; no core. *Surface (Interior):* as inner paste. *(Exterior):* as outer paste.
12.	Jar	G71, VI.NE34.278, No. 6 L. 34088	(No description)
13.	Jar	G70, VI.NE23.131, No. 7 L. 23056	*Technique:* Wheelmade. *Paste:* 7.5YR "light brown" 6/4; many small to some large organic, some small to medium iron, very small crystal and wadi gravel, few very small lime; core: 7.5YR "brown" 4/2; hard. *Surface (Interior):* 7.5YR "brown" 5/2. *(Exterior):* as paste.
14.	Jar	G71, VI.NE23.168, No. 7 L. 23-56	*Technique:* Wheelmade. *Paste:* 7.5YR "pinkish white" 8/2; many very small and few large wadi gravel, many very small crystal, some small to medium organic, few large lime; grey core; hard. *Surface (Interior):* as paste. *(Exterior):* as paste.
15.	Bowl	G70, VI.NE23.130, No. 7 L. 23056	*Technique:* Wheelmade. *Paste:* 5YR "reddish yellow" 7/6; many medium and few large wadi gravel, few large lime, small crystal and organic; grey core; hard. *Surface (Interior):* 5YR "pink" 7/4; 2.5YR "light red" 6/6 slip. *(Exterior):* 7.5YR "pink" 7/4.
16.	Bowl	G70,VI.NE23.130, No. 4 L. 23056	*Technique:* Wheelmade. *Paste:* 5YR "pinkish grey" 6/2; some very small wadi gravel, some very small and few small to medium lime, few large iron and very small crystal; no core; hard. *Surface (Interior):* 7.5YR "dark grey" N4/0. *(Exterior):* 7.5YR "pinkish grey" 7/2.
17.	Bowl	G70, VI.NE23.128, No. 7 L. 23056	*Technique:* Wheelmade. *Paste:* 5YR "reddish yellow" 7/6; some very small wadi gravel, few small to large lime, small and large iron and very small crystal; no core; hard. *Surface (Interior):* as pastge to 7.5YR "very dark grey" N3/0. *(Exterior):* as paste to 7.5YR "pinkish grey" 7/2.
18.	Bowl	G70, VI.NE23.131, No. 1 L. 23056	*Technique:* Wheelmade. *Paste:* 5YR "reddish yellow" 7/6; many very small and few large wadi gravel, few small and medium iron, very small to medium lime and very small crystal; light grey core; hard. *Surface (Interior):* as paste. *(Exterior):* as paste.
19.	Bowl	G71, VI.NE23.204, No. 7 L. 23056	*Technique:* Wheelmade. *Paste:* 5YR "reddish yellow" 6/6; some small to large lime, few small organic, few very small crystal; grey core; hard. *Surface (Interior):* as paste; radial burnished. *(Exterior):* as paste; slip on rim as interior; 10YR "red" 5/6 slip and wheel burnishing on rim.
20.	Bowl	G70, VI.NE23.129, No. 1 L. 23056	*Technique:* Wheelmade. *Paste:* 5YR "reddish yellow" 7/6; some very small wadi gravel, some very small and few small to large lime, few small and medium lime and very small crystal; grey core; hard. *Surface (Interior):* as paste. *(Exterior):* as paste.
21.	Cooking pot	G70, VI.NE23.130, No. 3 L. 23056	*Technique:* Wheelmade. *Paste:* 5YR "reddish brown" 5/3; some very small and few small wadi gravel, few very small to medium crystal, medium ceramic, small orgnaic; no core; hard. *Surface (Interior):* as paste. *(Exterior):* as paste.

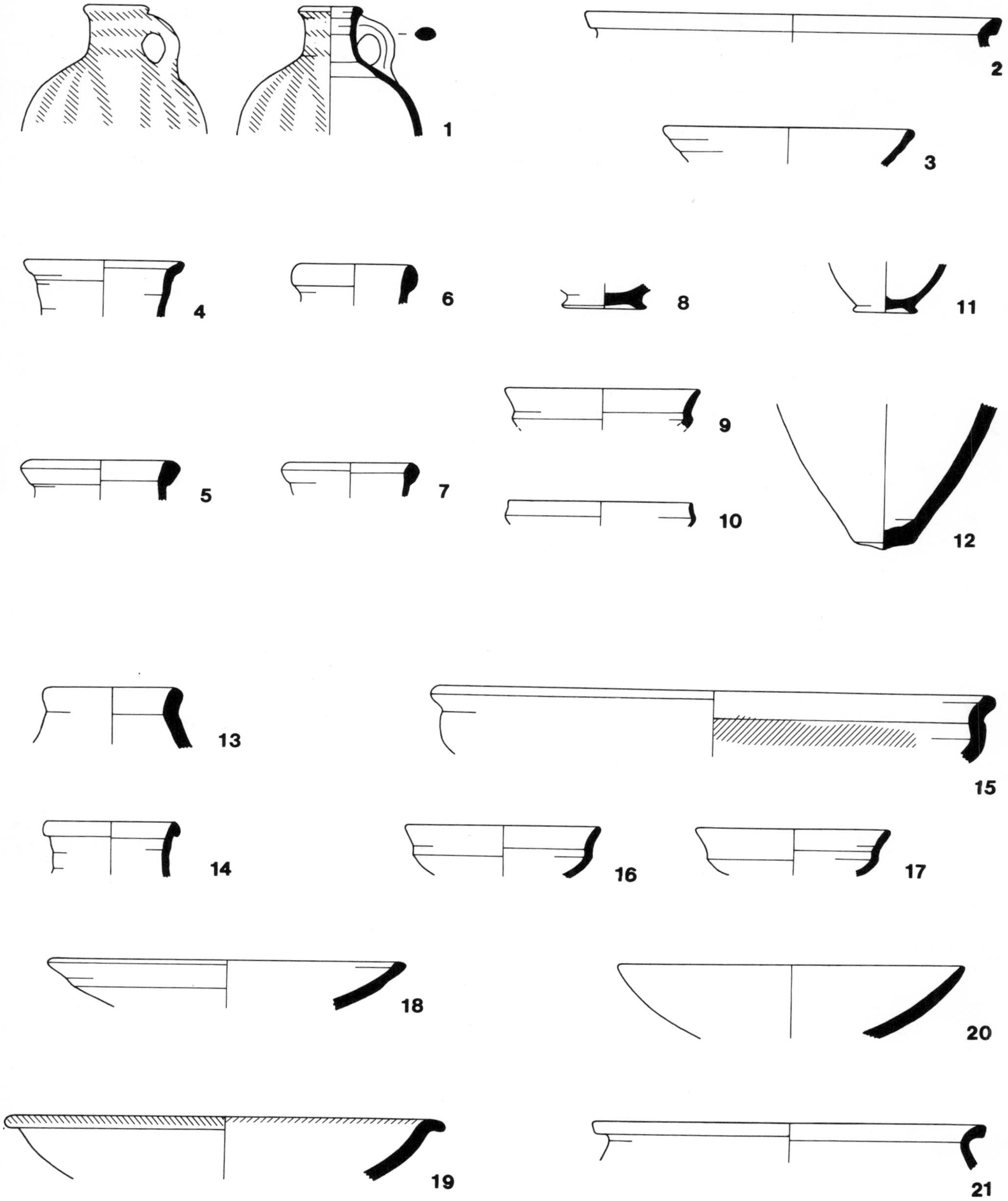
1
2
3
4
5
6
7
8
9
10
11
12
13
14
15
16
17
18
19
20
21

Plate Number	Pottery Type	Number and locus (see LOCUS INDEX)	Description (p. 277)
1.	Jar	G71, VI.NE23.169, No. 11 L. 23056	*Technique:* Wheelmade. *Paste:* 7.5YR "pink 7/4; many small to medium lime and calcite; grey core; hard. *Surface (Interior):* as paste. *(Exterior):* as paste.
2.	Jar	G70, VI.NE23.129, No. 8 L. 23056	*Technique:* Wheelmade. *Paste:* 7.5YR "pink 7/4; many small to medium lime and calcite; grey core; hard. *Surface (Interior):* as paste. *(Exterior):* as paste.
3.	Base	G70, VI.NE23.136, No. 1 L. 23056	*Technique:* Wheelmade. *Paste:* 7.5YR "pink"7/4; many small to medium lime and calcite; grey core; hard. *Surface (Interior):* as paste. *(Exterior):* as paste.
4.	Bowl	G70, VI.NE23.140, No. 7 L. 23056	*Technique:* Wheelmade. *Paste:* 5YR "reddish grey" 5/2; many small to medium lime; no core; hard. *Surface (Interior):* as paste. *(Exterior):* as paste.
5.	Bowl	G70, VI.NE23.140, No. 11 L. 23056	*Technique:* Wheelmade. *Paste:* 10YR "very pale brown" 7/4; many small to medium lime; slight grey core; hard. *Surface (Interior):* as paste. *(Exterior):* as paste.
6.	Bowl	G70, VI.NE23.135, No. 3 L. 23056	*Technique:* Wheelmade. *Paste:* 7.5YR "light brown" 6/6; many small to medium lime and calcite; grey core; hard. *Surface (Interior):* as paste. *(Exterior):* as paste.
7.	Cooking pot	G70, VI.NE23.140, No. 1 L. 23056	*Technique:* Wheelmade. *Paste:* 7.5YR "brown" 5/4; many medium to large white lime and grey wadi gravel; grey–black core; hard. *Surface (Interior):* 7.5YR "light brown" 6/4. *(Exterior):* as paste.
8.	Cooking pot	G70, VI.NE23.172, No. 3	*Technique:* Wheelmade. *Paste:* 5YR "reddish brown" 5/4; many medium to large white lime and grey wadi gravel, grey-black core; hard. *Surface (Interior):* 5YR "reddish brown" 5/4. *(Exterior):* as interior.
9.	Miniature pot (votive?)	G71, VI.NE24.371, No. 1 L. 24132	*Technique:* Wheelmade. *Paste:* 2.5YR "light red" 6/6; some to many small to medium and few large lime, few medium to large ceramic and wadi gravel and some very small to small crystal; no core; hard. *Surface (Interior):* as paste to 5YR "dark reddish brown" 3/2 on lip. *(Exterior):* as interior.
10.	Pithos	G71, VI.NE23.166, No. 4 L. 23049	*Technique:* Wheelmade. *Paste:* 7.5YR "pink" 7/4; many small to medium lime and calcite; grey core; hard. *Surface (Interior):* as paste. *(Exterior):* as paste.
11.	Jar	G71, VI.NE23.169, No. 14 L. 23049	*Technique:* Wheelmade. *Paste:* 7.5YR "pink" 7/4; many small to medium lime and calcite; grey core; hard. *Surface (Interior):* as paste. *(Exterior):* as paste.
12.	Jar	G71, VI.NE23.169, No. 13 L. 23049	*Technique:* Wheelmade. *Paste:* 7.5YR "pink" 7/4; many small to medium lime and calcite; grey core; hard. *Surface (Interior):* as paste. *(Exterior):* as paste.
13.	Cooking pot	G70, VI.NE23.169, No. 12 L. 23049	*Technique:* Wheelmade. *Paste:* 10YR "very pale brown" 7/4; many small to medium lime; slight grey core; hard. *Surface (Interior):* as paste. *(Exterior):* as paste.
14.	Bowl	G70, VI.NE23.127, No. 5 L. 23049	*Technique:* Wheelmade. *Paste:* 7.5YR "light brown" 6/6; many small to medium lime and calcite; grey core; hard. *Surface (Interior):* as paste. *(Exterior):* as paste.
15.	Bowl	G70, VI.NE23.165, No. 10 L. 23049	*Technique:* Wheelmade. *Paste:* 7.5YR "light brown" 6/6; many small to medium lime and calcite; grey core; hard. *Surface (Interior):* as paste; sporadic burnishing. *(Exterior):* as paste.
16.	Bowl	G70, VI.NE23.133, No. 1 L. 23049	*Technique:* Wheelmade. *Paste:* 7.5YR "light brown" 6/6; many small to medium lime and calcite; grey core; hard. *Surface (Interior):* as paste. *(Exterior):* as paste.
17.	Bowl	G70, VI.NE23.124, No. 7 L. 23049	*Technique:* Wheelmade. *Paste:* 7.5YR "reddish yellow" 7/6; many medium to large lime, calcite and wadi gravel; grey core; hard. *Surface (Interior):* as paste. *(Exterior):* as paste to mottled 10YR "very pale brown" 8/3.
18.	Jug	G71, VI.NE23.169, No. 1 L. 23049	*Technique:* Wheelmade. *Paste:* 2.5YR "white" 8/2; many small to medium lime and calcite; slight grey core; very hard. *Surface (Interior):* as paste. *(Exterior):* as paste.
19.	Cooking pot	G71, VI.NE25.300, No. 12 L. 25112	*Technique:* Wheelmade. *Paste:* 5YR "reddish brown" 5/4; some very small to medium and few large lime, few small to large wadi gravel and very small crystal; dark grey core; hard. *Surface (Interior):* as paste. *(Exterior):* as paste.
20.	Krater	G71, VI.NE25.267, No. 4 L. 25112	*Technique:* Wheelmade. *Paste:* 2.5YR "light red" 6/0; very many small lime, few medium organic and small ceramic; grey core; hard. *Surface (Interior):* as paste. *(Exterior):* 10YR "white" 8/2; slip raised band of incised rope decoration on rim; incised leaf decoration on body; burnish.
21.	Jar	G71, VI.NE23.251, No. 4 L. 25112	*Technique:* Wheelmade. *Paste:* 2.5YR "red" gravel and very small crystal; core: 7.5YR "brown" 5/4; hard. *Surface (Interior):* as paste. *(Exterior):* as paste.
22.	Cooking pot	G71, VI.NE25.307, No. 13 L. 25112	*Technique:* Wheelmade. *Paste:* 5YR "reddish brown" 5/3; some medium and large wadi gravel, few small to large lime and very small crystal; dark grey core; hard. *Surface (Interior):* as paste. *(Exterior):* as paste.

PLATE 12

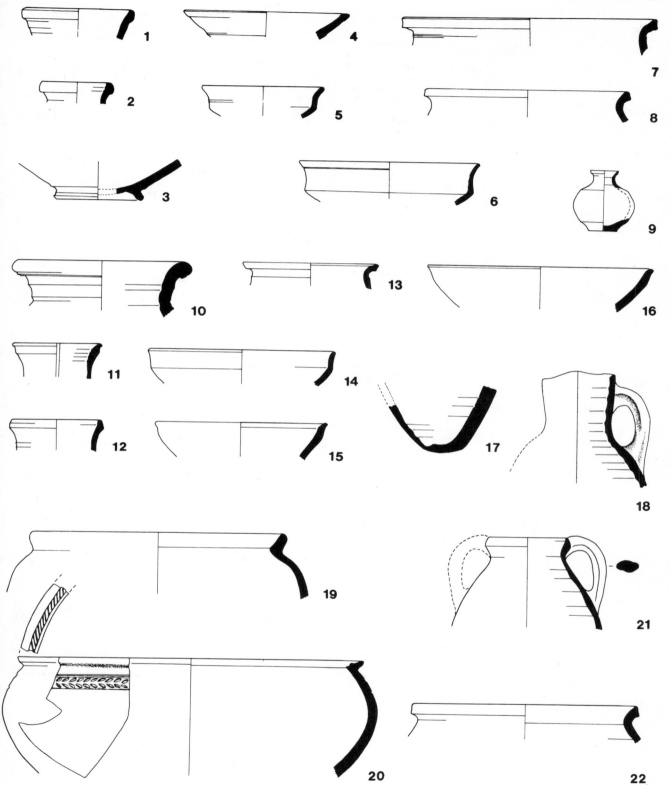

Plate Number	Pottery Type	Number and locus (see LOCUS INDEX)	Description (p. 277)
1.	Jar	G71, VI.NE25.300, No. 11 L. 25112	*Technique:* Wheelmade. *Paste:* 5YR "reddish yellow" 6/6; few large organic, very small to large lime, small wadi gravel and very small crystal; core: 5YR "dark reddish grey" 4/2; hard. *Surface (Interior):* as paste. *(Exterior):* as paste.
2.	Jar	G71, VI.NE25.307, No. 5 L. 25112	*Technique:* Wheelmade. *Paste:* 5YR "yellowish red" 5/6; some very small and few small to large lime, few small to large wadi gravel; no core; hard. *Surface (Interior):* as paste. *(Exterior):* as paste.
3.	Jar	G71, VI.NE25.315, No. 26 L. 25112	*Technique:* Wheelmade. *Paste:* 5YR "pink" 7/4; few very small to medium lime, small and medium wadi gravel and very small crystal; grey core; *Surface (Interior):* as paste. *(Exterior):* as paste to 5YR "reddish grey" 5/2.
4.	Jar	G71, VI.NE25.312, No. 28 L. 25112	*Technique:* Wheelmade. *Paste:* 7.5YR "light brown" 6/4; many very small and few medium lime, few medium ceramic and wadi gravel and very small crystal; light grey core; hard. *Surface (Interior):* as paste to 7.5YR "pink" 7/4. *(Exterior):* as interior.
5.	Jar	G71, VI.NE25.300, No. 6 L. 25112	*Technique:* Wheelmade. *Paste:* 7.5YR "light brown" 6/4; many very small and few medium lime, few medium ceramic and wadi gravel and very small crystal; light grey core; hard. *Surface (Interior):* as paste to 7.5YR "pink" 7/4. *(Exterior):* as interior.
6.	Jar	G71, VI.NE25.316, No. 2 L. 25112	*Technique:* Wheelmade. *Paste:* inner: 5YR "light reddish brown" 6/4; outer: 2.5YR "red" 5/6; some medium and few small and large lime, few small and medium wadi gravel and very small crystal; no core; hard. *Surface (Interior):* as inner and outer paste. *(Exterior):* as outer paste.
7.	Base	G71, VI.NE25.315, No. 1 L. 25112	*Technique:* Wheelmade. *Paste:* 7.5YR "light brown" 6/4; few small to large lime, large wadi gravel and medium ceramic; grey core; hard. *Surface (Interior):* as paste to 7.5YR "very dark grey" 3/2. *(Exterior):* as interior.
8.	Base	G71, VI.NE25.282, No. 11 L. 25112	*Technique:* Wheelmade. *Paste:* 2.5YR "red" 5/6; few large organic, small to large lime, very small and medium wadi gravel and very small crystal; grey core; hard. *Surface (Interior):* 7.5YR "light brown" 6/4. *(Exterior):* as paste.
9.	Cooking pot	G71, VI.NE25.312, No. 11 L. 25112	*Technique:* Wheelmade. *Paste:* 2.5YR "reddish brown" 4/4; few small to large lime, medium and large wadi gravel and very small crystal; grey core; hard. *Surface (Interior):* as paste. *(Exterior):* as paste.
10.	Cooking pot	G71, VI.NE25.306, No. 3 L. 25112	*Technique:* Wheelmade. *Paste:* 5YR "reddish brown" 5/4; few large and medium organic, very small to large lime, very small and small ceramic and very small crystal; dark grey core; hard. *Surface (Interior):* as paste. *(Exterior):* as paste.
11.	Krater	G71, VI.NE25.307, No. 21 L. 25112	*Technique:* Wheelmade. *Paste:* 5YR "reddish brown" 5/4; few large organic, small to large wadi gravel and small to medium lime; grey core; hard. *Surface (Interior):* as paste. *(Exterior):* as paste.
12.	Krater	G71, VI.NE25.300, No. 10 L. 25112	*Technique:* Wheelmade. *Paste:* 7.5YR "pink" 7/4; some very small wadi gravel, few small and large lime, small and medium organic and very small crystal; light grey core; hard. *Surface (Interior):* as paste. *(Exterior):* as paste.
13.	Bowl	G71, VI.NE25.312, No. 7 L. 25112	*Technique:* Wheelmade. *Paste:* 5YR "light reddish brown" 6/4; some very small and few medium lime, few very small wadi gravel, ceramic and crystal; grey core; hard. *Surface (Interior):* 5YR "very dark grey" 3/1; wheel brunish. *(Exterior):* as paste to 5YR "dark reddish brown" 3/2.
14.	Bowl	G71, VI.NE25.267, No. 5 L. 25112	*Technique:* Wheelmade. *Paste:* 2.5YR "light red" 6/8; few very small to large wadi gravel and lime, very small ceramic and crystal; grey core; hard. *Surface (Interior):* as paste. *(Exterior):* as paste.
15.	Bowl	G71, VI.NE25.312, No. 14 L. 25112	*Technique:* Wheelmade. *Paste:* 7.5YR "pink" 7/4; some very small and medium wadi gravel, few small and medium ceramic, very small and medium crystal and small lime; grey core; hard. *Surface (Interior):* as paste; wheel burnish. *(Exterior):* 7.5YR "pinkish grey" 6/2.
16.	Bowl	G71, VI.NE25.307, No. 9 L. 25112	*Technique:* Wheelmade. *Paste:* 5YR "reddish yellow" 6/6; few very small and large wadi gravel, small to large lime and very small crystal; no core; hard. *Surface (Interior):* as paste. *(Exterior):* as paste.
17.	Bowl	G71, VI.NE25.300, No. 8 L. 25112	*Technique:* Wheelmade. *Paste:* 5YR "reddish yellow" 6/6; few small to large lime, small and medium wadi gravel and small and very small crystal; grey core; *Surface (Interior):* as paste. *(Exterior):* as paste.
18.	Bowl	G71, VI.NE.307, No. 40 L. 25112	*Technique:* Wheelmade. *Paste:* 7.5YR "light brown" 6/4; few very small and small wadi gravel, crystal and lime; grey core; hard. *Surface (Interior):* as paste. *(Exterior):* as paste.
19.	Bowl	G71, VI.NE25.286, No. 7 L. 25112	*Technique:* Wheelmade. *Paste:* 7.5YR "pink" 8/4; some very small and few small lime, some very small wadi gravel; no core; hard. *Surface (Interior):* 2.5YR "light red" 6/6. *(Exterior):* 7.5YR "pink" 7/4 to 7.5YR "pinkish white" 8/2.
20.	Bowl	G71, VI.NE25.283, No. 22 L. 25112	*Technique:* Wheelmade. *Paste:* 5YR "reddish yellow" 6/6; few very small to large wadi gravel, small to large lime and very small crystal; light grey core; hard. *Surface (Interior):* as paste. *(Exterior):* as paste.
21.	Lamp	G71, VI.NE13.175, No. 3 L. 13042	*Technique:* Wheelmade. *Paste:* 10YR "very pale brown" 7/3; few medium to large wadi gravel, few medium lime and small organic, some small crystal; dark grey core; hard. *Surface (Interior):* as paste. *(Exterior):* as paste.

PLATE 13

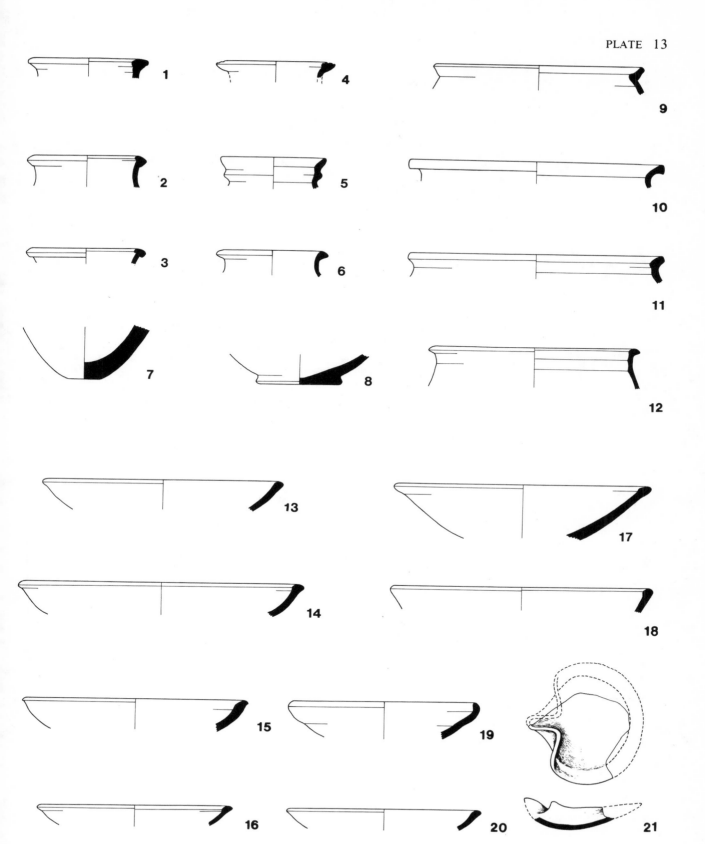

Plate Number	Pottery Type	Number and locus (see LOCUS INDEX)	Description (p. 277)
1.	Cooking pot	G70, VI.NE3.129, L. 3048	*Technique:* Wheelmade. *Paste:* 5YR "yellowish red" 5/6; many small crystal (quartz), few large limestone; no core; hard. *Surface (Interior):* as paste. *(Exterior):* as paste.
2.	Bowl	G70, VI.NE3.129, No. 9 L. 3048	*Technique:* Wheelmade. *Paste:* 5YR "pink" 7.4/ many small crystal (quartz); no core; hard. *Surface (Interior):* as paste. *(Exterior):* as paste.
3.	Krater	G71, VI.NE14.284, L. 14090	*Technique:* Wheelmade. *Paste:* 5YR "yellowish red" 5/8; some large organic, some very small to few large lime, few very small sand; dark grey core; hard. *Surface (Interior):* 10YR "very pale brown" 7/3. *(Exterior):* 5YR "pink" 8/3 to 5YR "light reddish brown" 6/4.
4.	Bowl	G71, VI.NE14.240, No. 2 L. 14090	*Technique:* Wheelmade. *Paste:* 2.5YR "red" 5/6 to 5YR "reddish yellow" 6/6; some to many very small crystal and lime, some small organic, few medium to large ceramic and lime; grey core; hard. *Surface (Interior):* 5YR "pink" 7/4 to 7.5YR "pinkish white" 8/2. *(Exterior):* as paste.
5.	Bowl	G71, VI.NE15.211, No. 7 L. 15158	*Technique:* Wheelmade. *Paste:* 7.5YR "pink" 8/4; many very small wadi gravel, few small iron, ceramic and lime; grey core; hard. *Surface (Interior):* 10YR "very pale brown" 8/4; wheel burnish on rim. *(Exterior):* as interior.
6.	Bowl (Imitation White Slip II)		*Technique:* Wheelmade. *Paste:* 5YR "pink" 7/4; some small and few large lime, few small ceramic and very small crystal; light grey ware; hard. *Surface (Interior):* as paste; wheel burnish. *(Exterior):* 10YR "white" 8/2 slip and 5YR "reddish brown" 4/3 organic paint decoration; wheel burnish.
7.	Jar	G71, VI.NE24.365, No. 9 L. 24098	*Technique:* Wheelmade. *Paste:* 2.5YR "light reddish brown" 6/4; very few tiny lime grits; no core; hard. *Surface (Interior):* as paste. *(Exterior):* as paste.
8.	Cooking pot	G71, VI.NE24.720. No. 10 L. 24098	*Technique:* Wheelmade. *Paste:* 7.5YR "light brown" 6/4; some small organic, few medium to large lime, small and very lage lime and very small crystal; dark grey core; hard. *Surface (Interior):* as paste. *(Exterior):* as paste.
9.	Dipper juglet (White Shaved)	G7., VI.NE24.270, No. 2 L. 24098	*Technique:* Wheelmade. *Paste:* 5YR "reddish brown" 5/3; some very small wadi gravel and lime, few medium ceramic, very small crystal and organic; no core; hard. *Surface (Interior):* as paste. *(Exterior):* 10YR "very pale brown" 7/3; knifeshaved.
10,	Chalice	G71, VI.NE24.311, No. 3 L. 24098	*Technique:* Wheelmade. *Paste:* 7.5YR "pinkish-white" 8/2; many small to medium lime grits; slight grey core; hard. *Surface (Interior):* as paste. *(Exterior):* as paste; 2.5YR "red" 5/6 paint.
11.	Bowl	G71, VI.NE24.270, No. 4 L. 24098	*Technique:* Wheelmade. *Paste:* 7.5YR "light reddish brown" 6/4; many very small wadi gravel, few large organic, small to large iron, small lime and ceramic crystal; light grey core; hard. *Surface (Interior):* as paste. *(Exterior):* as paste; wheel burnish below carination.
12.	Bowl	G71, VI.NE24.256, No. 8 L. 24098	*Technique:* Wheelmade. *Paste:* 7.5YR "light brown" 6/4; some small to medium organic, few to some very small to small crystal and lime, few medium ceramic; grey core; hard. *Surface (Interior):* as paste. *(Exterior):* as paste.
13.	Base	G71, VI.NE24.270, No. 7 L. 24098	*Technique:* Wheelmade. *Paste:* 7.5YR "reddish yellow" 8/56; many very small wadi gravel, few small organic and very large lime; no core; hard. *Surface (Interior):* 7.5YR "pinkish grey" 7/2. *(Exterior):* as paste; wet-smoothed.
14.	Krater	G71, VI.NE24.311, Nos. 5, 13, L. 24098	*Technique:* Wheelmade. *Paste:* 7.5YR "pinkish-white" 8/2; many small to medium lime grits; slight grey core; hard. *Surface (Interior):* as paste. *(Exterior):* as paste.
15.	Krater	G71, VI.NE24.283, No. 4 L. 24127	*Technique:* Wheelmade. *Paste:* 7.5YR "pinkish white" 8/2; some very small and large lime and wadi gravel, few very small and small ceramic; no core; hard. *Surface (Interior):* as paste. *(Exterior):* as paste.
16.	Bowl	G71, VI.NE24.280, No. 3 L. 24127	*Technique:* Wheelmade. *Paste:* 7YR "pink" 7/6; few large iron, very small to large lime, very small to medium ceramic, very small and small wadi gravel and very small crystal; light grey core; hard. *Surface (Interior):* as paste. *(Exterior):* as paste.
17.	Krater	G71, VI.NE24.291, No. 2 L. 24127	*Technique:* Wheelmade. *Paste:* 5YR "reddish hellow" 7/6; few large organic and iron, very small to large lime, medium ceramic, very small to medium wadi gravel and very small crystal; grey core; hard. *Surface (Interior):* as paste. *(Exterior):* 7.5YR "pinkish white" 8/2; vertical burnish; horizontal burnish.
18.	Goblet/ Chalice	G871, VI.NE24.329, No. 8 L. 24135	*Technique:* Wheelmade. *Paste:* 5YR "reddish yellow" 7/6; some small organic and very small wadi gravel and crystal, few medium to large lime, large iron and medium ceramic; dark grey; hard. *Surface (Interior):* as paste. *(Exterior):* as paste; 5YR "dark reddish grey" 4/2 and 10YR "red" 4/6 organic paint decoration.
19.	Jar	G71, VI.NE34.279, No. 6 L. 34086	*Technique:* Wheelmade. *Paste:* 7.6YR "pinkish white" 8/2; many small to medium lime grits; slight grey core; hard. *Surface (Interior):* as paste. *(Exterior):* as paste; 2.5YR "red" 5/6 paint.

PLATE 14

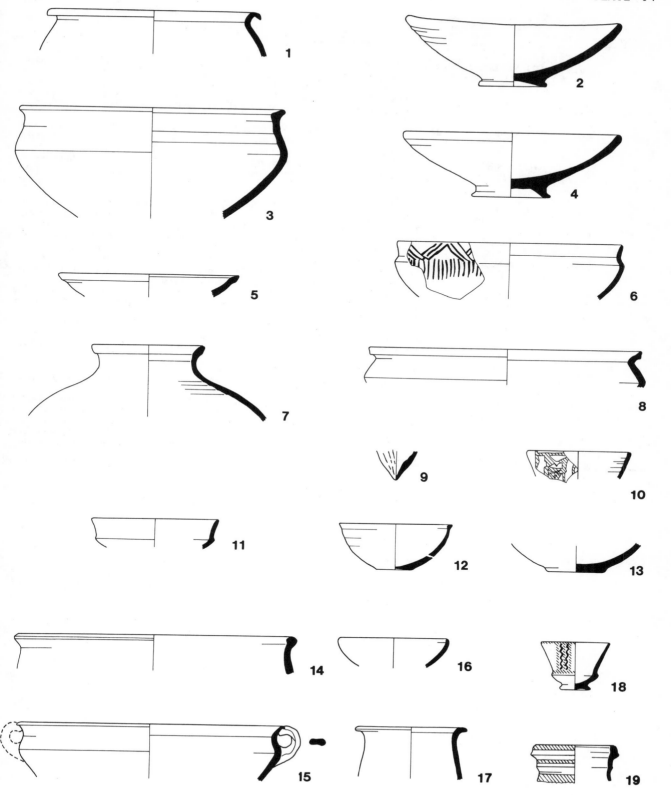

Plate Number	Pottery Type	Number and locus (see LOCUS INDEX)	Description (p. 277)
1.	Jar	G71, VI.NE25.311, No. 2 L. 25097	*Technique:* Wheelmade. *Paste:* 5YR "reddish brown" 4/4; some small and few medium to large lime, few medium to large wadi gravel, small ceramic, and very small crystal; grey core; hard. *Surface (Interior):* a paste. *(Exterior):* 10YR "light grey" 7/2.
2.	Bowl	G71, VI.NE25.266, No. 26 L. 25097	*Technique:* Wheelmade. *Paste:* 7.5YR "light brown" 6/4; many very small crystal, few small ceramic and organic and medium wadi gravel; grey core; hard. *Surface (Interior):* as paste. *(Exterior):* as paste.
3.	Bowl	G71, VI.NE25.264, No. 24 L. 25097	*Technique:* Wheelmade. *Paste:* 5YR "reddish brown" 4/4; many very small to few medium crystal, few medium organic and large lime; dark grey core; hard. *Surface (Interior):* 5YR "yellowish red" 5/6; wheel burnish. *(Exterior):* as interior.
4.	Krater	G71, VI.NE25.269, No. 1 L. 25097	*Technique:* Wheelmade. *Paste:* 5YR "reddish yellow" 6/6; some small and few medium lime, few small ceramic and very small crystal; core: 7.5YR "light brown" 6/4; hard. *Surface (Interior):* 10YR "very pale brown" 8/3 slip. *(Exterior):* as interior and bands of 5YR "dark reddish grey" 4/2 organic paint.
5.	Juglet	G71, VI.NE25.269, No. 22 L. 25097	*Technique:* Wheelmade. *Paste:* 2.5YR "light red" 6/6; few small lime, organic and crystal; no core; hard. *Surface (Interior):* as paste. *(Exterior):* 10YR "very pale brown" 7/3 slip; hand burnish.
6.	Base	G71, VI.NE26.272, No. 5 L. 26086	*Technique:* Wheelmade. *Paste:* 5YR "reddish yellow" 7/6; some very small and few small to large lime, few large wadi gravel and organic, small to large ceramic; grey core; hard. *Surface (Interior):* as paste. *(Exterior):* as paste.
7.	Bowl	G71, VI.NE26.262, No. 2 L. 26086	*Technique:* Wheelmade. *Paste:* 5YR "pink" 7/4; some very small crystal, some very small and few small and medium lime, few large iron and wadi gravel, small to large ceramic, and small organic; grey core; hard. *Surface (Interior):* as paste. *(Exterior):* as paste.
8.	Bowl	G71, VI.NE26.262A, No. 1 L. 26086	*Technique:* Wheelmade. *Paste:* 7.5YR "light brown" 6/4; many very small crystal, few small to large lime, few small wadi grvel, few medium ceramic, few small and large organic; light grey core; hard. *Surface (Interior):* as paste. *(Exterior):* as paste.
9.	Krater	G71, VI.NE26.272, No. 2 L. 26086	*Technique:* Wheelmade. *Paste:* 5YR "reddish yellow" 7/6; some very small and few small to medium lime, few large iron, very small to large ceramic, medium organic and very small crystal; grey core; hard. *Surface (Interior):* as paste. *(Exterior):* as paste, 7.5YR "pinkish white" 8/2 and 5YR "grey" 5/1.
10.	Krater	G71, VI.NE26.231, No. 1 L. 26086	*Technique:* Wheelmade. *Paste:* 10YR "white" 8/2; few very small and medium to large lime, very small sand, small organic and small to large ceramic; no core; hard. *Surface (Interior):* as paste. *(Exterior):* as paste.
11.	Goblet/ Chalice	G71, VI.NE34.321, No. 1 L. 34086	*Technique:* Wheelmade. *Paste:* inner: 7.5YR "pink" 8/4; outer: 5YR "reddish yellow" 9/6; few small and medium lime, small organic, very small wadi gravel and crystal; grey core; hard. *Surface (Interior):* as outer paste. *(Exterior):* as outer paste; 10YR "red" 4/6 organic paint decoration.
12.	Jar	G70, VI.N34.175, No. 1 L. 34072P	*Technique:* Wheelmade. *Paste:* 5YR "reddish yellow" 7/6; some very small and few small to large lime, few large wadi gravel and organic, small to large ceramic; grey core; hard. *Surface (Interior):* as paste. *(Exterior):* as paste.

PLATE 15

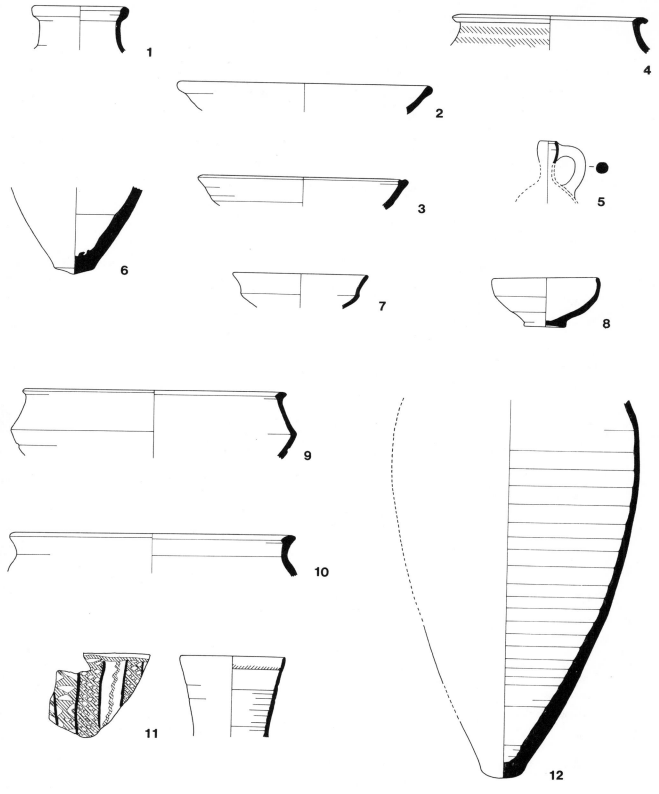

Plate Number	Pottery Type	Number and locus (see LOCUS INDEX)	Description (p. 277)
1.	Jar	G71, VI.NE34.285, No. 1 L. 34086	*Technique:* Wheelmade. *Paste:* 5YR "reddish yellow" 6/6; some very small wadi gravel, few small to large lime, small organic and very small crystal; no core; hard. *Surface (Interior):* as paste. *(Exterior):* as paste.
2.	Jar	G71, VI.NE34.308, No. 17 L. 34086	*Technique:* Wheelmade. *Paste:* 5YR "reddish yellow" 7/6; many very small and few medium wadi gravel, few medium iron, small and medium lime and ceramic and very small crystal; no core; hard. *Surface (Interior):* as paste. *(Exterior):* as paste.
3.	Jar	G71, VI.NE34.260, No. 10 L. 34086	*Technique:* Wheelmade. *Paste:* 5YR "grey" 5/1; some small organic and very small lime, few very large iron and small wadi gravel and ceramic; no core; hard. *Surface (Interior):* 7.5YR "light brown" 6/4. *(Exterior):* as interior.
4.	Jar	G71, VI.NE34.303, No. 15 L. 34086	*Technique:* Wheelmade. *Paste:* 5YR "reddish yellow" 7/6; some very small and few small to large lime, few to some very small wadi gravel and few very small crystal; grey core; hard. *Surface (Interior):* as paste. *(Exterior):* as paste.
5.	Jar	G71, VI.NE34.209, No. 1 L. 34086	*Technique:* Wheelmade. *Paste:* 5YR "light reddish brown" 6/4; some very small wadi gravel, few very small to large lime, few very small ceramci and crystal; light grey core; hard. *Surface (Interior):* as paste. *(Exterior):* 10YR "white" 8/2; bands of 10YR "weak red" 4/4 organic paint.
6.	Jar	G71, VI.NE34.265, No. 14 L. 34086	*Technique:* Wheelmade. *Paste:* 7.5YR "light brown" 6/4; some very small and few medium lime, few small to large ceramic, very small and medium wadi gravel, and very small crystal; grey core; hard. *Surface (Interior):* as paste. *(Exterior):* as paste; bands of 10YR "weak red" 4/4 and 10YR "dark reddish grey" 3/1 organic paint; wheel burnish on rim.
7.	Jar	G71, VI.NE34.295, No. 6 L. 34086	*Technique:* Wheelmade. *Paste:* 2.5YR "light red" 6/6; some very small organic, few very small wadi gravel and crystal; core: 10YR "very pale brown" 7/3; hard. *Surface (Interior):* 5YR "reddish yellow" 7/6. *(Exterior):* as interior.
8.	Base	G71, VI.NE34.314, No. 1 L. 34086	*Technique:* Wheelmade. *Paste:* 5YR "reddish yellow" 7/6; some very small wadi gravel, few medium ceramic and iron, small to large organic, very small and small crystal; grey core; hard. *Surface (Interior):* as paste. *(Exterior):* as paste.
9.	Bowl	G71, VI.NE34.253, No. 1 L. 34086	*Technique:* Wheelmade. *Paste:* 5YR "reddish yellow" 7/6; some small organic and very small wadi gravel, few small and medium lime and medium iron; light grey core; hard. *Surface (Interior):* as paste. *(Exterior):* as paste.
10.	Bowl	G71, VI.NE34.314, No. 12 L. 34086	*Technique:* Wheelmade. *Paste:* 7.5YR "light brown" 6/4; few small to large lime, medium wadi gravel and iron, small organic and very small crystal; dark grey core; hard. *Surface (Interior):* as paste. *(Exterior):* as paste.
11.	Bowl	G71, VI.NE34.325, No. 5 L. 34086	*Technique:* Wheelmade. *Paste:* 5YR "pink" '7/4; few small and large organic, few very small and small lime, small ceramic and very small wadi gravel and crystal; grey core; hard. *Surface (Interior):* as paste. *(Exterior):* as paste.
12.	Bowl	G71, VI.NE34.253, No. 20 L. 34086	*Technique:* Wheelmade. *Paste:* 2.5YR "light red" 6/8; some small lime and very small organic and crystal; grey core; hard. *Surface (Interior):* as paste to as exterior. *(Exterior):* 5YR "pinkish white" 8/2.
13.	Bowl	G71, VI.NE34.260, No. 3 L. 34086	*Technique:* Wheelmade. *Paste:* 5YR "reddish yellow" 7/6; some very small and few small and medium lime, few small and medium ceramic, and very small wadi gravel and crystal; no core; hard. *Surface (Interior):* as paste. *(Exterior):* as paste.
14.	Bowl	G71, VI.NE34.302, No. 5 L. 34086	*Technique:* Wheelmade. *Paste:* 5YR "reddish yellow" 6/6; few very small to medium lime, wadi gravel and crystal; grey core; hard. *Surface (Interior):* as paste; 10YR "red" 5/6 slip on rim. *(Exterior):* as paste; slip on rim as interior.
15.	Bowl (White Slip II)	G71, VI.NE34.253 L. 34086	*Technique:* Handmade. *Paste:* 5YR "reddish brown" 5/4; many very small and small lime, some small organic, few very small crystal; 7.5YR "grey" 6/0; metallic. *Surface (Interior):* 10YR "dark greyish brown" 4/2 slip; hand burnish. *(Exterior):* 10YR "pale brown" 6/3 slip; hand burnish; 5YR "dark reddish brown" 3/3 organic paint decoration.
16.	Bowl (White Slip II)	G71, VI.NE34.253 L. 34086	*Technique:* Wheelmade. *Paste:* Handmade. *Paste:* 5YR "reddish brown" 5/4; many very small and small lime, some small organic, few very small crystal; 7.5YR "grey" 6/0; metallic. *Surface (Interior):* 10YR "dark greyish brown" 4/2 slip; hand burnish. *(Exterior):* 10YR "pale brown" 6/3 slip; hand burnish; 5YR "dark reddish brown" 3/3 organic paint decoration.
17.	Krater	G70, VI.NE35.117, No. 6 L. 35035	*Technique:* Handmade? *Paste:* inner: 5YR "reddish brown" 4/4; outer: 10YR "white" 8/1 (thick layer of slip?); some very small organic few very small crystal and lime; core: 7.5YR "grey" 5/0; metallic. *Surface (Interior):* 2.5YR "very dark grey"; 3.0 slip; hand burnish. *(Exterior):* slip as interior; hand burnish; 5YR "light reddish brown" 6/4 lozenge – small square decoration in reserve slip technique.
18.	Jar	G71, VI.NE35.368, No. 7 L. 35069	*Technique:* Wheelmade. *Paste:* 5YR "reddish brown" 4/4; few very small to large lime, medium and very small crystal, and small ceramic; grey core; hard. *Surface (Interior):* as paste to 5YR "dark grey" 4/1. *(Exterior):* as interior.
19.	Jar	G71, VI.NE35.366, No. 14 L. 35069	*Technique:* Wheelmade. *Paste:* 2.5YR "light red" 6/6; some very small lime and wadi gravel, few small ceramic and very small crystal; grey core; hard. *Surface (Interior):* as paste to 2.5YR "grey" N5/0. *(Exterior):* as paste.
20.	Base	G71, VI.NE35.354, No. 6 L. 35069	*Technique:* Wheelmade. *Paste:* 5YR "light reddish brown" 6/4; some very small and few small to large lime, few small and very small crystal; no core; hard. *Surface (Interior):* as paste. *(Exterior):* as paste.
21.	Cooking pot	G71, VI.NE35.352, No. 6 L. 35069	*Technique:* Wheelmade. *Paste:* 2.5YR "light red" 6/6; some small organic and very small crystal, few small and some medium lime; grey core; hard. *Surface (Interior):* as paste. *(Exterior):* as paste.
22.	Krater	G71, VI.NE25.346, No. 6 L. 35069	*Technique:* Wheelmade. *Paste:* 10YR "white" 8/2; few medium iron, very small to medium lime and ceramic, and very small wadi gravel; no core; hard. *Surface (Interior):* as paste. *(Exterior):* as paste.
23.	Baking tray	G71, VI.NE35.378, No. 1 L. 35069	*Technique:* Wheelmade. *Paste:* inner: 5YR "reddish yellow" 7/6; outer: 2.5YR "light red" 6/6; some medium and few large wadi gravel, few small to large lime; no core; hard. *Surface (Interior):* as outer paste to 5YR "dark grey" 4/1. *(Exterior):* as outer paste.
24.	Bowl	G71, VI.NE35.363, No. 3 L. 35069	*Technique:* Wheelmade. *Paste:* 5YR "reddish yellow" 6/6; some very small wadi gravel, few very small to large lime, small and medium iron, very small ceramic and crystal; light grey core; hard. *Surface (Interior):* 7.5YR "pink" 8/4. *(Exterior):* as interior.
25.	Bowl	G71, VI.NE35.352, No. 4 L. 35069	*Technique:* Wheelmade. *Paste:* 7.5YR "pink" 7/4; some very small and few medium and large lime, few small ceramic; light grey core; hard. *Surface (Interior):* 7.5YR "pinkish white" 8/2. *(Exterior):* as interior.
26.	Bowl	G71, VI.NE35.366, No. 8 L. 35069	*Technique:* Wheelmade. *Paste:* 2.5YR "light red" 6/6; few to some very small and few medium and large lime, few medium and large wadi gravel and very small and medium crystal; light grey core; hard. *Surface (Interior):* as paste. *(Exterior):* as paste.

PLATE 16

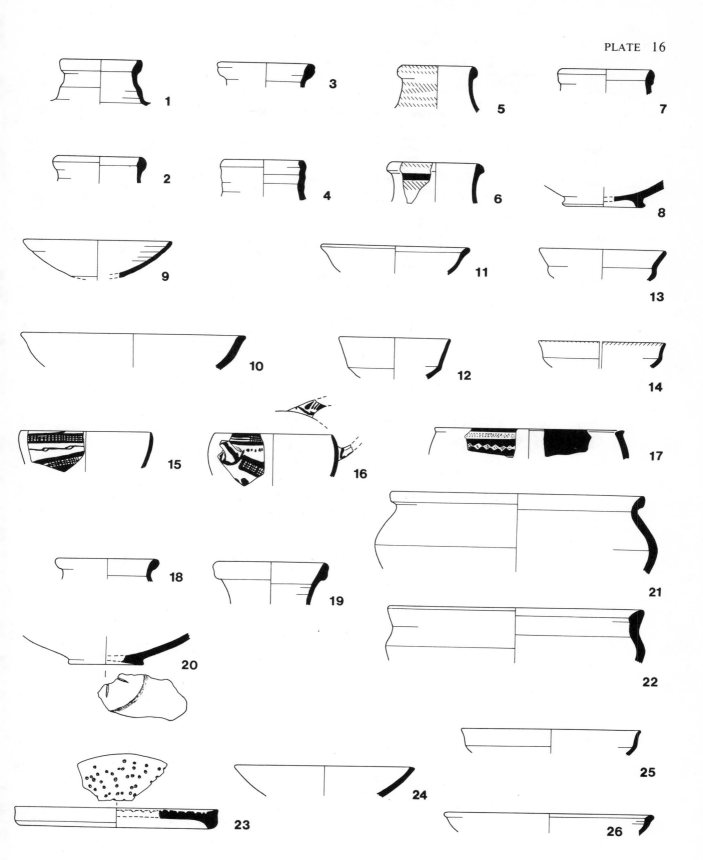

Plate Number	Pottery Type	Number and locus (see LOCUS INDEX)	Description (p. 277)
1.	Jar	G71, VI.NE25.276, No. 19 L. 25115	*Technique:* Wheelmade. *Paste:* 5YR "light reddish brown" 6/4; few very small to large lime, medium to large wadi gravel, small organic and very small sand; grey core;hard. *Surface (Interior):* as paste. *(Exterior):* as paste.
2.	Base	G71, VI.NE25.273, No. 13 L. 25115	*Technique:* Wheelmade. *Paste:* 5YR "reddish brown" 5/4; some small to large lime, large wadi gravel, few large ceramic; core: 5YR "reddish brown" 5/3; hard. *Surface (Interior):* as paste. *(Exterior):* as paste.
3.	Base	G71, VI.NE25.276, No. 7 L. 25115	*Technique:* Wheelmade. *Paste:* 5YR "light reddish brown" 6.4; many very small crystal, few very small lime and ceramic and wadi gravel; no core; hard. *Surface (Interior):* 10YR "white" 8/2. *(Exterior):* as interior.
4.	Base	G71, VI.NE25.273, No. 12 L. 25115	*Technique:* Wheelmade. *Paste:* 5YR "pink" 7/4; some very small to small and few medium to large lime, few large wadi gravel and small ceramic and organic; grey core; hard. *Surface (Interior):* as paste. *(Exterior):* as paste to 7.5YR "dark brown" 4/2.
5.	Jug	G71, VI.NE25.273, No. 14 L. 25115	*Technique:* Wheelmade. *Paste:* 5YR "reddish yellow" 6/6; many small crystal, few small to large lime and organic and small and large ceramic; grey core; hard. *Surface (Interior):* as paste. *(Exterior):* 10YR "white" 8/2.
6.	Bowl	G71, VI.NE25.276, No. 1 L. 25115	*Technique:* Wheelmade. *Paste:* 5YR "pink" 7/4; many very small crystal, few small lime, small to medium ceramic and medium to large wadi gravel; light grey core; hard. *Surface (Interior):* as paste. *(Exterior):* as paste.
7.	Cooking pot	G71, VI.NE25.276, No. 10 L. 25115	*Technique:* Wheelmade. *Paste:* 5YR "reddish brown" 4/4; many small to some large crystal, some medium organic; dark grey core; hard. *Surface (Interior):* as paste. *(Exterior):* as paste.
8.	Cooking pot	G71, VI.NE25.273, No. 5 L. 25115	*Technique:* Wheelmade. *Paste:* 5YR "reddish brown" 5/4; some large wadi gravel and medium lime, few small to medium crystal; no core; hard. *Surface (Interior):* as paste. *(Exterior):* as paste.
9.	Cooking pot	G71, VI.NE25.273, No. 3 L. 25115	*Technique:* Wheelmade. *Paste:* 5YR "reddish brown" 5/4; few large wadi gravel, medium to large lime and organic, and very small crystal; grey core; hard. *Surface (Interior):* as paste. *(Exterior):* as paste.
10.	Bowl	G70, VI.NE33.105, No. 10 L. 33047	*Technique:* Wheelmade. *Paste:* 7.5YR "light brown" 6/4; some very small and very large organic, few small wadi gravel, very small lime and crystal; grey core; hard. *Surface (Interior):* as paste. *(Exterior):* as paste
11.	Bowl	G70, VI.NE33.105, No. 6 L. 33047	*Technique:* Wheelmade. *Paste:* 2.5YR "light red" 6/8; few small ime, ceramic and organic and very small crystal; grey core; hard. *Surface (Interior):* 5YR "pink" 8/3. *(Exterior):* as paste to interior.
12.	Jar	G70, VI.NE33.107, No. 1 L. 33047	*Technique:* Wheelmade. *Paste:* 5YR "reddish bown" 5/3; some very small wadi gravel and crystal, few small organic; no core; hard. *Surface (Interior):* as paste. *(Exterior):* as paste.
13.	Base	G70, VI.NE33.107, No. 8 L. 33047	*Technique:* Wheelmade. *Paste:* 7.5YR "pink" 8/4; some small organic, few large iron, medium wadi gravel, small lime and very small crystal; grey core; hard. *Surface (Interior):* as paste. *(Exterior):* as paste.
14.	Bowl	G70, VI.NE33.99, No. 18 L. 33047	*Technique:* Wheelmade. *Paste:* 5YR "grey" 5/1; few small lime and very small organic; no core; hard. *Surface (Interior):* as paste. *(Exterior):* 7.5YR "light brown" 6/4.
15.	Cup or beaker	G70, VI.NE33.98, No. 11 L. 33047	*Technique:* Wheelmade. *Paste:* 5YR "reddish yellow" 6/6; few very small crystal, organic and wadi gravel; no core; hard. *Surface (Interior):* 7.5YR "pink" 7/4. *(Exterior):* as interior; band of 10YR "dusky red" 3/4 organic paint.
16.	Bowl (White Slip II)	G70, VI.NE33.97, No. 21 L. 33047	*Technique:* Handmade. *Paste:* inner: 2.5YR "dark grey" N4/0; outer: 2.5YR "red" 4/6; few very small crystal, wadi gravel, lime and small ceramic; no core; metallic. *Surface (Interior):* 10YR "light grey" 7/1 slip inside rim; hand burnish. *(Exterior):* 10YR "grey" 6/1 slip; hand burnish; 5YR "dark reddish brown" 3/3 organic paint decoration.
17.	Bowl	G70, VI.NE33.94, No. 4 L. 33047	*Technique:* Wheelmade. *Paste:* 5YR "reddish yellow" 7/6; some small organic, few very small to medium lime, very small wadi gravel and crystal; grey core; hard. *Surface (Interior):* 7.5YR "pink" 8/4. *(Exterior):* as interior.
18.	Cooking pot	G70, VI.NE33.94, No. 3 L. 33047	*Technique:* Wheelmade. *Paste:* 5YR "reddish brown" 5/4; some small organic and crystal, few small wadi gravel; dark grey core; hard. *Surface (Interior):* as paste. *(Exterior):* as paste.
19.	Cooking pot	G70, VI.NE33.107, No. 10 L. 33047	*Technique:* Wheelmade. *Paste:* 5YR "light reddish brown" 6/4; many medium wadi gravel, some organic, few small lime; dark grey core; hard. *Surface (Interior):* as paste. *(Exterior):* as paste.
20.	Cooking pot	G70, VI.NE33.105, No. 13 L. 33047	*Technique:* Wheelmade. *Paste:* 5YR "reddish yellow" 7/6; few small and some large lime, some very small and few small crystal, some small organic; dark grey core; hard. *Surface (Interior):* 5YR "pinkish grey" 7/2. *(Exterior):* as interior.
21.	Bowl	G70, VI.NE33.105, No. 17 L. 33047	*Technique:* Wheelmade. *Paste:* 5YR "pink" 7/4; few small and medium organic, very small to medium lime, very small wadi gravel and crystal and small ceramic; dark grey core; hard. *Surface (Interior):* as paste. *(Exterior):* as paste.
22.	Bowl	G70, VI.NE33.105, No. 11 L. 33047	*Technique:* Wheelmade. *Paste:* 5YR "light reddish brown" 6/4; few small and large lime, small and medium organic, small wadi gravel and very small crystal; grey core; hard. *Surface (Interior):* as paste; traces of 2.5YR "red" 5/6 organic paint. *(Exterior):* as paste.
23.	Krater	G70, VI.NE33.97, No. 4 L. 33047	*Technique:* Wheelmade. *Paste:* 2.5YR "light red" 6/8; many very small crystal, few small and medium wadi gravel and small organic; grey core; hard. *Surface (Interior):* as paste to 5YR "pink" 8/3. *(Exterior):* 5YR "white" 8/1.
24.	Krtater	G70, VI.NE33.105, No. 3 L. 33047	*Technique:* Wheelmade. *Paste:* 7.5YR "light brown" 6/4; some very small and small organic, few small and medium wadi gravel and very small lime; grey core; hard. *Surface (Interior):* as paste. *(Exterior):* as paste.

PLATE 17

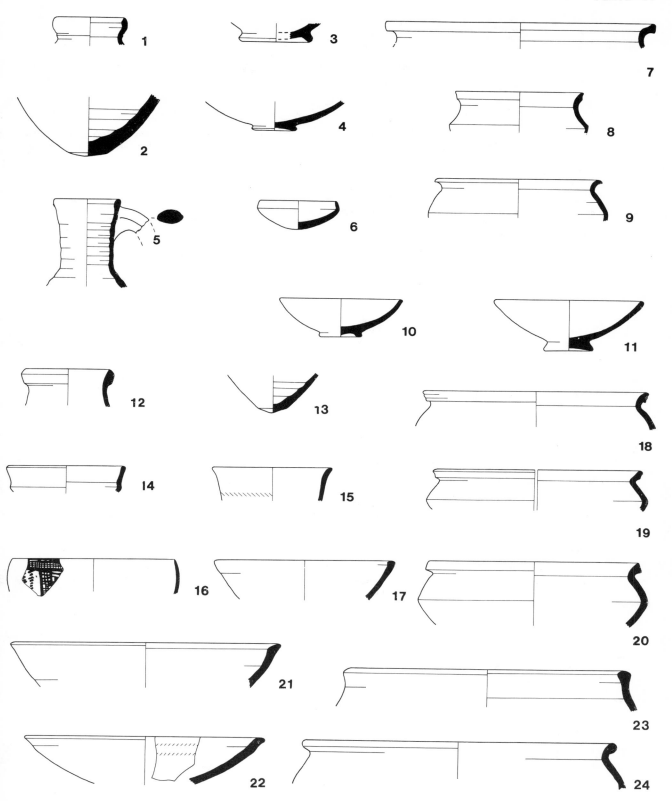

Plate Number	Pottery Type	Number and locus (see LOCUS INDEX)	Description (p. 277)
1.	Krater or bowl	G71, VI.NE23.263, No. 10 - L. 23089	*Technique:* Wheelmade. *Paste:* 5YR "reddish yellow" 7/6; few small and medium lime, small organic, very small crystal and wadi gravel; grey core; hard. *Surface (Interior):* as paste; 10YR "dark red" 3/6 slip on rim. *(Exterior):* as paste; slip on rim as interior.
2.	Jar	G70, VI.NE34,168, No. 11 L. 34058	*Technique:* Wheelmade. *Paste:* inner: 7.5YR "pink" 7/4; outer: 2.5YR "light red" 6/8; some very small wadi gravel and lime, few medium iron small ceramic and very small crystal; grey core; hard. *Surface (Interior):* as inner paste. *(Exterior):* as inner paste.
3.	Jar	G70, VI.NE34.153, No. 8 L. 34058	*Technique:* Wheelmade. *Paste:* 5YR "reddish yellow" 7/6; very many very small and many small organic, few small lime and very small crystal; dark grey core; hard. *Surface (Interior):* as paste. *(Exterior):* as paste.
4.	Bowl	G70, VI.NE34,167, No. 12 L. 34058	*Technique:* Wheelmade. *Paste:* 5YR "pink" 7/4; some very small wadi gravel, few very small and small lime and ceramic; grey core; hard. *Surface (Interior):* as paste. *(Exterior):* as paste.
5.	Bowl	G70, VI.NE34,168, No. 1 L. 34058	*Technique:* Wheelmade. *Paste:* 5YR "reddish yellow" 6/6; many very small wadi gravel, few small organic and very small crystal; no core; hard. *Surface (Interior):* as paste. *(Exterior):* as paste.
6.	Bowl	G70, VI.NE34.165, No. 17 L. 34058	*Technique:* Wheelmade. *Paste:* 5YR "reddish yellow" 7/6; many small to large organic, few very small crytal; dark grey core; hard. *Surface (Interior):* 7.5YR "pinkish grey" 7/2. *(Exterior):* as paste.
7.	Bowl	G70, VI.NE34.117, No. 8 L. 34058	*Technique:* Wheelmade. *Paste:* 5YR "reddish yellow" 7/6; some very small and few small to large organic, very small to medium crystal and ceramic; grey core; hard. *Surface (Interior):* as paste to 5YR "dark grey" 4/1. *(Exterior):* as paste to 7.5YR "pinkish grey" 7/2.
8.	Base	G70, VI.NE34.167, No. 13 L. 34058	*Technique:* Wheelmade. *Paste:* 5YR "reddish yellow" 7/6; some very small wadi gravel, few large iron, small to large lime and small ceramic; dark grey core; hard. *Surface (Interior):* as paste. *(Exterior):* 7.5YR "pink" 8/4.
9.	Krater	G70, VI.NE34.147, No. 4 L. 34058	*Technique:* Wheelmade. *Paste:* 5YR "reddish yellow" 7/6; many very small wadi gravel, some small and few medium organic, few medium lime and small ceramic; light grey core; hard. *Surface (Interior):* 5YR "pinkish grey" 7/2. *(Exterior):* as interior.
10.	Krater	G71, VI.NE34.202, No. 10 L. 34058	*Technique:* Wheelmade. *Paste:* 7.5YR "pink" 7/4; many very small wadi gravel, few very small and medium lime and very small crystal; grey core; hard. *Surface (Interior):* as paste. *(Exterior):* as paste.
11.	Krater	G70, VI.NE34.91, No. 18 L. 34058	*Technique:* Wheelmade. *Paste:* 5YR "reddish yellow" 6/6; many very small lime, some very small and few medium ceeramic, few medium organic; grey core; hard. *Surface (Interior):* as paste. *(Exterior):* as paste.
12.	Krater	G70, VI.NE34.117, No. 5 L. 34058	*Technique:* Wheelmade. *Paste:* 5YR "reddish yellow" 6/6; some very small and few small wadi, few small lime and very small crystal; light grey core; hard. *Surface (Interior):* as paste. *(Exterior):* as paste.
13.	krater	G70, VI.NE34.117, No. 6 L. 34058	*Technique:* Wheelmade. *Paste:* 5YR "reddish yellow" 7/6; some very small and few large wadi gravel and lime, very small ceramic and crystal; no core; hard. *Surface (Interior):* as paste; 10YR "red" 4/4 slip on rim. *(Exterior):* as paste; slip on rim as interior.
14.	Bowl	G70, VI.NE34.153, No. 11 L. 34058	*Technique:* Wheelmade. *Paste:* 5YR "reddish yellow" 7/6; some very small wadi gravel, few small lime and ceramic; grey core; hard. *Surface (Interior):* as paste. *(Exterior):* as paste.
15.	Bowl	G70, VI.NE34.117, No. 4 L. 34058	*Technique:* Wheelmade. *Paste:* 5YR "pink" 7/4; some very small and few medium lime, few small and large ceramic and very small wadi gravel; light grey core; hard. *Surface (Interior):* as paste. *(Exterior):* as paste.
16.	Bowl	G70, VI.NE34.167, No. 9 L. 34058	*Technique:* Wheelmade. *Paste:* 5YR "yellowish red" 5/6; some very small and few small wadi gravel, few very small to large lime, large organic and very small crystal; grey core; hard. *Surface (Interior):* as exterior. *(Exterior):* 2.5YR "light red" 6/6.
17.	Chalice	G70, VI.NE34.158, No. 5 L. 34058	*Technique:* Wheelmade. *Paste:* 5YR "reddish yellow" 7/6; some very small wadi gravel and crystal, few small and large organic, few small iron and lime; *Surface (Interior):* as paste. *(Exterior):* 2.5YR "red" 5/6 slip.
18.	Bowl	G70, VI.NE34.153, No. 3 L. 34058	*Technique:* Wheelmade. *Paste:* 5YR "pink" 7/4; many very small wadi gravel, few small and medium lime; light grey core; hard. *Surface (Interior):* as paste. *(Exterior):* as paste.
19.	Cooking pot	G70, VI.NE34.153, No. 7 L. 34058	*Technique:* Wheelmade. *Paste:* 5YR "reddish brown" 5/4; large wadi gravel, very small and large lime and very small crystal; no core; hard. *Surface (Interior):* as paste. *(Exterior):* as paste.
20.	Bowl	G71, VI.NE26.249, No. 9 L. 34058	*Technique:* Wheelmade. *Paste:* 5YR "reddish yellow" 7/6; some medium and large organic, few very small to medium lime, very small ceramic and very small wadi gravel; grey core; hard. *Surface (Interior):* as paste; 10YR "red" 5/6 slip on rim. *(Exterior):* 7.5YR "pink" 7/4 slip on rim as interior.
21.	Bowl	G70, VI.NE34.170, No. 9 L. 34058	*Technique:* Wheelmade. *Paste:* 5YR "pink" 7/4; some very small and few very large wadi gravel, some medium organic, few large iron and very small crystal; dark grey core; hard. *Surface (Interior):* as paste. *(Exterior):* as paste

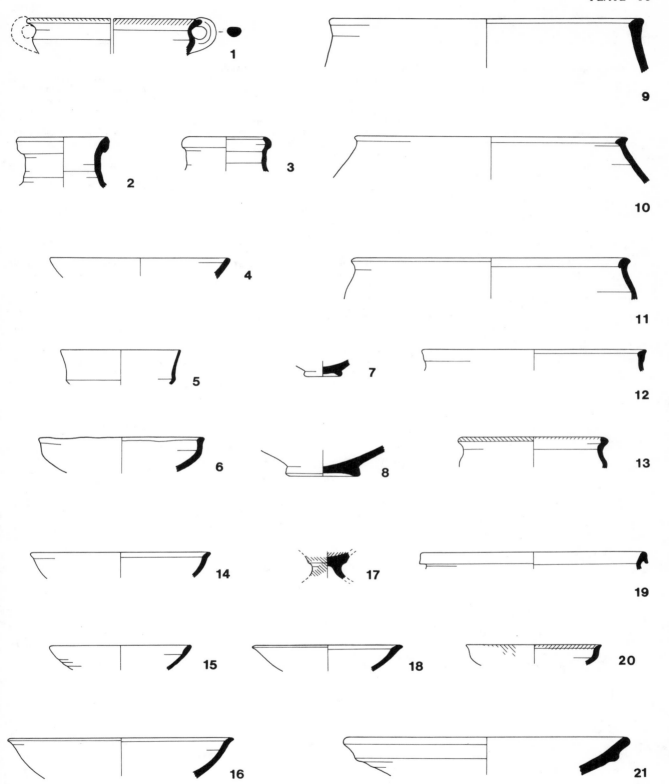

PLATE 18

Plate Number	Pottery Type	Number and locus (see LOCUS INDEX)	Description (p. 277)
1.	Cooking pot	G70, VI.NE4.139, No. 10 L 4057	*Technique:* Wheelmade. *Paste:* 5YR "dark reddish grey" 4/2; few very small to large lime and crystal, and medium organic; no core; hard. *Surface (Interior):* as paste. *(Exterior):* as paste.
2.	Krater	G70, VI.NE4.124, No. 1 L. 4057	*Technique:* Wheelmade. *Paste:* 5YR "reddish brown" 5'4; some very small and few medium lime and crystal, few very small wadi gravel; grey core; hard. *Surface (Interior):* 7.5YR "pinkish white" 8/2 to 7.5YR "grey" N5/0; traces of wheel burnish on rim. *(Exterior):* bands of 10YR "white" 8/2 and 5YR "light reddish brown" 6/4 organic paint; traces of burnish.
3.	Bowl	G70, VI.NE4.128, No. 17 L. 4057	*Technique:* Wheelmade. *Paste:* 5YR "pink" 7/4; many very small and few medium lime, few very small ceramic and crystal; grey core; hard. *Surface (Interior):* 7.5YR "pinkish white" 8/2; 5YR "dusky red" 3/4 slip on rim. *(Exterior):* as paste; as interior.
4.	Bowl	G71, VI.NE6.188, No. 6 L. 6102	*Technique:* Wheelmade. *Paste:* 7.5YR "pinkish grey" 7/2; some small and medium wadi gravel and lime, few small and medium crystal, small organic; grey core; hard. *Surface (Interior):* as paste. *(Exterior):* as paste.
5.	Jar	G70, VI.NE13.180, No. 8 L. 13043	*Technique:* Wheelmade. *Paste:* 5YR "light reddish brown" 6/4; some very small crystal, few small and large lime, small ceramic and organic; grey core; hard. *Surface (Interior):* as paste. *(Exterior):* as paste.
6.	Jar	G70, VI.NE13.209, No. 6 L. 13043	*Technique:* Wheelmade. *Paste:* 2.5YR "light reddish brown" 6/4; some very small wadi gravel very small and few very large lime, few small organic and iron and very small crytal, large wood sliver; no core; hard. *Surface (Interior):* 7.5YR "pink" 8/4. *(Exterior):* as interior.
7.	Jar	G70, VI.NE13.180, No. 6 L. 13043	*Technique:* Wheelmade. *Paste:* 5YR "reddish yellow" 7/6; many very small lime, few large wadi gravel, few very small and medium ceramic and very small crystal; light grey core; hard. *Surface (Interior):* as paste. *(Exterior):* as paste.
8.	Jar	G70, VI.NE13.172, No. 8 L. 13043	*Technique:* Wheelmade. *Paste:* 7.5YR "light brown" 6/4; very many very small and few very large wadi gravel, few small and large lime, medium organic, small ceramic, very small crystal; grey core; hard. *Surface (Interior):* as paste. *(Exterior):* as paste.
9.	Krater	G70, VI.NE13.180, No. 9 L. 13043	*Technique:* Wheelmade. *Paste:* 5YR "pink" 8/4; some very small wadi gravel, few small, large and very large lime, large iron, very small crystal and organic; grey core; hard. *Surface (Interior):* as paste. *(Exterior):* as paste to 10YR "very pale brown" 8/3.
10.	Cooking jug?	G70, VI.NE13.209, No. 1 L. 13043	*Technique:* Wheelmade. *Paste:* 2.5YR "light red" 6/6; many small to medium lime, few very small crystal; grey core; hard. *Surface (Interior):* as paste. *(Exterior):* as paste.
11.	Cooking jug	G70, VI.NE13.172, No. 10 L. 13043	*Technique:* Wheelmade. *Paste:* 5YR "pink" 7/4; many very small wadi gravel, few large lime, small iron and organic and very small crystal; light grey core; hard. *Surface (Interior):* as paste to 10YR "white" 8/2. *(Exterior):* as interior.
12.	Krater	G70, VI.NE13.178, No. 7 L. 13043	*Technique:* Wheelmade. *Paste:* 5YR "pink" 7/4; may very small wadi gravel, few medium and very large iron, small lime and organic and small and very small crystal; grey core; hard. *Surface (Interior):* as paste. *(Exterior):* as paste.
14.	Bowl	G70, VI.NE13.172, No. 7 L. 13043	*Technique:* Wheelmade. *Paste:* 10YR "very dark grey" 3/1; some small to large organic, very small wadi gravel, few large iron, small to large lime, and very small crystal; no core; hard. *Surface (Interior):* 7.5YR "pink" 7/4. *(Exterior):* as interior.
13.	Krater	G70, VI.NE13.175, No. 2 L. 13043	*Technique:* Wheelmade. *Paste:* 7.5YR "pink" 7.4; many very small and few medium and large lime, few medium wadi gravel and very small ceramic; no core; hard. *Surface (Interior):* as paste. *(Exterior):* 10YR "white" 8/2 slip on rim and body; 5YR "reddish brown" 5/3 organic paint decoration.
15.	juglet	G70, VI.NE13.178, No. 2 L. 13043	*Technique:* Wheelmade. *Paste:* 5YR "reddish yellow" 7/6; some small and few large wadi gravel, few very small crystal; core; 7.5YR "light brown" 6/4; hard. *Surface (Interior):* 7.5YR "pink" 8/4. *(Exterior):* as interior.
16.	Base	G70, VI.NE13.176, No. 2 L. 13043	*Technique:* Wheelmade. *Paste:* inner: 7.5YR "pink" 7/4; outer: 5YR "reddish yellow" 7/6; many very small wadi gravel, few small to large lime, very small organic and crystal; no core; hard *Surface (Interior):* as inner paste. *(Exterior):* as outer paste to 7.5YR "pinkish white" 8/2.
17.	Pilgrim flask	G70, VI.NE13.175, No. 10 L. 13043	*Technique:* Wheelmade. *Paste:* 7.5YR "grey" N6/0; outer: 7.5YR "pinkish grey" 7/2; some very small and few medium lime, few medium lime, few medium wadi gravel, medium and small ceramic and small organic; no core; hard. *Surface (Interior):* as innner paste. *(Exterior):* as outer paste; 5YR "reddish brown" 5/4 organic paint decoration.
18.	Bowl	G70, VI.NE13.175, No. 1 L. 13043	*Technique:* Wheelmade. *Paste:* 2.5YR "light red" 6/8; few very small to large lime, very small ceramic and crystal; grey core; hard. *Surface (Interior):* as paste. *(Exterior):* as paste to 10YR "white" 8/2.
19.	Bowl or cup	G70, VI.NE13.178, No. 22 L. 13043	*Technique:* Wheelmade. *Paste:* 5YR "reddish yellow" 7/6; many very small wadi gravel, few small organic; no core; hard. *Surface (Interior):* as paste; patches of 7.5YR "pinkish white" 8/2. *(Exterior):* as paste with slip on rim as interior.
20.	Base	G70, VI.NE13.172, No. 5 L. 13043	*Technique:* Wheelmade. *Paste:* 7.5YR "light brown" 6/4; many very small and few medium lime, few very small ceramic; no core; hard. *Surface (Interior):* as paste. *(Exterior):* as paste.
21.	Krater	G69, VI.NE14.77, 78, Nos. 2–4 L. 14057	*Technique:* Wheelmade. *Paste:* 5YR "pink" 7/3; some to many crystal; no core; hard. *Surface (Interior):* as paste. *(Exterior):* as paste.
22.	Flask	G70, VI.NE14.157, No. 9 L. 14057	*Technique:* Wheelmade. *Paste:* 2.5YR "light red" 6/6; many very small and few small to large lime, few very small ceramic and crystal; core: 10YR "very pale brown" 7/3; hard. *Surface (Interior):* as paste; organic paint on rim as exterior. *(Exterior):* 10YR "white" 8/2 slip and band of 10YR "dusky red" 3/4 organic paint on rim.
23.	Juglet	G71, VI.NE14.249, No. 1 L. 14095	*Technique:* Wheelmade. *Paste:* 5YR "reddish yellow" 7/6; some small wadi gravel, few small lime and crystal, and very small to medium organic; grey core; hard. *Surface (Interior):* as exterior; drippings of organic paint as exterior. *(Exterior):* as paste to 10YR "white" 8/2; irregular hand burnish; 2.5YR "dark red" 3/6 organic paint decoration.

PLATE 19

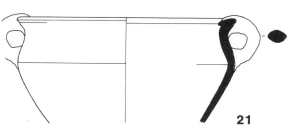

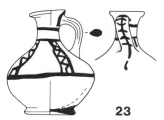

Plate Number	Pottery Type	Number and locus (see LOCUS INDEX)	Description (p. 277)
1.	Cooking pot	G71, VI.NE16.260, No. 4 L. 16112	*Technique:* Wheelmade. *Paste:* 5YR "reddish yellow" 5/3; few large lime and wadi gravel and very small, medium and large crytal; grey core; hard. *Surface (Interior):* as paste. *(Exterior):* as paste.
2.	Krater	G70, VI.NE34.144, No. 14 L. 34053.1	*Technique:* Wheelmade. *Paste:* 5YR "reddish yellow" 7/6; few medium iron and wadi gravel, small and medium organic, very small crystal; grey core; hard. *Surface (Interior):* as paste. *(Exterior):* as paste.
3.	Bowl	G71, VI.NE34.221, No. 2 L. 34072.1	*Technique:* Wheelmade. *Paste:* 7.5YR "dark brown" 4/2; many very small lime, few small and medium wadi gravel and ceramic, very small crystal; core: 7.5YR "brown" 5/2; hard. *Surface (Interior):* bands of 10YR "light grey" 7/2, 7.5YR "dark brown" 3/2, and 10YR "red" 5/6 organic paint; wheel burnish. *(Exterior):* 10YR "very pale brown" 7/3 to 10YR "grey" 6/1.
4.	Cooking pot	G70, VI.NE34.164, No. 10 L. 34072	*Technique:* Wheelmade. *Paste:* 5YR "light reddish brown" 6/4; some small and medium organic, some small lime, few very small and small crystal; dark grey core; hard. *Surface (Interior):* as paste. *(Exterior):* as paste.
5.	Bowl	G70, VI.NE24.162, No. 9 L. 34072P	*Technique:* Wheelmade. *Paste:* 5YR "pink" 8/4; very many very small wadi gravel, some small organic and very small crystal, few small ceramic and lime; light grey core; hard. *Surface (Interior):* as paste. *(Exterior):* as paste.
6.	Bowl	G70, VI.NE34.99, No. 8 L. 34022.1	*Technique:* Wheelmade. *Paste:* 5YR "reddish yellow" 7/8; some small organic and very small crystal, few small lime and ceramic; grey core; hard. *Surface (Interior):* 5YR "pink" 8/4; 2.5YR "reddish brown" 5/4 to 7.5YR "dark brown" 3/2 slip on rim. *(Exterior):* 10YR "white" 8/2 slip on rim as interior.
7.	Jar	G71, VI.NE16.205, No. 2 L. 16082	*Technique:* Wheelmade. *Paste:* 7.5YR "light brown" 6/4; some very small and few medium lime, some very small crystal, few medium iron; core: 7.5YR "brown" 5.2; hard. *Surface (Interior):* as exterior. *(Exterior):* 7.5YR "pink" 7/4.
8.	Jar	G71, VI.NE16.203, No. 4 L. 16082	*Technique:* Wheelmade. *Paste:* 7.5YR "light brown" 6.4; some very small and few medium lime, some very small crystal, few small wadi gravel, very small ceramic and large organic; grey core; hard. *Surface (Interior):* as paste. *(Exterior):* traces of 10YR "white" 8/1 slip, bands of 10YR "red" 4/4 organic paint.
9.	Bowl	G71, I.NE16.204, No. 15 L. 16082	*Technique:* Wheelmade. *Paste:* 5YR "reddish brown" 5/4; some very small and few medium lime, few medium organic, very small to medium ceramic and very small crystal; grey core; hard. *Surface (Interior):* as paste to 5YR "reddish grey" 5/2. *(Exterior):* 7.5YR "pinkish grey" 6/2.
10.	Bowl	G71, VI.NE16.207, No. 3 L. 16082	*Technique:* Wheelmade. *Paste:* 5YR "yellowish red" 5/6; few very small and medium lime and wadi gravel, adn very small ceramic and crystal; core: 5YR "reddish brown" 5/3; hard. *Surface (Interior):* as exterior: *(Exterior):* 7.5YR "pink" 7/4.
11.	Bowl	G71, VI.NE16.206, No. 2 L. 16082	*Technique:* Wheelmade. *Paste:* 7.5YR "pink" 8/4; some very small and few small and large ceramic and lime, few small organic and very small crystal; no core; hard. *Surface (Interior):* as paste. *(Exterior):* 10YR "white" 8/2.
12.	Bowl	G71, VI.NE16.204, No. 6 L. 16082	*Technique:* Wheelmade. *Paste:* 7.5YR "reddish yellow" 7/6; few very small lime, ceramic and crystal; light grey core; hard. *Surface (Interior):* as paste. *(Exterior):* as paste.
13.	Bowl	G71, VI.NE16.202, No. 3 L. 16082	*Technique:* Wheelmade. *Paste:* 5YR "reddish yellow" 6/6; some very small and few large lime, few very small and medium crystal and very small and small ceramic; no core; hard. *Surface (Interior):* 5YR "pinkish grey" 7/2; 10YR "weak red" 5/4 slip on rim and decoration. *(Exterior):* as interior: slip on rim as interior.
14.	Cooking pot	G71, VI.NE16.207, No. 36 L. 16082	*Technique:* Wheelmade. *Paste:* 5YR "reddish brown" 5/4; few very small to large lime and very small crystal; dark grey core; hard. *Surface (Interior):* as paste. *(Exterior):* as paste.
15.	Cooking pot	G71, VI.NE16.202, No. 9 L. 16082	*Technique:* Wheelmade. *Paste:* 2.5YR "light red" 6/6; some large and few very small lime, few very small crystal; dark grey core; hard. *Surface (Interior):* as paste. *(Exterior):* as paste.
16.	Krater	G71, VI.NE16.203, No. 10	*Technique:* Wheelmade. *Paste:* 5YR "reddish yellow" 6/6; some very small wadi gravel, few very small and medium to large lime, medium iron and very small crystal; grey core; hard. *Surface (Interior):* as paste. *(Exterior):* as paste.
17.	Krater	G71, VI.NE16.207, No. 22 L. 16082	*Technique:* Wheelmade. *Paste:* 5YR "reddish yellow" 6/6; many very small and few medium and large lime, few very small ceramic and crystal; no core hard. *Surface (Interior):* as paste. *(Exterior):* 10YR "white" 8/2.
18.	Base	G71, VI.NE16.208, No. 11 L. 16082	*Technique:* Wheelmade. *Paste:* 7.5YR "light brown" 6/4; some very small and few medium and large lime, some very small crystal, few medium organic and large iron and wadi crystal; grey core; hard. *Surface (Interior):* as paste. *(Exterior):* as paste.
19.	Bowl or cup	G71, VI.NE23.243, No. 7 L. 23054	*Technique:* Wheelmade. *Paste:* 7.5YR "light brown" 6/4; some small and few medium and large lime, few very small crystal; no core; hard. *Surface (Interior):* as paste. *(Exterior):* as paste; band of 10YR "white" 8/2 organic paint.
20.	Cup- and-saucer	G21, VI.NE16.203, No. 6 L. 16082	*Technique:* Wheelmade. *Paste:* 5YR "pink" 7/4; some small and few very large organic, some medium wadi gravel and very small crystal, few medium and very large lime, and very large iron; grey core; hard. *Surface (Interior):* 7.5YR "reddish yellow" 8/6. *(Exterior):* 10YR "very pale brown" 7/3.
21.	Cup- and-Saucer	G71, VI.NE16.210, No. 17 L. 16082	*Technique:* Wheelmade. *Paste:* 7.5YR "pink" 7/4; many very small wadi gravel, few small and medium lime, medium ceramic and very small crystal; no core; hard. *Surface (Interior):* as paste. *(Exterior):* as paste.

PLATE 20

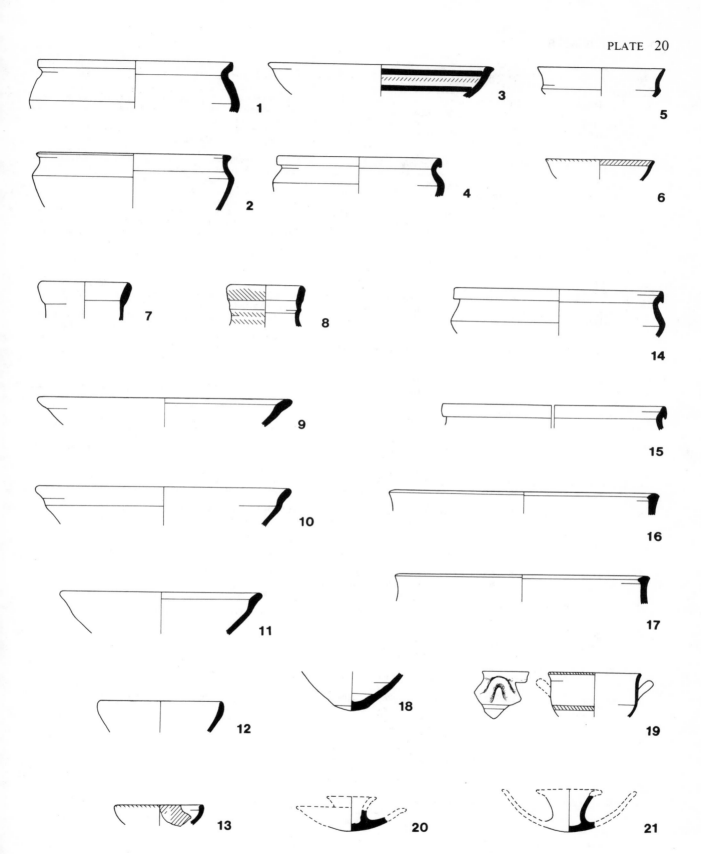

Plate Number	Pottery Type	Number and locus (see LOCUS INDEX)	Description (p. 277)
1.	Jar	G71, VI.NE16.272, No. 11 L. 16110	*Technique:* Wheelmade. *Paste:* 5YR "reddish yellow" 7/6; some very small and few medium wadi gravel, few small and medium iron, very small and small lime and very small crystal; core: 7.5YR "light brown" 6/4; hard. *Surface (Interior):* as paste. *(Exterior):* as paste.
2.	Jar	G71, VI.NE16.257, No. 11 L. 16110	*Technique:* Wheelmade. *Paste:* 2.5YR "red" 5/6; few very small to large lime, very small wadi gravel and crystal; core: 5YR "light reddish brown" 6/4; hard. *Surface (Interior):* as paste. *(Exterior):* as paste.
3.	Jar	G71, VI.NE16.265, No. 2 L. 16110	*Technique:* Wheelmade. *Paste:* 5YR "reddish yellow" 7/6; few large organic, very small to medium lime, very small and small ceramic and very small wadi gravel and crystal; core: 7.5YR "light brown" 6/4; hard. *Surface (Interior):* as paste and core. *(Exterior):* as paste.
4.	Bowl	G71, VI.NE16.302, No. 5 L. 16110	*Technique:* Wheelmade. *Paste:* 7.5YR "light brown" 6/4; many very small and few large wadi gravel; no core; hard. *Surface (Interior):* as paste; wheel burnish. *(Exterior):* as paste.
5.	Bowl	G71, VI.NE16.265, No. 18 L. 16110	*Technique:* Wheelmade. *Paste:* 7.5YR "pinkish grey" 6/2; some very small wadi gravel, few very small to medium lime, small iron and very small ceramic and crystal; no core; hard. *Surface (Interior):* as paste; 5YR "reddish brown" 4/3 slip on rim; wheel burnish. *(Exterior):* as paste; slip on rim as interior.
6	Krater	G71, VI.NE16.272, No. 16 L. 16110	*Technique:* Wheelmade. *Paste:* 2.5YR "light red" 6/6; few very small to medium lime, very small and small iron and very small wadi gravel and crystal; light grey core; hard. *Surface (Interior):* as paste. *(Exterior):* 7.5YR "pinkish white" 8/2.
7.	Krater	G71, VI.NE16.272, No. 8 L. 16110	*Technique:* Wheelmade. *Paste:* 7.5YR "light brown" 6/4; few to some very small wadi gravel, few medium ceramic, small to medium lime and iron and very small crystal; no core; hard. *Surface (Interior):* 10YR "white" 8/2. *(Exterior):* as interior.
8.	Cooking pot	G71, VI.NE16.265, No. 1 L. 16110	*Technique:* Wheelmade. *Paste:* 5YR "reddish brown" 5/3; some large and few small to medium lime, few small and large organic, medium and large wadi gravel and very small crystal; grey core; hard. *Surface (Interior):* as paste. *(Exterior):* as paste.
9.	Bowl	G71, VI.NE16.257, No. 1 L. 16110	*Technique:* Wheelmade. *Paste:* 5YR "light reddish brown" 6/4; many very small and few medium wadi gravel, few small lime and ceramic and very small crystal; grey core; hard. *Surface (Interior):* as paste. *(Exterior):* as paste.
10.	Bowl	G71, VI.NE16.302, No. 6 L. 16110	*Technique:* Wheelmade. *Paste:* 7.5YR "pinkish grey" 6/2; some very small and few medium wadi gravel, few to large lime and iron, very small crystal; no core; hard. *Surface (Interior):* as paste. *(Exterior):* as paste.
11.	Bowl	G71, VI.NE16.301, No. 13 L. 16110	*Technique:* Wheelmade. *Paste:* 5YR "reddish yellow" 7/6; few very small to medium lime, very small and small to medium lime, very small and small crystal; very small wadi gravel; light grey core; hard. *Surface (Interior):* as paste; traces of wheel burnish. *(Exterior):* as paste; 2.5YR "red" 4/6 organic paint decoration on rim and body; wheel burnish.
12.	Jar	G70, VI.NE23.101, No. 17 L. 23036	*Technique:* Wheelmade. *Paste:* 5YR "light reddish brown" 6/4; some very small and few small to large lime, few large iron, very small and medium ceramic and very small crystal; grey core; hard. *Surface (Interior):* as paste. *(Exterior):* as paste.
13.	Bowl or cup	G71, VI.NE23.350, No. 2 L. 23036	*Technique:* Wheelmade. *Paste:* 7.5YR "pink" 7/4; some very small wadi gravel, few medium lime, small organic, very small crystal; grey core; hard. *Surface (Interior):* as paste and core. *(Exterior):* as paste.
14.	Krater	G70, VI.NE23.101, No. 19 L. 23036	*Technique:* Wheelmade. *Paste:* 5YR "light reddish brown" 6/4; few very small to large lime, very small to medium ceramic and very small crystal; grey core; hard. *Surface (Interior):* as paste. *(Exterior):* as paste.
15.	Bowl	G70, VI.NE23.94, No. 2 L. 23036	*Technique:* Wheelmade. *Paste:* 5YR "reddish yellow" 7/6; many very small wadi gravel, some very small and large crystal, few small and medium lime, small ceramic and organic; light grey core; hard. *Surface (Interior):* as paste. *(Exterior):* as paste.
16.	Juglet	G69? VI.NE23.98, L. 23036	*Technique:* Wheelmade. *Paste:* 7.5YR "reddish yellow" 6/6; few medium lime and wadi gravel, few small to medium crystal; no core; hard. *Surface (Interior):* as paste. *(Exterior):* as paste; traces of 7.5YR "light grey" 7/0 slip (?).
17.	Cooking pot	G70, VI.NE23.101, No. 3 L. 23036	*Technique:* Wheelmade. *Paste:* 5YR "yellowish red" 5/8; many small to large lime some small organic few small wadi gravel and very small crystal; dark grey core; hard. *Surface (Interior):* 5YR "light reddish brown" 6/4. *(Exterior):* as interior.
18.	Bowl	G70, VI.NE23.101, No. 2 L. 23036	*Technique:* Wheelmade. *Paste:* 5YR "pink" 7/4; many very small wadi gravel, few small lime and very small crystal and organic; light grey core; hard. *Surface (Interior):* 10YR "white" 8/2 slip; 10YR "weak red" 5/4 organic paint on rim and decoration. *(Exterior):* slip as interior.
19.	Bowl or cup	G71, VI.NE23.351, No. 4 L. 23036	*Technique:* Wheelmade. *Paste:* 5YR "reddish yellow" 6/6; few very small to small lime, crystal and ceramic; core: 7.5YR "light brown" 6/4; hard. *Surface (Interior):* as paste; slip on rim as exterior. *(Exterior):* 10YR "white" 8/1 slip and 5YR "reddish black" 2/1 organic paint decoration.
20.	Sherd	G70, VI.NE23.101, No. 1 L. 23036	*Technique:* Wheelmade. *Paste:* 5YR "reddish yellow" 7/6; many very small wadi gravel, few medium and small organic, small iron and very small crystal; grey core; hard. *Surface (Interior):* as paste. *(Exterior):* 7.5YR "pinkish white" 8/2 slip; 7.5YR "dark brown" 3/2 and 10YR "weak red" 4/4 organic paint decoration.
21.	Jar	G70, VI.NE24.220, No. 3 L. 24087	*Technique:* Wheelmade. *Paste:* 5YR "reddish yellow" 6/6; some very small crystal, few medium lime, medium and large wadi gravel and large iron; light grey core; hard. *Surface (Interior):* as paste. *(Exterior):* as paste.
22.	Base	G70, VI.NE24.220, No. 18 L. 24087	*Technique:* Wheelmade. *Paste:* 5YR "light reddish brown" 6/6; many small and few large lime, few medium organic and very small crystal; no core; hard. *Surface (Interior):* as paste. *(Exterior):* as paste.
23.	Bowl or cup	G70, VI.NE24.220, No. 20 L. 24087	*Technique:* Wheelmade. *Paste:* 2.5YR "red" 5/6; some very small and few medium and large lime, few large wadi gravel, medium organic, small ceramic and very small crystal; grey core; hard. *Surface (Interior):* as paste. *(Exterior):* 7.5YR "white" 8/2 slip; band of 10YR "red" 5/6 organic paint on rim and decoration.
24.	Cooking pot	G70, VI.NE24.210, No. 2 L. 24087	*Technique:* Wheelmade. *Paste:* 5YR "yellowish red" 5/6; some very small and small and few medium and large crystal, few medium and large wadi gravel; no core; hard. *Surface (Interior):* as paste. *(Exterior):* as paste
25.	Cooking pot	G70, VI.NE24.207, 22 L. 24087	*Technique:* Wheelmade. *Paste:* 5YR "reddish brown" 4/4; few very small to some large lime, few small ceramic and very small crystal; dark grey core; hard. *Surface (Interior):* as paste. *(Exterior):* as paste

PLATE 21

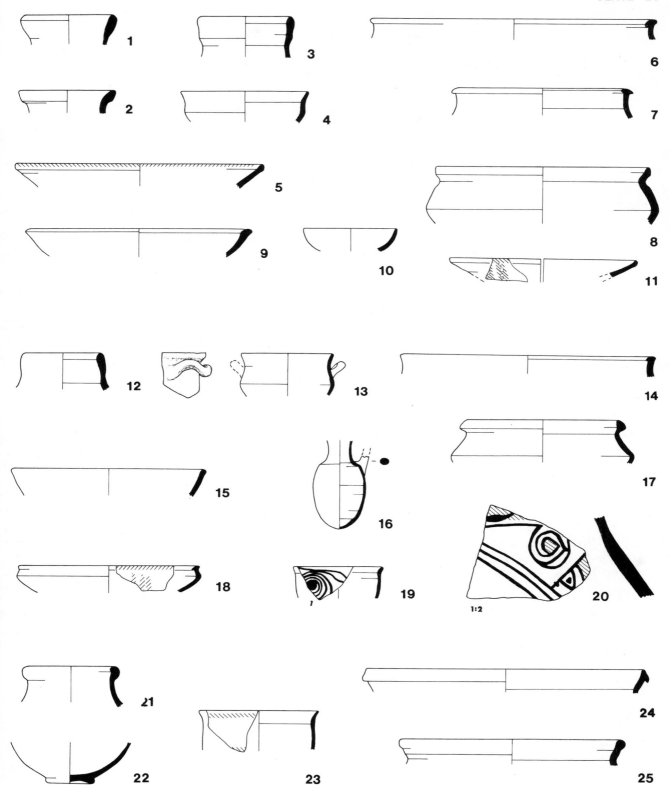

Plate Number	Pottery Type	Number and locus (see LOCUS INDEX)	Description (p. 277)
1.	Bowl	G70, VI.NE24.207, No. 6 L. 24087	*Technique:* Wheelmade. *Paste:* 5YR "reddish yellow" 6/2; many very small and few medium to large lime, few large wadi gravel and iron, small and medium ceramic and very small crystal; grey core; hard. *Surface (Interior):* as paste; 2.5YR "red" 5/6 organic paint decoration. *(Exterior):* as paste.
2.	Bowl	G70, VI.NE24.207, 209, No. 2, L. 24087	*Technique:* Wheelmade. *Paste:* 5YR "reddish yellow" 6/6; many very small and few medium to large lime, few large wadi gravel and iron, small and medium ceramic and very small crystal; grey core; hard. *Surface (Interior):* as paste; 2.5YR "red" 5/6 organic paint decoration. *(Exterior):* as paste.
3.	Krater	G70, VI.NE24.204, No. 11 L. 24087	*Technique:* Wheelmade. *Paste:* 7.5YR "light brown" 6/4; few medium lime, very small crystal and wadi gravel; grey core; hard. *Surface (Interior):* as paste. *(Exterior):* as paste.
4.	Krater	G70, VI.NE24.207, No. 7 L. 24086	*Technique:* Wheelmade. *Paste:* 7.5YR "light brown" 4/4; many very small and few medium and large lime, few small ceramic and organic and very small crystal; grey core; hard. *Surface (Interior):* as paste. *(Exterior):* as paste.
5.	Bowl or cup	G70, VI.NE24.207, No. 26 L. 24087	*Technique:* Wheelmade. *Paste:* 5YR "reddish yellow" 6/6; few medium ceramic, very small and medium wadi gravel, small organic and very small crystal; grey core; hard. *Surface (Interior):* as paste. *(Exterior):* as paste; bands of 10YR "weak red" 4/3 organic paint.
6.	Pilgrim flask	G70, VI.NE24.223, No. 13 L. 24087	*Technique:* Wheelmade. *Paste:* 5YR "pink" 7/4; some small to large lime, few very small crystal; no core; hard. *Surface (Interior):* as paste. *(Exterior):* as paste.
7.	Bowl	G70, VI.NE24.220, No. 9 L. 24087	*Technique:* Wheelmade. *Paste:* 5YR "reddish yellow" 7/6; many very small and few large lime, some large organic and few small to medium ceramic and very small crystal; grey core; hard. *Surface (Interior):* as paste; 10YR "dusky red" 3/2 organic paint decoration. *(Exterior):* as paste.
8.	Bowl or cup	G70, VI.NE24.184, No. 3 L. 24087	*Technique:* Wheelmade. *Paste:* 5YR "reddish yellow" 6/6; few medium ceramic, very small and medium wadi gravel, small organic and very small crystal; grey core; hard. *Surface (Interior):* as paste. *(Exterior):* as paste; bands of 10YR "weak red" 4/3 organic paint.
9.	Cooking pot	G70, VI.NE24.208, No. 15 L. 24087	*Technique:* Wheelmade. *Paste:* 5YR "reddish brown" 5/4; some medium and large and few very small lime, few medium organic and very small crystal; dark grey core; hard. *Surface (Interior):* as paste. *(Exterior):* as paste.
10.	Bowl	G70, VI.NE24.220, No. 4 L. 24087	*Technique:* Wheelmade. *Paste:* 5YR "reddish brown" 7/6; many very small and few small to large lime, few very small crystal; core: 7.5YR "light brown" 6/4; hard. *Surface (Interior):* as paste; 10YR "red" 4/8 slip on rim. *(Exterior):* as paste.
11.	Jug	G70, VI.NE24.207, No. 3 L. 24087	*Technique:* Wheelmade. *Paste:* 5YR "reddishyellow" 6/6; many very small crystal, few small to large lime, and medium organic; grey core; hard. *Surface (Interior):* as paste. *(Exterior):* as paste.
12.	Lamp	G70, VI.NE25.125, No. 2 · L. 25063	*Technique:* Wheelmade. *Paste:* 5YR "reddish yellow" 7/6; many small sand, few small to large ceramic; no core; hard. *Surface (Interior):* as paste. *(Exterior):* as paste.
13.	Bowl	G70, VI.NE25.125, No. 1 L. 25063	*Technique:* Wheelmade. *Paste:* 2.5YR "light reddish brown" 6/4; few small crystal, few small to medium lime; dark grey core; hard. *Surface (Interior):* as paste. *(Exterior):* as paste.
14.	Jar	G71, VI.NE25.157, No. 16 L. 25063	*Technique:* Wheelmade. *Paste:* 5YR "pink" 7/4; few very small to medium lime and crystal and small ceramic; core: 7.5YR "pink" 8/4; hard. *Surface (Interior):* as paste. *(Exterior):* as paste.
15.	Jar	G71, VI.NE25.173, No. 10 L. 25063	*Technique:* Wheelmade. *Paste:* 7.5YR "light brown" 6/4; some very small and few medium crystal, few large iron, very small lime and wadi gravel; no core; hard. *Surface (Interior):* as paste. *(Exterior):* as paste.
16.	Cooking pot	G71, VI.NE25.149, No. 2 L. 25063	*Technique:* Wheelmade. *Paste:* 5YR "dark reddish grey" 4/2; few very small to large lime, large wadi gravel, medium and large oranic, medium ceramic and very small crystal; grey core; hard. *Surface (Interior):* as paste. *(Exterior):* as paste.
17.	Bowl	G71, VI.NE25.149, No. 3 L. 25063	*Technique:* Wheelmade. *Paste:* 5YR "reddish yellow" 5/6; many very small and few small to large lime, some very small crystal; few small ceramic and wadi gravel; grey core; hard. *Surface (Interior):* as paste and exterior. *(Exterior):* 7.5YR "pinkish white" 8/2.
18.	Lamp	G71, VI.NE25.213, No. 2 L. 25091.1	*Technique:* Wheelmade. *Paste:* 5YR "pink" 7/4; few small to large lime, some medium wadi gravel, no core; hard. *Surface (Interior):* as paste to 7.5YR "pink" 8/4. *(Exterior):* as paste.
19.	Bowl	G71, VI.NE25.213, No. 1 L. 25091.1	*Technique:* Wheelmade. *Paste:* 7.5YR "reddish yellow" 8/6; few small to large lime, few large ceramic and organic; no core; hard. *Surface (Interior):* as paste. *(Exterior):* as paste.

PLATE 22

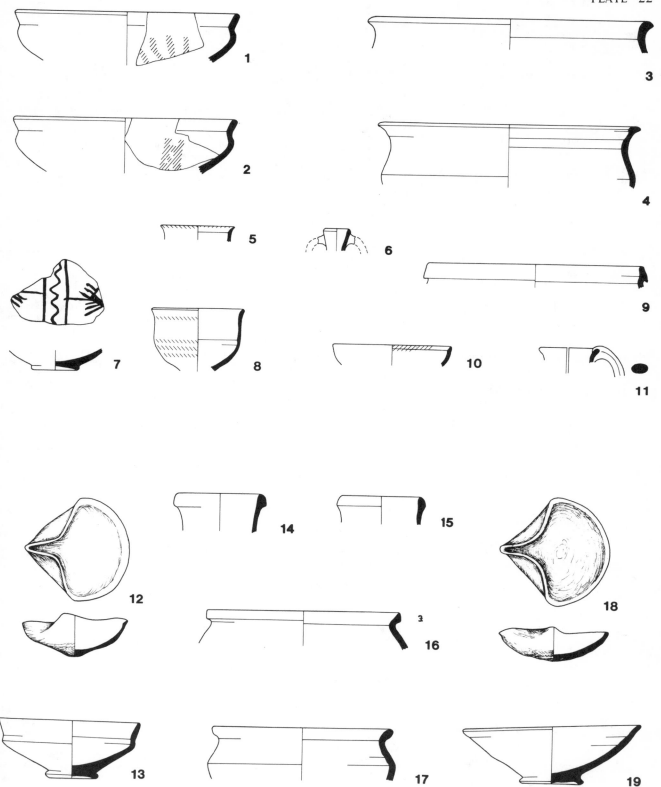

Plate Number	Pottery Type	Number and locus (see LOCUS INDEX)	Description (p. 277)
1.	Jar	G71, VI.NE16.277, No. 2 L. 16095.1	*Technique:* Wheelmade. *Paste:* 7.5YR "pinkish white" 8/2; some very small, few large wadi gravel, few very small to large lime and very small crystal; no core; hard. *Surface (Interior):* as paste. *(Exterior):* as paste; 10YR "white" 8/1 band.
2.	Jar	G71, VI.NE16.263, No. 7 L. 16095.1	*Technique:* Wheelmade. *Paste:* 5YR "reddish yellow" 7/6; some very small sand, few very small wadi gravel and very small and small lime; core; 7.5YR "light brown" 6/4; hard. *Surface (Interior):* as paste. *(Exterior):* as paste.
3.	Krater	G72, VI.NE16.263, No. 12 L. 16095	*Technique:* Wheelmade. *Paste:* 5YR "reddish yellow" 7/6; some very small and few small and large lime, few small to large organic, few very small and small ceramic and very small crystal; grey core; hard. *Surface (Interior):* as paste. *(Exterior):* as paste.
4.	Sherd	G71, VI.NE16.277, No. 4 L. 16095.1	*Technique:* Wheelmade. *Paste:* 7.5YR "pink" 7/4; few very small and small lime, small iron and very small wadi gravel, ceramic and crystal; no core; hard. *Surface (Interior):* as paste. *(Exterior):* as paste; 5YR "reddish brown" 5/4 and 2.5YR "very dusky red" 2.5/2 organic paint decoration; hand burnish.
5.	Jar	G70, VI.NE23.84A, No. 4 L. 23031	*Technique:* Wheelmade. *Paste:* 7.5YR "light brown" 6/4; many very small wadi gravel, few medium to large organic and very small crystal; dark grey core; hard. *Surface (Interior):* as paste. *(Exterior):* as paste.
6.	Cooking pot	G71, VI.NE16.263, No. 2 L. 10095.1	*Technique:* Wheelmade. *Paste:* 5YR "reddish brown" 5/4; few very small to large crystal, small and large organic and medium ceramic; grey core; hard. *Surface (Interior):* as paste. *(Exterior):* as paste.
7.	Jar	G70, VI.NE34.90, No. 10 L. 34022.1	*Technique:* Wheelmade. *Paste:* 5YR "reddish yellow" 7/6; many very small lime, some very small and few medium crystal, few very small ceramic; light grey core; hard. *Surface (Interior):* as paste. *(Exterior):* as paste.
8.	Jar	G70, VI.NE34.108C, No. 17, L. 34043.1	*Technique:* Wheelmade. *Paste:* 5YR "reddish yellow" 6/6; some very small and medium and few large lime, few very small ceramic; grey core; hard. *Surface (Interior):* as paste. *(Exterior):* as paste.
9.	Jug or jar	G70, VI.NE34.112A, No. 3 L. 34043.1	*Technique:* Wheelmade. *Paste:* 5YR "light reddish brown" 6/4; few very small lime, ceramic and crystal; no core; hard. *Surface (Interior):* as paste. *(Exterior):* 10YR "white" 8/1 slip; 10YR "weak red" 4/3 slip on rim.
10.	Bowl	G70, VI.NE23.84A, No. 1 L. 23031	*Technique:* Wheelmade. *Paste:* 5YR "reddish yellow" 7/6; some very small and few small to medium lime, some very small wadi gravel, few very small and medium ceramic; light grey core; hard. *Surface (Interior):* as exterior. *(Exterior):* 10YR "white" 8/2 to 7.5YR "pink" 8/4 slip.
11.	Cooking jug?	G70, VI.NE34.112B, No. 3 L. 34043.1	*Technique:* Wheelmade. *Paste:* 5YR "yellowish red" 5/6; few very small to medium lime and very small and small crystal; no core; hard. *Surface (Interior):* as paste and exterior. *(Exterior):* 10YR "light grey" 7/2.
12.	Jar	G70, VI.NE3.84, No. 5 L. 3020	*Technique:* Wheelmade. *Paste:* 2.5YR "red" 6/6; many very small to small crystal, few small wadi gravel, lime and ceramic; grey core; hard. *Surface (Interior):* as paste. *(Exterior):* as paste.
13.	Juglet	G70, VI.NE3.84, No. 20 L. 3020	*Technique:* Wheelmade. *Paste:* 7.5YR "light brown" 7/2; very many small to some large lime, some small to medium ceramic, few very small crystal, few small wadi gravel; no core; hard. *Surface (Interior):* as paste. *(Exterior):* as paste; 7.5YR "pinkish white" 8/2 wet smoothed, body vertically shaved.
14.	Krater	G71, VI.NE5.145, No. 3 L. 5059.1	*Technique:* Wheelmade. *Paste:* 5YR "reddish yellow" 6/6; some very small and few medium lime, few small to medium ceramic, few large wadi gravel; grey core; hard. *Surface (Interior):* 2/5YR "red" 5/6; wheel burnish. *(Exterior):* as interior; burnish as interior.
15.	Amphora	G69, VI.NE13.186, No. 1 L. 13038.1	*Technique:* Wheelmade. *Paste:* 5YR "pink" 7/3; some small crystal (quartz); no core; hard. *Surface (Interior):* as paste. *(Exterior):* as paste.
16.	Krater	G70, VI.NE14.164, No. 4 L. 14061	*Technique:* Wheelmade. *Paste:* 7.5YR "pink" 7/4; some very small and few large lime, few small ceramic; no core; hard. *Surface (Interior):* as paste. *(Exterior):* as paste.
17.	Bowl or cup	G70, VI.NE14.164, No. 3 L. 14061	*Technique:* Wheelmade. *Paste:* 5YR "reddish yellow" 6/6; many very small and few medium and large lime, few medium and large ceramic, medium wadi gravel and very small crystal; grey core; hard. *Surface (Interior):* as paste. *(Exterior):* as paste; 10YR "weak red" 4/4 slip on rim.
18.	Bowl	G70, VI.NE14.157, No. 3 L. 14061	*Technique:* Wheelmade. *Paste:* 5YR "reddish yellow" 6/6; some very small crystal, few small and medium ceramic and lime and small organic; grey core; hard. *Surface (Interior):* as paste. *(Exterior):* as paste.
19.	Bowl	G70, VI.NE14.153, 164, No. 12 L. 15061	*Technique:* Wheelmade. *Paste:* 5YR "reddish yellow" 6/6; some small and few medium and large lime, few medium and large wadi gravel, small to large ceramic and very small crystal; grey core; hard. *Surface (Interior):* as paste to 7.5YR "pink" 8/3. *(Exterior):* as paste.
20.	Bowl	G71, VI.NE16.213, No. 2 L. 16088	*Technique:* Wheelmade. *Paste:* 7.5YR "pink" 7/4; some very small and few medium wadi gravel, few small lime and organic and very small crystal; dark grey core; hard. *Surface (Interior):* as paste. *(Exterior):* as paste.
21.	Bowl	G71, VI.NE16.234, No. 2 L. 16088	*Technique:* Wheelmade. *Paste:* 5YR "yellowish red" 6/6; very many very small crystal; few medium and large wadi gravel and lime, some medium and large organic few small ceramic; grey core; hard. *Surface (Interior):* as paste. *(Exterior):* 7.5YR "pink" 7/4 to 7/5YR "dark grey" 4/0.
22.	Cooking pot	G71, VI.NE16.213, No. 15 L. 16088	*Technique:* Wheelmade. *Paste:* 5YR "reddish brown" 5/3; some medium lime, small organic, few small and medium wadi gravel, medium iron, very small crystal; grey core; hard. *Surface (Interior):* 5YR "light reddish brown" 6/4. *(Exterior):* as interior.
23.	Bowl	G71, VI.NE23.228, No. 7 L. 23054B	*Technique:* Wheelmade. *Paste:* 5YR "reddish yellow" 7/6; many very small, some small and few medium to large lime, few very small crystal; no core; hard. *Surface (Interior):* as paste to 7.5YR "pinkish white" 8/2; 10YR "red" 4/4 organic paint on rim and decorations. *(Exterior):* as paste; organic paint on rim and traces on body as interior.
24.	Bowl or cup	G71, VI.NE23.194, 203, No. 4, L. 23054B	*Technique:* Wheelmade. *Paste:* 7.5YR "pink" 7/4; some very small lime and ceramic, few small wadi gravel and very small crystal; no core; hard. *Surface (Interior):* as paste; organic paint on rim as exterior. *(Exterior):* as paste; 10YR "dusky red" 3/4 organic paint decoration.

PLATE 23

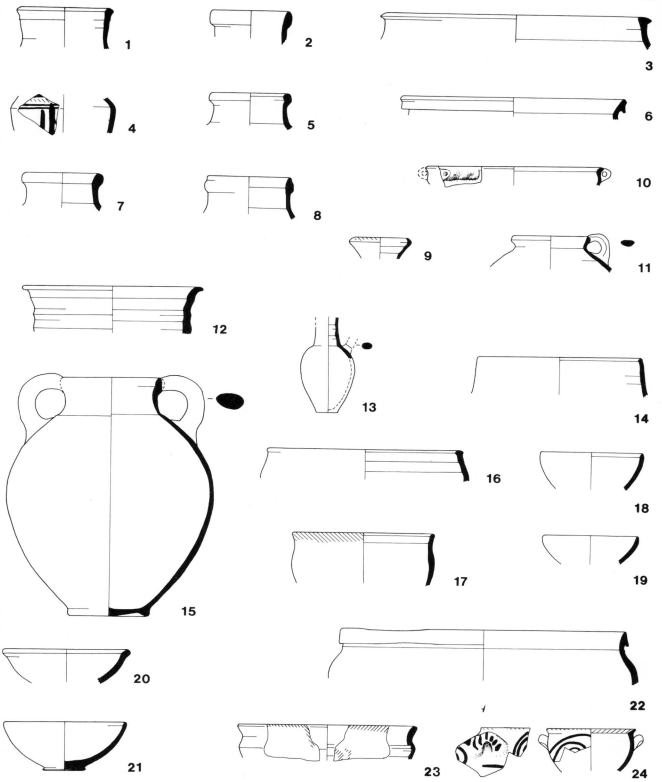

Plate Number	Pottery Type	Number and locus (see LOCUS INDEX)	Description (p. 277)
1.	Jar	G70, VI.NE23.60, No. 5 L. 23027	*Technique:* Wheelmade. *Paste:* 5YR "reddish yellow" 6/6; many very small lime, few very small ceramic; light grey core; hard. *Surface (Interior):* as paste. *(Exterior):* as paste.
2.	Jar	G70, VI.NE23.61, No. 12 L. 23027	*Technique:* Wheelmade. *Paste:* 7.5YR "light brown" 6/4; many very small crystal, few very small and large lime, medium ceramic; no core; hard. *Surface (Interior):* as paste. *(Exterior):* as paste.
3.	Krater	G70, VI.NE23.60, No. 9 L. 23027	*Technique:* Wheelmade. *Paste:* 5YR "reddish yellow" 6/6; many very small and few small to large lime, few medium and large wadi gravel, very small to medium ceramic and very small crystal; grey core; hard. *Surface (Interior):* as paste. *(Exterior):* as paste.
4.	Bowl	G70, VI.NE23.60, No. 1 L. 23027	*Technique:* Wheelmade. *Paste:* 7.5YR "pink" 7/4; some very small and few medium and large lime, few large wadi gravel and iron, very small to medium ceramic and very small crytal; hard. *Surface (Interior):* as paste; band of 10YR "weak red" 5/4 organic paint on rim and decoration. *(Exterior):* as paste.
5.	Bowl	G70, VI.NE23.61, No. 1 L. 23027	*Technique:* Wheelmade. *Paste:* 5YR "reddish yellow" 7/6; many small organic, some small wadi gravel, few small ceramic, lime, and very small wadi gravel, few small ceramic, lime, and very small crystal; light grey core; hard. *Surface (Interior):* as paste; band of 10YR "red" 4/6 organic paint on rim and decoration. *(Exterior):* as paste.
6.	Bowl	G70, VI.NE23.80, No. 14 L. 23027	*Technique:* Wheelmade. *Paste:* 5YR "reddish yellow" 5/6; some very small and few medium lime, few very small and medium organic, wadi gravel and ceramic and very small crystal; grey core; hard. *Surface (Interior):* as paste; 10YR "red" 4/6 slip on rim. *(Exterior):* as paste; slip on rim as interior.
7.	Bowl	G70, VI.NE23.60, No. 17 L. 23027	*Technique:* Wheelmade. *Paste:* 7.5YR "light brown" 6/4; many very small and few small to large lime, few very small and medium ceramic and very small crystal; no core; hard. *Surface (Interior):* 10YR "white" 8/2; 10YR "weak red" 4/4 slip on rim. *(Exterior):* as interior; slip on rim as interior.
8.	Bowl or cup	G70, VI.NE23.60, No. 2 L. 23027	*Technique:* Wheelmade. *Paste:* 7.5YR "pink" 7/4; some very small lime, few very small crystal and ceramic; no core; hard. *Surface (Interior):* as paste; band of 10YR "dark red" 4/6 organic paint on rim. *(Exterior):* as paste to organic paint decoration as interior.
9.	Chalice	G70, VI.NE23.60, No. 11 L. 23027	*Technique:* Wheelmade. *Paste:* 7.5YR "pink" 8/4; outer: 5YR "grey" 6/1; very many very small wadi gravel, few large lime, medium ceramic and organic and very small crystal; no core; hard. *Surface (Interior):* as inner paste; 2.5YR "reddish brown" 5/4 slip on rim. *(Exterior):* as outer paste.
10.	Chalice base	G70, VI.NE23.69, No. 4 L. 23027	*Technique:* Wheelmade. *Paste:* 5YR "reddish yellow" 7/6; few medium organic, small lime, very small wadi gravel and crystal; grey core; hard. *Surface (Interior):* 10YR "very pale brown" 8/4 to 10YR "grey" 6/1. *(Exterior):* 7.5YR "pink" 7/4.
11.	Krater	G70, VI.NE23.69, No. 10 L. 23027	*Technique:* Wheelmade. *Paste:* 7.5YR "light brown// 6.4; few large wadi gravel, small ceramic, very small lime and crystal; grey core; hard. *Surface (Interior):* as paste. *(Exterior):* as paste.
12.	Krater	G70, VI.NE23.77, No. 3 L. 23027	*Technique:* Wheelmade. *Paste:* 5YR "reddish brown" 5/4; some very small lime and crystal, few small ceramic; grey core; hard. *Surface (Interior):* as paste. *(Exterior):* 7.5YR "pink" 7/4.
13.	Krater	G70, VI.NE23.83, No. 3 L. 23027	*Technique:* Wheelmade. *Paste:* 5YR "reddish yellow" 7/6; some very small wadi gravel, few medium iron, small organic and lime and very small crystal; grey core; hard. *Surface (Interior):* as paste. *(Exterior):* as paste.
14.	Bowl	G70, VI.NE23.80, No. 15, L. 23027	*Technique:* Wheelmade. *Paste:* inner: 5YR "reddish yellow" 7/6; outer: 7.5YR "pink" 7/4; many very small and few small to large lime, few medium ceramic, and large; grey core; hard. *Surface (Interior):* as paste; inner: 10YR "weak red" 4/4 slip on rim. *(Exterior):* as outer paste.
15.	Krater	G70, VI.NE23.81, No. 6 L. 23027	*Technique:* Wheelmade. *Paste:* 5YR "reddish yellow" 7/6; some very small crystal, few small to large lime, large iron and very small ceramic; light grey core; hard. *Surface (Interior):* as paste; slip and band of organic paint on rim as exterior. *(Exterior):* 10YR "white" 8/1 slip, organic paint; 10YR "red" 4/6 band; 10YR "dark reddish grey" 3/1 decoration.
16.	Krater	G70, VI.NE23.81, No. 15 L. 23027	*Technique:* Wheelmade. *Paste:* 5YR "light reddish brown" 6/4; some very small lime, wadi gravel and ceramic and few large lime; no core; hard. *Surface (Interior):* as paste; organic paint on rim as exterior. *(Exterior):* 7.5YR "pink" 8/4 band of 10YR "red" 4/6 organic paint on rim; 10YR "reddish black" 2.5/1 organic paint decoration.
17.	Bowl	G70, VI.NE23.77, No. 20 L. 23027	*Technique:* Wheelmade. *Paste:* 7.5YR "light brown" 6/4; few very small to large lime, very small and medium ceramic, and very small crystal; core; 7.5YR "pink" 8/4; hard. *Surface (Interior):* 7.5YR "pink" 8/4; 10YR "weak red" 4/4 slip on rim. *(Exterior):* 10YR "white" 8/2 slip onrim as interior.
18.	Bowl or cup	G70, VI.NE23.59, No. 11 L. 23027	*Technique:* Wheelmade. *Paste:* a2.5YR "light red" 6/6; some very small wadi gravel, few very small and small organic and very small crystal; core: 5YR "reddish yellow" 7/6; hard. *Surface (Interior):* 10YR "white" 8/1 slip; possible trace of band of 10YR "red" 4/6 organic paint on rim. *(Exterior):* slip as interior; 10YR "dusky red" 3/2 organic paint decoration.
19.	Cooking pot	G70, VI.NE23.83, No. 4 L. 23027	*Technique:* Wheelmade. *Paste:* 5YR "reddish yellow" 6/6; very many very small to large crystal, some medium lime and organic; dark grey core; hard. *Surface (Interior):* as paste. *(Exterior):* as paste.
20.	Cooking pot	G70, VI.NE23.81, No. 24 L. 23027	*Technique:* Wheelmade. *Paste:* 5YR "reddish brown" 5/4; some very small and few medium and large lime, few large organic; grey core; hard. *Surface (Interior):* as paste. *(Exterior):* as paste.
21.	Krater	G70 VI.NE23.59, No. 2 L. 23027	*Technique:* Wheelmade. *Paste:* 7.5YR "pink" 7/4; some large organic and very small wadi gravel, few small iron and crystal; dark grey core;hard. *Surface (Interior):* as paste. *(Exterior):* as paste; 2.5YR "light red" 6/6 slip on rim.
22.	Bowl or cup	G70, VI.NE23.59, No. 7 L. 23027	*Technique:* Wheelmade. *Paste:* 5YR "reddish yellow" 6/6; many very small wadi gravel, few small organic and lime and very small crystal; core: 7.5YR "light brown" 6/4; hard. *Surface (Interior):* 7.5YR "pinkish white" 8/2 slip. *(Exterior):* slip as interior; 5YR "dark reddish brown" 2.5/2 organic paint decoration traces of 10YR " red" 5/6 organic paint on rim.
23.	Jug	G70, VI.NE23.80, No. 23 L. 23-27	*Technique:* Wheelmade. *Paste:* 5YR "pink" 7/4; some medium organic and very small wadi gravel, few small and large lime and very small crystal; core: 7.5YR "pink" 7/4; hard. *Surface (Interior):* as paste. *(Exterior):* as paste.

PLATE 24

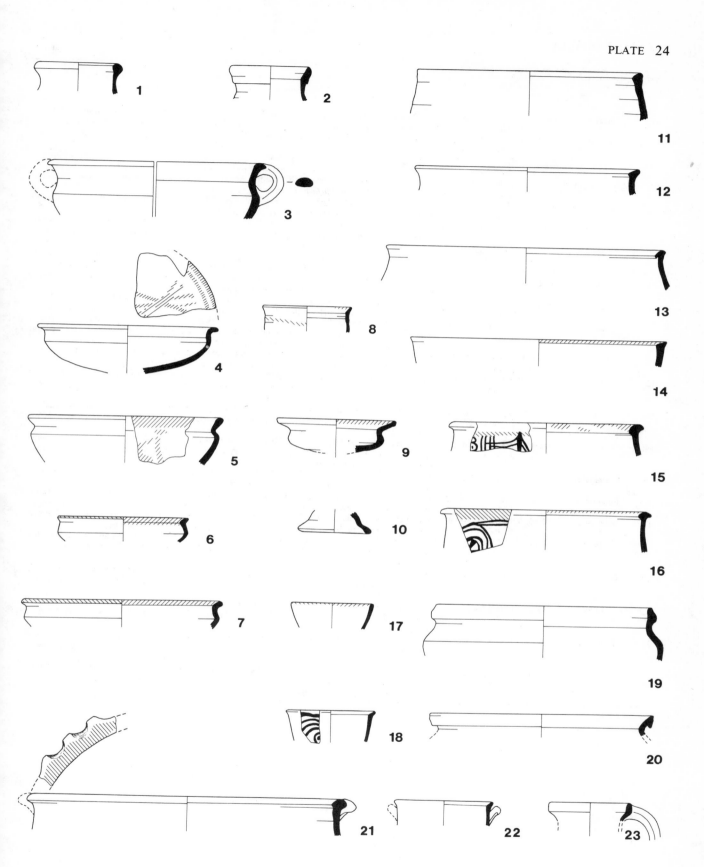

Plate Number	Pottery Type	Number and locus (see LOCUS INDEX)	Description (p. 277)
1.	Krater	G69, VI.NE24.54, No. 5 L. 24028	*Technique:* Wheelmade. *Paste:* 5YR "pink" 7/4; few medium organic, small to medium ceramic, very small wadi gravel and crystal; grey core. *Surface (Interior):* as paste. *(Exterior):* as paste.
2.	Krater	G69, VI.NE24.47/54 No. 1–7, L. 24028/24029	*Technique:* Wheelmade. *Paste:* 5YR "pink" 7/4; some small calcite and crystal; no core; hard. *Surface (Interior):* as paste. *(Exterior):* 10YR "dark red" 3/6 slip.
3.	Bowl	G69, VI.NE24.54, No. 3 L. 24028	*Technique:* Wheelmade. *Paste:* 5YR "pink" 7/3; many small crystal, few medium to large ceramic; no core; hard. *Surface (Interior):* as paste. *(Exterior):* as paste.
4.	Cooking pot	G70, VI.NE34.93, No. 3 L. 24032	*Technique:* Wheelmade. *Paste:* 5YR "reddish brown" 5/4; few small to large lime and very small crystal; grey core; hard. *Surface (Interior):* as paste. *(Exterior):* as paste.
5.	Cooking pot	G70, VI.NE34.53, No. 9 L. 34032	*Technique:* Wheelmade. *Paste:* 5YR "reddish brown" 5/4; few small to large lime and very small crystal; no core; hard. *Surface (Interior):* as paste. *(Exterior):* as paste.
6.	Krater	G69, VI.NE34.66, No. 4 L. 34032	*Technique:* Wheelmade. *Paste:* 5YR "reddish brown" 7/6; some small wadi gravel, few small organic and very small crystal; dark grey core; hard. *Surface (Interior):* as paste. *(Exterior):* as paste.
7.	Jar	G70, VI.NE34.162, 165, No. 12 L. 34032	*Technique:* Wheelmade. *Paste:* 5YR "reddish yellow" 7/6; some very small wadi gravel, few small and medium lime and small organic; "light brown" 6/4; hard. *Surface (Interior):* as paste; paint on rim as exterior. *(Exterior):* as paste; bands of 10YR "weak red" 5/4 organic paint.
8.	Pyksis	G70, VI.NE34.93, L. 34032	*Technique:* Wheelmade. *Paste:* 7.5YR "light brown" 6/4; few small to medium lime and black grits; no core; medium. *Surface (Interior):* as paste. *(Exterior):* as paste.
9.	Jar	G69, VI.NE3.34, No. 3 L. 3003	*Technique:* Wheelmade. *Paste:* 7.5YR "light brown" 6/4; many very small to small crystal, few small lime and organic, light grey core; hard. *Surface (Interior):* as paste. *(Exterior):* as paste.
10.	Base	G69, VI.NE3.31, No. 20 L. 3003	*Technique:* Wheelmade. *Paste:* inner: 7.5YR "very dark grey" 3/0; outer: 7.5YR "light brown" 6/4; some very small to small crystal, few small and large wadi gravel and lime and small and medium ceramic; grey core; hard. *Surface (Interior):* as inner paste. *(Exterior):* as outer paste.
11.	Krater	G69, VI.NE3.34, No. 8 L. 3003	*Technique:* Wheelmade. *Paste:* 5YR "pink" 7/4; some small crystal, few medium and large wadi gravel and lime, no core, hard. *Surface (Interior):* as paste. *(Exterior):* as paste.
12.	Bowl	G69, VI.NE3.31, No. 15 L. 3003	*Technique:* Wheelmade. *Paste:* 7.5YR "light brown" 6/4; some small wadi gravel, few small lime and crystal, large iron; no core; hard. *Surface (Interior):* as paste to 10YR "white" 8/2. *(Exterior):* as interior.
13.	Base	G69, VI.NE3.30, No. 18 L. 3003	*Technique:* Wheelmade. *Paste:* 2.5YR "light brown" 6/4; many very small crystal, few small to large lime and large wadi gravel; grey core; hard. *Surface (Interior):* as paste. *(Exterior):* 10YR "white" 8/2.
14.	Cooking pot	G69, VI.NE3.31, No. 18 L. 3003	*Technique:* Wheelmade. *Paste:* 5YR "light reddish brown" 6/4 to 5YR "reddish brown" 4/3; many small to large lime, some small organic, few very small crystal; light grey core; hard. *Surface (Interior):* as paste. *(Exterior):* as paste.
15.	Cooking pot	G69, VI.NE3.39, No. 15 L. 3003	*Technique:* Wheelmade. *Paste:* 2.5YR "red" 5/6; some medium and large, few small lime; dark grey core; hard. *Surface (Interior):* as paste. *(Exterior):* as paste.
16.	Bowl or cup	G69, VI.NE3.35, No. 22 L. 3003	*Technique:* Wheelmade. *Paste:* 7.5YR "pink" 7/4; some very small wadi gravel, few small ceramic and very small crystal and lime; no core; hard. *Surface (Interior):* as paste. *(Exterior):* as paste.
17.	Bowl or cup	G69, VI.NE3.39, No. 9 L. 3003	*Technique:* Wheelmade. *Paste:* 7.5YR "light brown" 6/4; few small organic, very small wadi gravel and crystal; no core; hard. *Surface (Interior):* 5YR "pink" 8/4. *(Exterior):* as interior.
18.	Base	G70, VI.NE3.50, No. 5 L. 3042	*Technique:* Wheelmade. *Paste:* 7.5YR "reddish yellow" 7/6; many very small wadi gravel, few medium iron and lime, very small crystal; core; 10YR "very pale brown" 7/3; hard. *Surface (Interior):* as paste. *(Exterior):* as paste.
19.	Bowl or cup	G69, VI.NE3.32, No. 3 L. 3003	*Technique:* Wheelmade. *Paste:* 7.5YR "light brown" 6/4; many small and few very small crystal, few small wadi gravel and small to medium lime; no core; hard. *Surface (Interior):* as paste. *(Exterior):* as paste.
20	Krater	G70, VI.NE3.50, No. 2 L. 3004.1	*Technique:* Wheelmade. *Paste:* 7.5YR "light brown" 6/4; few medium iron and lime, very small wadi gravel and crystal; grey core; hard. *Surface (Interior):* 10YR "very pale brown" 7/3. *(Exterior):* 10YR "white" 8/1.
21.	Bowl or cup	G70, VI.NE3.50, No. 6 L. 3004.1	*Technique:* Wheelmade. *Paste:* 7.5YR "light brown" 6/4; some very small crystal, many very small wadi gravel, few small organic; light grey core; hard. *Surface (Interior):* 10YR "very pale brown" 8/3; 10YR "white" 8/1 slip on rim. *(Exterior):* as interior; slip on rim as interior.
22.	Bowl	G69, VI.NE3.39, No. 18 L. 3042	*Technique:* Wheelmade. *Paste:* 7.5YR "light brown" 6/4; many very small crystal, few medium organic and wadi gravel and very small and medium ceramic; dark grey core; hard. *Surface (Interior):* as paste. *(Exterior):* as paste.

PLATE 25

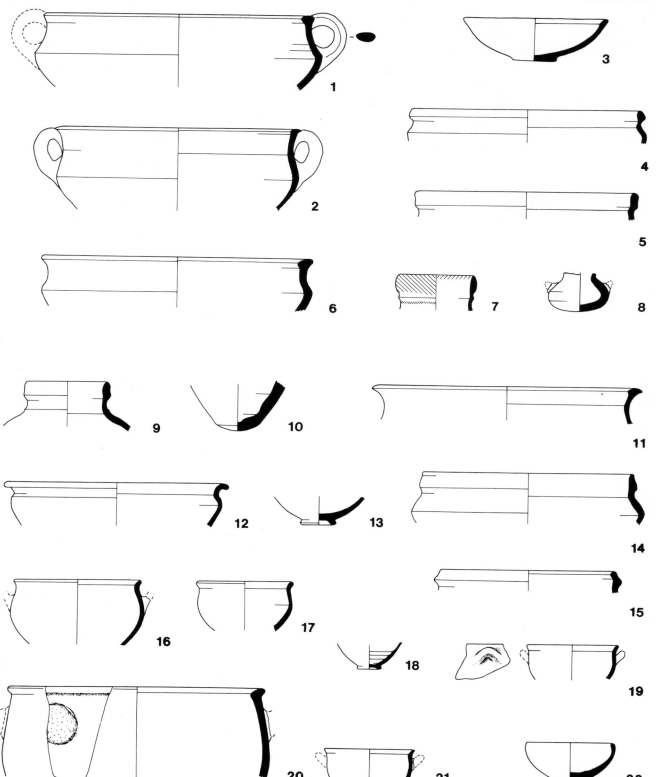

Plate Number	Pottery Type	Number and locus (see LOCUS INDEX)	Description (p. 277)
1.	Jar	G69, VI.NE13.96, No. 7 L. 13030	*Technique:* Wheelmade: *Paste:* 5YR "pink" 7/3; many small crystal; no core; hard. *Surface (Interior):* as paste. *(Exterior):* as paste.
2.	Juglet	G70, VI.NE13.155, No. 5 L. 13030	*Technique:* Wheelmade. *Paste:* 7.5YR "pink" 7/4; very many very small to small crystal, few lime and wadi gravel; no core; hard. *Surface (Interior):* as paste. *(Exterior):* as paste.
3.	Jar	G69, VI.NE13.96, L. 13030	*Technique:* Wheelmade. *Paste:* 5YR "pink" 7/4; some small crystal (?); no core to light grey core; hard. *Surface (Interior):* as paste. *(Exterior):* as paste.
4.	Bowl	G71, VI.NE5.135, No. 2 L. 5052	*Technique:* Wheelmade. *Paste:* 2.5YR "brown" 5/4; some small to large lime, some very small crystal, few small wadi gravel; no core; hard. *Surface (Interior):* 10YR "white" 8/2 to 7.5YR "pink" 7/4. *(Exterior):* 10YR "white" 8/2.
5.	Bowl	G71, VI.NE5.141, No. 29 L. 5052	*Technique:* Wheelmade. *Paste:* 7.5YR "light brown" 6/4; many very small to small crystal, few medium and large lime, few large ceramic; no core; hard. *Surface (Interior):* as paste. *(Exterior):* as paste.
6.	Bowl	G71, VI.NE5.135, No. 1 L. 5052	*Technique:* Wheelmade. *Paste:* 7.5YR "pink" 7/4; few small lime, few very small to small ceramic, few very small crystal, few medium wadi gravel; light grey core; hard. *Surface (Interior):* 10YR "white" 8/2. *(Exterior):* as interior.
7.	Bowl	G71, VI.NE5.168, No. 13 L. 5072	*Technique:* Wheelmade. *Paste:* 5YR "reddish yellow" 6/6; few large wadi gravel, some medium to large lime, few medium to large ceramic, few very small crystal; no core; hard. *Surface (Interior):* as paste. *(Exterior):* as paste.
8.	Krater	G70, VI.NE13.57, Nos. 1, 3 L. 13030	*Technique:* Wheelmade. *Paste:* 5YR "pink" 7/3; small, medium, and large limestone grits; slightly grey core; hard.? *Surface (Interior):* as paste. *(Exterior):* as paste.
9.	Juglet	G69, VI.NE13.91, Nos. 13–12 L. 13030	*Technique:* Wheel and handmade. *Paste:* 10YR "brown" 5/3; some small wadi gravel; no core; hard. *Surface (Interior):* as paste. *(Exterior):* 10YR "white" 8/2; lines: 5YR "reddish brown" 5/3.
10.	Jar	G69, VI.NE13.95, L. 13030	*Technique:* Wheelmade. *Paste:* 5YR "pink" 7/4; many small crystal; light grey core, hard. *Surface (Interior):* as paste. *(Exterior):* as paste.

PLATE 26

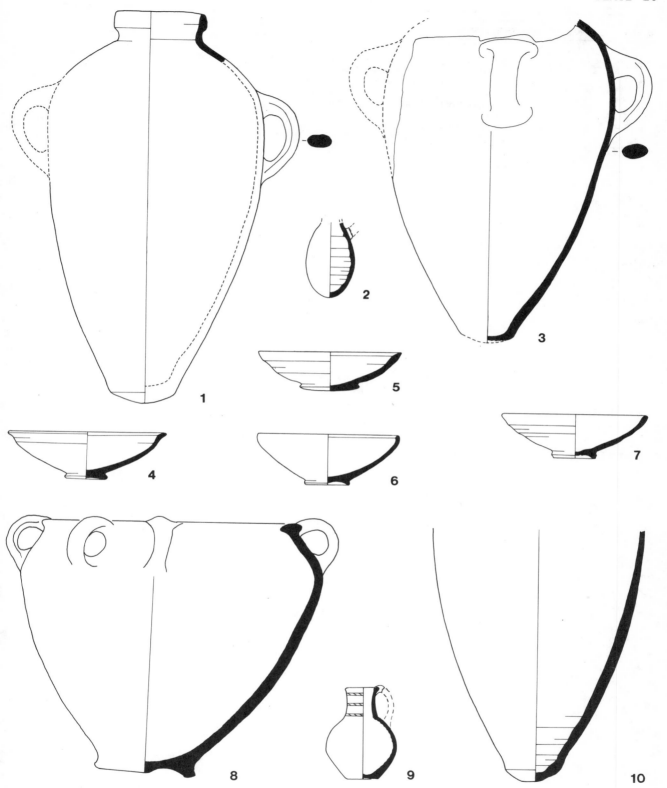

Plate Number	Pottery Type	Number and locus (see LOCUS INDEX)	Description (p. 277)
1.	Jar	G69, VI.NE13.97, No. 1 L. 13030	*Technique:* Wheelmade. *Paste:* 7.5YR "pink" 7/4; many small crystal; no core; hard. *Surface (Interior):* as paste. *(Exterior):* as paste.
2.	Jar	G69, VI.NE13.99, No. 1 L. 13030	*Technique:* Wheelmade. *Paste:* 5YR "pink" 7/3; some to many small crystal; light grey core; hard. *Surface (Interior):* as paste. *(Exterior):* as paste.
3.	Jar	G69, VI.NE13.98, No. 1 L. 13030	*Technique:* Wheelmade. *Paste:* 5YR "pink" 7/4; some to many ceramics, crystal; no core; hard. *Surface (Interior):* as paste. *(Exterior):* as paste.
4.	Jar	G69, VI.NE13.93, No. 1 L. 13037	*Technique:* Wheelmade. *Paste:* 7.5YR "pink" 7/4 – 5YR "pink" 7/3; some small to medium ceramics; grey core; hard. *Surface (Interior):* as paste. *(Exterior):* as paste.

PLATE 27

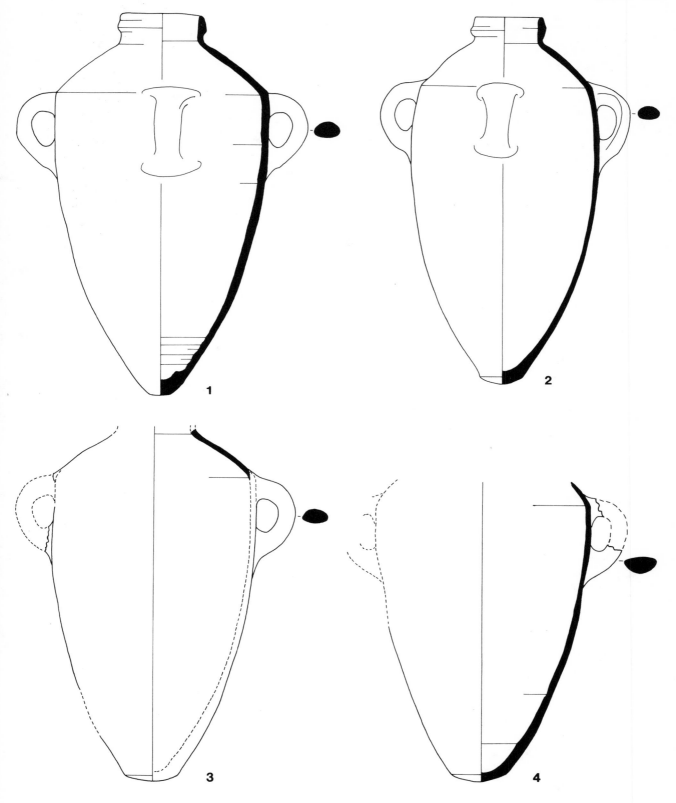

Plate Number	Pottery Type	Number and locus (see LOCUS INDEX)	Description (p. 277)
1.	Jar	G69, VI.NE13.94, No. 2 L. 13037	*Technique:* Wheelmade. *Paste:* 5YR "pink" 7/4; some small crystal and ceramic; grey core; hard. *Surface (Interior):* as paste. *(Exterior):* as paste.
2.	Jar	G69, VI.NE13.94, No. 1 L. 13037	*Technique:* Wheelmade. *Paste:* 5YR "reddish yellow" 7/6 – 6/6; some large crystal and lime; light grey core; hard. *Surface (Interior):* as paste. *(Exterior):* as paste.
3.	Juglet	G69, VI.NE13.117, L. 13038P	*Technique:* Wheelmade. *Paste:* 2.5YR "red" 5/6; many very small and few small to large lime, few large wadi gravel and iron, some very small crystal; grey core; hard. *Surface (Interior):* as paste. *(Exterior):* 7YR "pink" 7/4 to 5YR "very dark grey" 3/2.
4.	Bowl	G70, VI.NE13.166, No. 7 L. 13038P	*Technique:* Wheelmade. *Paste:* 5YR "pink" 7/4; some very small crystal, few small lime and wadi gravel; grey core; hard. *Surface (Interior):* as paste; 10YR "red" 4/8 slip on rim. *(Exterior):* as paste to 7.5YR "pinkish white" 8/2 slip on rim as interior.
5.	Beerjug	G69, VI.NE13.114, No. 9 L. 13038	*Technique:* Wheelmade. *Paste:* 5YR "pink" 7/4; many small crystal (quartz); light grey core; hard. *Surface (Interior):* as paste. *(Exterior).* 2.5YR "red" 5/6; painted decorative line 2.5YR "dusky red"3/2; 5YR "pinkish white" 8/2.
6.	Bottle	G69, VI.NE13.145, No. 1 L. 13038P	*Technique:* Wheelmade. *Paste:* 7.5YR "pinkish grey"6/2; many very small and few large lime, few large iron, medium wadi gravel and very small crystal; grey core; hard. *Surface (Interior):* as paste. *(Exterior):* 10YR "white" 8/2.
7.	Krater	G70, VI.NE13.166, No. 13 L. 13038P	*Technique:* Wheelmade. *Paste:* inner: 7.5YR "pink" 8/4; outer: 2.5YR "light red" 6/6; many very small crystal, few small and large lime, large organic and small wadi gravel; grey core; hard. *Surface (Interior):* 5YR "white" 8/1. *(Exterior):* as interior.
8.	Krater	G70, VI.NE13.166, No. 10 L. 13038P	*Technique:* Wheelmade. *Paste:* inner: 7.5YR "pink" 8/4; outer: 2.5YR "light red" 6/6; many small wadi gravel, few small and large lime, small organic and iron, very small crystal; light grey core; hard. *Surface (Interior):* 7.5YR "pinkish white" 8/2. *(Exterior):* as interior.
9.	Krater	G69, VI.NE13.111, No. 27 L. 13038P	*Technique:* Wheelmade. *Paste:* 7.5YR "pink" 7/4; few very small and medium lime and very small ceramic and crystal; light grey core; hard. *Surface (Interior):* as paste. *(Exterior):* as paste.
10.	Krater	G70, VI.NE13.157, No. 5 L. 13038P	*Technique:* Wheelmade. *Paste:* 5YR "reddish yellow" 7/6; some very small wadi gravel, few small lime, iron, organic and ceramic, very small crystal; grey core; hard. *Surface (Interior):* as paste. *(Exterior):* 2.5YR "white" slip; band of 2.5YR "pale yellow" 8/4 organic paint on rim; 7.5YR "brown" 5/2 organic paint decoration.

PLATE 28

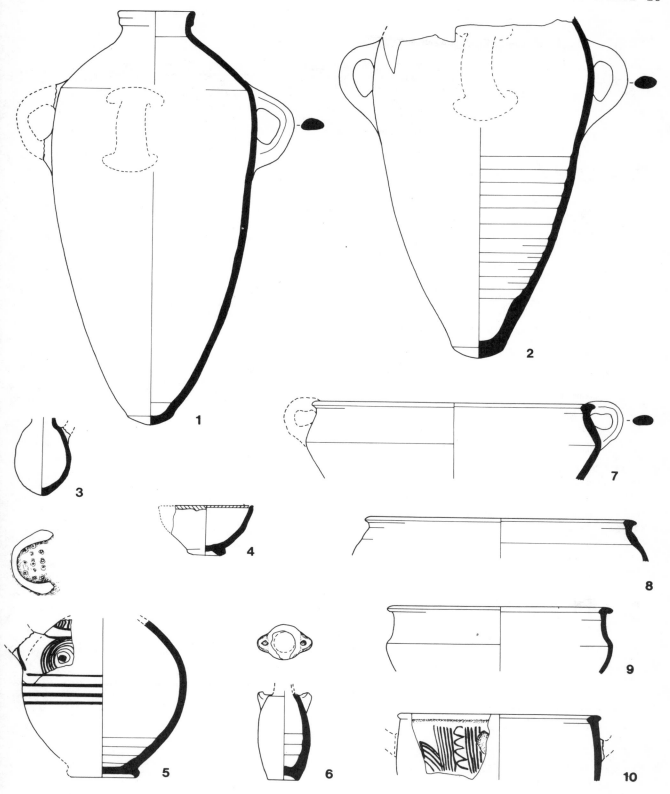

Plate Number	Pottery Type	Number and locus (see LOCUS INDEX)	Description (p. 277)
1.	Jar	G70, VI.NE13.128, No. 3 L. 13038P	*Technique:* Wheelmade. *Paste:* 7.5YR "pinkish grey" 7/2; some very small wadi gravel, small to few large organic, few small and very large lime and very small crystal; dark grey core; hard. *Surface (Interior):* as paste. *(Exterior):* as paste.
2.	Jar	G70, VI.NE13.166, No. 9 L. 13038P	*Technique:* Wheelmade. *Paste:* 5YR "reddish yellow" 6/6; many very small and few small wadi gravel, some very small crystal, few medium lime; no core; hard. *Surface (Interior):* 7.5YR "pink" 7/4. *(Exterior):* as interior.
3.	Bowl	G70, VI.NE13.176, No. 6 L. 13038P	*Technique:* Wheelmade. *Paste:* 5YR "reddish yellow" 7/6; many very small and few small wadi gravel, few small and medium organic, small lime and very small crystal; core: 7.5YR "pinkish grey" 7/2; hard. *Surface (Interior):* 7.5YR "pink" 8/4. *(Exterior):* as interior.
4.	Bowl	G70, VI.NE13.12, No. 6 L. 13038P	*Technique:* Wheelmade. *Paste:* 7.5YR "pink" 7/4; many very small and few medium wadi gravel, few small and medium lime, few small organic and very small crystal; grey core; hard. *Surface (Interior):* as paste. *(Exterior):* as paste.
5.	Bowl	G69, VI.NE13.112, No. 18 L. 13038P	*Technique:* Wheelmade. *Paste:* 5YR "reddish yellow" 7/6; many very small and few large lime, few large wadi gravel, small ceramic and very small crystal; grey core; hard. *Surface (Interior):* as paste. *(Exterior):* as paste.
6.	Bowl	G70, VI.NE13.12, No. 10 L. 13038P	*Technique:* Wheelmade. *Paste:* 7.5YR "light brown" 6/4; many very small and medium wadi gravel, few large iron and very small crystal; light grey core; hard. *Surface (Interior):* as paste. *(Exterior):* as paste.
7.	Flask	G70, VI.NE13.157, No. 2 L. 13038P	*Technique:* Wheelmade. *Paste:* 7.5YR "pink" 7/4; many very small wadi gravel, some small organic, few very small lime and crystal; grey core; hard. *Surface (Interior):* 10YR "light grey" 7/2. *(Exterior):* as interior.
8.	Base	G69, VI.NE14.80, No. 5 L. 14015	*Technique:* Wheelmade. *Paste:* inner: 7.5YR "pink" 7/4; outer: 2.5YR "light red" 6/6; some very small and few small and medium lime, few medium and large organic, very small and medium crystal; no core; hard. *Surface (Interior):* as inner paste. *(Exterior):* as paste to 10YR "white" 8/1.
9.	Jug	G69, VI.NE14.51, No. 1 L. 14015	*Technique:* Wheelmade. *Paste:* 5YR "pink" 7/4; some small crystal and ceramic; light grey core; hard. *Surface (Interior):* as paste. *(Exterior):* as paste; decorative lines 2.5YR "red" 5/6.
10.	Jug	G69, VI.NE13.148, L. 13038P	*Technique:* Wheelmade. *Paste:* 5YR "pink" 7/1; some large lime; no core; hard. *Surface (Interior):* as paste. *(Exterior):* as paste.
11.	Cooking pot	G70, VI.NE13.157, No. 3 L. 13038P	*Technique:* Wheelmade. *Paste:* 5YR "reddish brown" 5/3; few very small to large lime and very small crystal; dark grey core; hard. *Surface (Interior):* as paste. *(Exterior):* as paste.
12.	Cooking pot	G70, VI.NE13.157, No. 15 L. 13038P	*Technique:* Wheelmade. *Paste:* 5YR "light reddish brown" 6/4; few small and many medium and large wadi gravel, few small and some medium lime; no core; hard. *Surface (Interior):* as paste. *(Exterior):* 2.5YR "light red" 6/6.
13.	Cooking pot	G69, VI.NE13.131, No. 6 L. 13038P	*Technique:* Wheelmade. *Paste:* 5YR "reddish brown" 5/4; some very small crystal, few small to large lime; grey core; hard. *Surface (Interior):* as paste. *(Exterior):* as paste.
14.	Cooking pot	G69, VI.NE13.112, No. 11 L. 13038P	*Technique:* Wheelmade. *Paste:* 5YR "reddish brown" 5/4; few very small to large lime and crystal, few large wadi gravel and medium organic; grey core; hard. *Surface (Interior):* as paste. *(Exterior):* as paste.
15.	Cooking pot	G70, VI.NE13.164A, No. 2 L. 13038P	*Technique:* Wheelmade. *Paste:* 2.5YR "light red" 6/6; some very small to few medium lime, few small to some medium wadi gravel, few small to medium organic, very small crystal; grey core; hard. *Surface (Interior):* as paste. *(Exterior):* as paste.
16.	Amphora	G69, VI.NE14.33, No. 9 L. 14015	*Technique:* Wheelmade. *Paste:* 5YR "pink" 7/4; many small wadi gravel, mostly quartz; no core; hard. *Surface (Interior):* as paste. *(Exterior):* as paste.
17.	Bowl or cup	G69, VI.NE14.37, No. 4 L. 14015	*Technique:* Wheelmade. *Paste:* 5YR "light reddish brown" 6/4; some very small sand, few medium ceramic, small wadi gravel, very small crystal; dark grey core; hard. *Surface (Interior):* 5YR "reddish yellow" 7/6; band of 10YR "red" 4/6 slip on rim. *(Exterior):* as interior.
18.	Pyxis	G69, VI.NE14.85, 90, No. 3, L. 14015	*Technique:* Wheelmade. *Paste:* 5YR "reddish yellow" 6/6; some very small and medium and large lime, few medium and large organic, very small to large ceramic and small crystal; grey core; hard. *Surface (Interior):* as paste. *(Exterior):* as paste.
19.	Krater	G69, VI.NE14.31, No. 10 L. 14015	*Technique:* Wheelmade. *Paste:* 5YR "pink" 7/4; many very small to few large wadi gravel, few medium ceramic, small organic and very small crystal; light grey core; hard. *Surface (Interior):* as paste. *(Exterior):* as paste.
20.	Bowl	G70, VI.NE14.153, No. 6 L. 14015	*Technique:* Wheelmade. *Paste:* 5YR "reddish yellow" 6/6; many very small crystal, few very small and small ceramic, small organic and medium; lime; dark grey core; hard. *Surface (Interior):* 7.5YR "pink" 7/4; band of 2.5YR "red" 5/6 organic paint on rim and decoration. *(Exterior):* as interior; paint on rim as interior.
21.	Bowl or cup	G70, VI.NE14.153, No. 8 L. 14015	*Technique:* Wheelmade. *Paste:* 2.5YR "light red" 6/6; some small and few medium and large lime, few small wadi gravel and ceramic and very small crystal; core: 7.5YR "pink" 7/4; hard. *Surface (Interior):* as paste; band of 2.5YR "red" 4/6 slip on rim. *(Exterior):* as paste; slip on rim as interior.

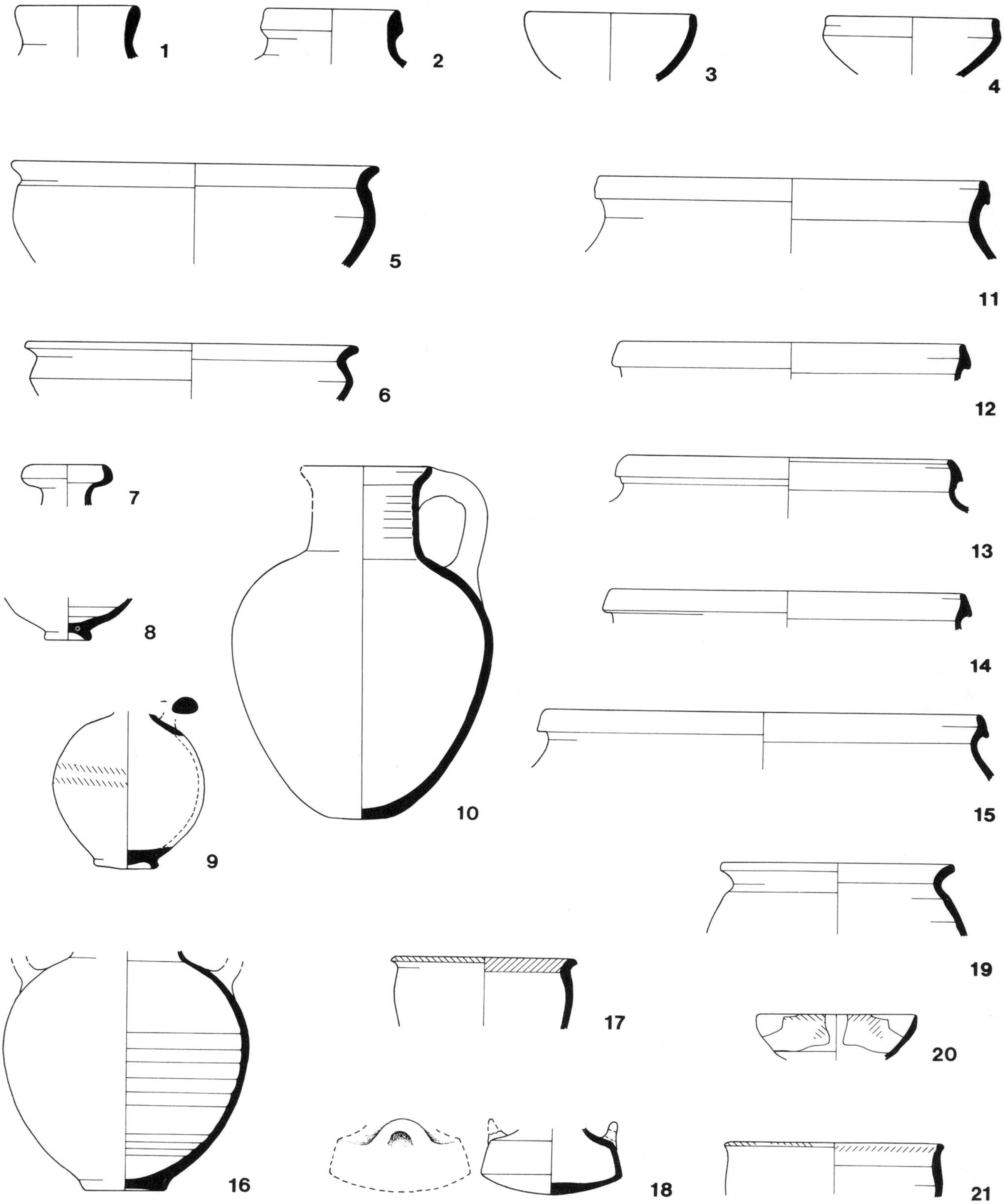
1
2
3
4
5
11
6
12
7
13
8
14
9
10
15
19
16
17
20
18
21

Plate Number	Pottery Type	Number and locus (see LOCUS INDEX)	Description (p. 277)
1.	Jar	G69, VI.NE14.33, L. 14015	*Technique:* Wheelmade. *Paste:* 5YR "light reddish brown" 6/4; many small crystal; no core; hard. *Surface (Interior):* as paste. *(Exterior):* as paste.
2.	Jar	G69, VI.NE14.59, L. 14015	*Technique:* Wheelmade. *Paste:* 5YR "pink" 7/4; many small crystal (quartz); light grey core; hard. *Surface (Interior):* as paste. *(Exterior):* as paste.
3.	Jar	G69, VI.NE14.36, No. 9 L. 14015	*Technique:* Wheelmade. *Paste:* 5YR "pink" 7/4; many small crystal, few large limestone; no core; hard. *Surface (Interior):* as paste. *(Exterior):* as paste.
4.	Bowl	G69, VI.NE14.33, Nos. 2,7, L. 14015	*Technique:* Wheelmade. *Paste:* 7.5YR "pink" 7/4; some to many small crystal (quartz): no core; hard. *Surface (Interior):* lines: 10YR "dusky red" 3/4. *(Exterior):* as paste.
5.	Bowl	G69, VI.NE14.28, No. 14 L. 14015	*Technique:* Wheelmade. *Paste:* inner: 7.5YR "pink" 8/4; outer: 5YR "reddish yellow" 7/6; very many very small and few medium and large lime, few very small ceramic and crystal; no core; hard. *Surface (Interior):* as inner paste; 10YR "dusky red" 3/4 organic paint decoration. *(Exterior):* 7.5YR "pinkish white" 8/2.
6.	Bowl	G69, VI.NE14.38, Nos. 5, 9 L. 14015	*Technique:* Wheelmade. *Paste:* 5YR "reddish yellow" 7/6; many small wadi gravel, mostly quartz; light grey core; hard. *Surface (Interior):* 10YR "red" 5/6 decorative slip. *(Exterior):* as paste.

PLATE 30

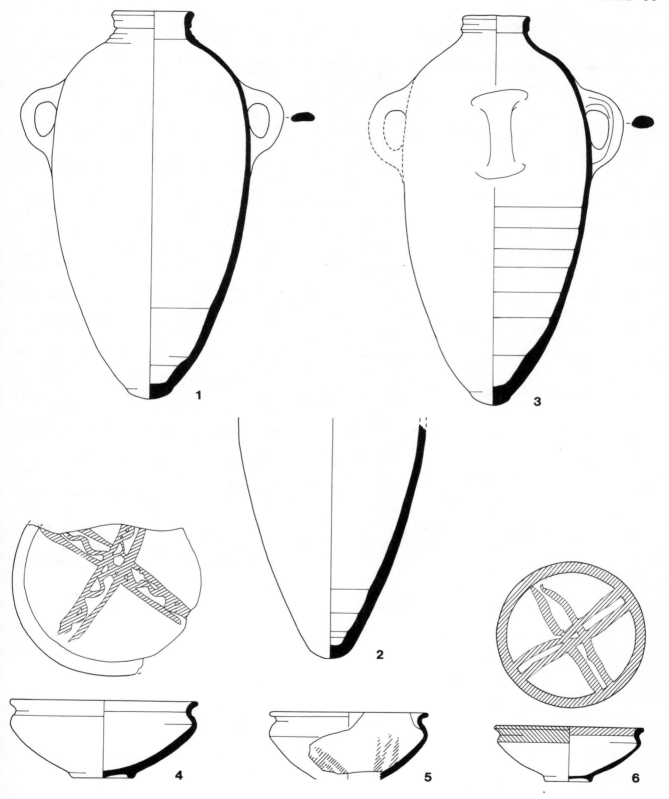

Plate Number	Pottery Type	Number and locus (see LOCUS INDEX)	Description (p. 277)
1.	Amphora(?)	G69, VI.NE37, No. 6 L. 14015	*Technique:* Wheelmade. *Paste:* 5YR "pink" 7/4; some to many small crystal (quartz); no core; hard. *Surface (Interior):* as paste. *(Exterior):* as paste.
2.	Krater	G69, VI.NE14.37, No. 1 L. 14015	*Technique:* Wheelmade. *Paste:* 7.5YR "pink" 7/4; many very small to small crystal and wadi gravel, some small to medium organic and few large wadi gravel and lime; grey core; hard. *Surface (Interior):* 5YR "reddish yellow" 7/6. *(Exterior):* 7.5YR "pink" 8/2 slip with bands of 2.5YR "red" 5/6 organic paint and 2.5YR "black" N2.5/0 organic paint decoration.
3.	Krater	G69, VI.NE14.33, No. 8 L. 14015	*Technique:* Wheelmade. *Paste:* 5YR "reddish yellow" 7/6; some medium to large organic, few very small to medium wadi gravel, small lime, very small ceramic and crystal; grey core; hard. *Surface (Interior):* as paste. *(Exterior):* as paste.
4.	Krater	G69, VI.NE14.63, No. 3 L. 14015	*Technique:* Wheelmade. *Paste:* 5YR "reddish yellow" 6/6; some very small and few small and medium lime, some very small crystal, few small and medium ceramic; grey core; hard. *Surface (Interior):* as paste. *(Exterior):* as paste.
5.	Cooking pot	G69, VI.NE14.80, No. 5 L. 14015	*Technique:* Wheelmade. *Paste:* 5YR "reddish brown" 5/4; some medium and few small and large lime, few very small and medium crystal, small to large ceramic and large wadi gravel; dark grey core; hard. *Surface (Interior):* as paste. *(Exterior):* as paste.
6.	Cooking pot	G69, VI.NE14.44, No. 15 L. 14015	*Technique:* Wheelmade. *Paste:* 5YR "reddish brown" 5/4; some medium to few large wadi gravel, few very small to large lime; grey core; hard. *Surface (Interior):* as paste. *(Exterior):* as paste.
7.	Krater	G69, VI.NE14.63, No. 5 L. 14015	*Technique:* Wheelmade. *Paste:* 5YR "reddish yellow" 7/6; few very small to medium lime, small to large organic, medium wadi gravel, large iron and very small crystal; core: 7.5YR "light brown" 6/4; hard. *Surface (Interior):* as paste *(Exterior):* 10YR "white" 8/1 slip; bands of 10YR "red" 4/4 organic paint on rim and body.
8.	Krater	G70, VI.NE14.153, No. 3 L. 14032.1	*Technique:* Wheelmade. *Paste:* 7.5YR "light brown" 6/4; many very small crystal, few small ceramic and organic and small to large lime and large wadi gravel; light grey core; hard. *Surface (Interior):* as paste. *(Exterior):* as paste.
9.	Bowl	G70, VI.NE23.44, No. 7 L. 23014P	*Technique:* Wheelmade. *Paste:* 5YR "reddish yellow" 7/6; some very small and few medium to large lime, few medium ceramic and very small crystal; core: 7.5YR "pink" 7/4; hard. *Surface (Interior):* as paste. *(Exterior):* as paste
10.	Chalice	G70, VI.NE23.19, No. 12 L. 23010	*Technique:* Wheelmade. *Paste:* 7YR "light reddish brown" 6/4; many very small wadi gravel, some very small crystal, few small and large lime, medium iron and small organic; grey core; hard. *Surface (Interior):* as paste; 5YR "weak red" 4/4 slip on rim. *(Exterior):* as paste; slip on rim as interior.
11.	Bowl	G71, VI.NE26.223, No. 3 L. 26076	*Technique:* Wheelmade. *Paste:* 7.5YR "light brown" 6/4; some very small and few small to large lime, few small to large organic, small ceramic and wadi gravel and very small crystal; grey core; hard. *Surface (Interior):* as paste to 7.5YR "pinkish grey" 6/2; 2.5YR "red" 5/6 slip on rim. *(Exterior):* as interior; traces of slip on rim as interior.
12.	Bowl	G71, VI.NE26.227, No. 20 L. 26076	*Technique:* Wheelmade. *Paste:* 5YR "reddish yellow" 7/6; few very small to large lime, large wadi gravel, very small and small ceramic, very small wadi gravel and crystal; light grey core; hard. *Surface (Interior):* as paste. *(Exterior):* as paste.
13.	Chalice	G70, VI.NE23,24.88, No.12, L. 23014P	*Technique:* Wheelmade. *Paste:* 5YR "reddish yellow" 7/6; some very small to few very large lime, few small to medium ceramic and very small crystal; grey core; hard. *Surface (Interior):* as paste to 7.5YR "pinkish white" 8/2. *(Exterior):* as interior.
14.	Juglet	G70, VI.NE23,24.88, L. 23014P	*Technique:* Wheelmade. *Paste:* 5YR "reddish yellow" 6/6; may very small to few medium lime, few small wadi gravel, few small ceramic, feww very small crystal; no core; hard. *Surface (Interior):* as paste. *(Exterior):* as paste.
15.	Jar	G71, VI.NE26.228, No. 22 L. 26076	*Technique:* Wheelmade. *Paste:* 7.5YR "pink" 7/4; some very small and few small and large lime, few large iron, very small and large wadi gravel, very small to medium ceramic and very small crystal; grey core; hard. *Surface (Interior):* 10YR "very pale brown" 8/4; 2.5YR "weak red" 4/2 slip on rim. *(Exterior):* as paste; 2.5YR "red" 5/6 slip on rim; bands of 10YR "white" 8/1 organic paint.

PLATE 31

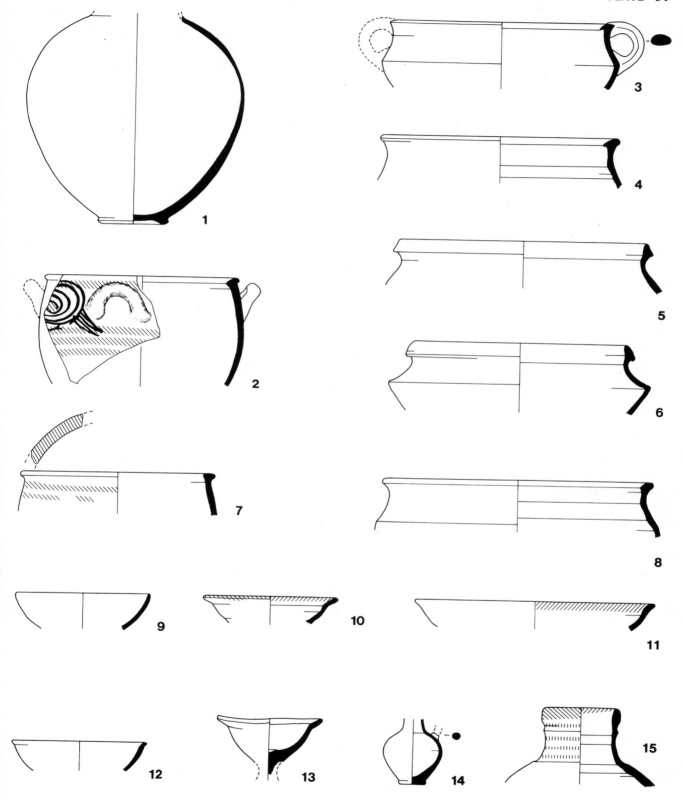

Plate Number	Pottery Type	Number and locus (see LOCUS INDEX)	Description (p. 277)
1.	Jar	G69, VI.NE24.67, No. 1 L. 24039	*Technique:* Wheelmade. *Paste:* 7.5YR "strong brown" 5/6; many very small crystal, few medium and large lime, organic and wadi gravel; grey core; hard. *Surface (Interior):* as paste. *(Exterior):* as paste.
2.	Krater	G69, VI.NE24.93, No. 6 L. 24039	*Technique:* Wheelmade. *Paste:* 7.5YR "pink" 7/4; few medium organic, small ceramic and very small crystal; dark grey core; hard. *Surface (Interior):* as paste; traces of 5YR "reddish yellow" 6/6 slip. *(Exterior):* as paste.
3.	Bowl	G69, VI.NE24.93, No. 5 L. 24039	*Technique:* Wheelmade. *Paste:* 5YR "reddish yellow" 7/6; some very small crystal, few large lime, small ceramic and very small organic; grey core; hard. *Surface (Interior):* as paste. *(Exterior):* as paste.
4.	Bowl	G69, VI.NE24.93, No. 16 L. 24039	*Technique:* Wheelmade. *Paste:* 7.5YR "pink" 7/4; some small organic and very small wadi gravel, few very small crystal; light grey core; hard. *Surface (Interior):* 5YR "reddish yellow" 10YR "dusky red" 3/4 slip on rim. *(Exterior):* 7.5YR "pink" 8/4; slip on rim as interior.
5.	Bowl	G69, VI.NE24.81, L. 24042	*Technique:* Wheelmade. *Paste:* 5YR "pink" 7/4; many small crystal and ceramic; light grey core; hard. *Surface (Interior):* as paste. *(Exterior):* 7.5YR "pinkish white" 8/2; 5YR "dark reddish brown" 3/2; 2.5YR "red" 4/6; slip, polished and painted decorative lines.
6.	Bowl	G69, VI.NE24.78, No. 5 L. 24042	*Technique:* Wheelmade. *Paste:* 5YR "reddish yellow" 6/6; many very small and few medium lime, few medium ceramic and very small crystal; core: 7.5YR "light brown" 6/4; hard. *Surface (Interior):* as paste. *(Exterior):* as paste.
7.	Krater	G69, VI.NE24.89, No. 14 L. 24042	*Technique:* Wheelmade. *Paste:* 5YR "reddish yellow" 7/6; few small wadi gravel, lime and organic and very small crystal; dark grey core; hard. *Surface (Interior):* as paste. *(Exterior):* as paste.
8.	Krater	G69, VI.NE24.78, No. 1 L. 24042	*Technique:* Wheelmade. *Paste:* 5YR "pink" 7/4; some small wadi gravel, few small ceramic and very small crystal; dark grey core; hard. *Surface (Interior):* as paste. *(Exterior):* as paste.
9.	Bowl	G69, VI.NE24.89, No. 8 L. 24042	*Technique:* Wheelmade. *Paste:* 5YR "reddish yellow" 6/6; some very small and few medium and large lime, few small and medium ceramic and very small crystal; light grey core; hard. *Surface (Interior):* as paste; band of 10YR "red" 4/6 slip on rim. *(Exterior):* as paste.
10.	Bowl	G69, VI.NE24.78, No. 10 L. 24042	*Technique:* Wheelmade. *Paste:* 5YR "pink" 7/3; many very small wadi gravel, few very small to large lime; light grey core; hard. *Surface (Interior):* 10YR "white" 8/2; 2.5YR "reddish brown" 5/4 slip on rim. *(Exterior):* as interior.
11.	Krater	G69, VI.NE24.84, No. 2 L. 24042	*Technique:* Wheelmade. *Paste:* 5YR "reddish yellow" 7/6; few large iron, medium ceramic, small lime and organic and very small crystal; grey core; hard. *Surface (Interior):* as paste. *(Exterior):* 7.5YR "pinkish white" 8/2 slip; bands of 10YR "red" 4/6 organic paint and 5YR "dark reddish brown" 3/2 organic paint decoration.
12.	Bowl	G69, VI.NE24.130, No. 1 L. 24049P	*Technique:* Wheelmade. *Paste:* 2.5YR "light red" 6/8; some small to very large lime, few small organic and very small crystal; light grey core; hard. *Surface (Interior):* as paste; 7.5YR "pinkish white" 8/2 slip, 5YR "dusky red" 3/4 organic paint decoration. *(Exterior):* as paste to 10YR "very pale brown" 8/4.
13.	Jar	G69, VI.NE24.130, No. 14 L. 24049P	*Technique:* Wheelmade. *Paste:* 5YR "reddish yellow" 6/6; few small ceramic, very small crystal, lime and wadi gravel; very light grey core; hard. *Surface (Interior):* 5YR "reddish yellow" 7/6. *(Exterior):* as paste.
14.	Krater	G69, VI.NE24.130, No. 2 L. 24049P	*Technique:* Wheelmade. *Paste:* 5YR "reddish yellow" 7/6; some medium organic, very small to small wadi gravel, few medium lime and very small crystal; dark grey core; hard. *Surface (Interior):* 10YR "very pale brown" 8/3. *(Exterior):* as paste.
15.	Krater	G69, VI.NE24.130, No. 7 L. 24049P	*Technique:* Wheelmade. *Paste:* 5YR "reddish yellow" 7/6; few very large to small lime, small organic, very small crystal; dark grey core; hard. *Surface (Interior):* 10YR "very pale brown" 8/3. *(Exterior):* as paste.

PLATE 32

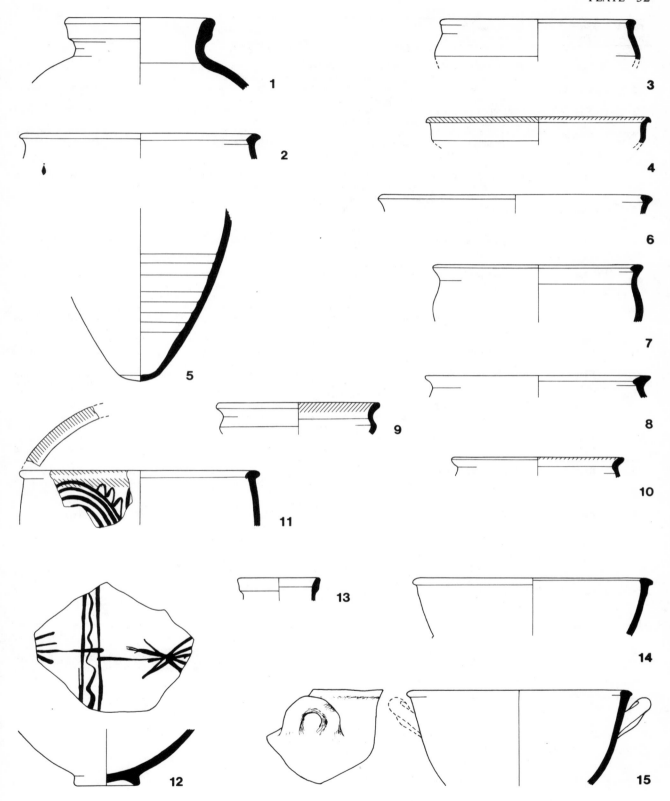

Plate Number	Pottery Type	Number and locus (see LOCUS INDEX)	Description (p. 277)
1.	Lamp	G69, VI.NE24.59, No. 4 L. 24039	*Technique:* Wheel and Handmade. *Paste:* 5YR "pink" 7/4; many small quartz; light grey core; hard. *Surface (Interior):* as paste. *(Exterior):* as paste.
2.	Cooking pot	G69, VI.NE24.93, No. 20 L. 24039	*Technique:* Wheelmade. *Paste:* 5YR ";reddish brown" 5/4; few small to large lime and very small crystal; grey core;hard. *Surface (Interior):* as paste. *(Exterior):* as paste.
3.	Cooking pot	G69, VI.NE24.73, No. 8 L. 24039	*Technique:* Wheelmade. *Paste:* 5YR "yellowish red" 5/6; many small to large lime, few very small crystal; no core; hard. *Surface (Interior):* as paste. *(Exterior):* as paste.
4.	Cooking pot	G69, VI.NE24.78, No. 20 L. 24039	*Technique:* Wheelmade. *Paste:* 5YR "reddish brown" 5/4; few small to large lime and crystal and large wadi gravel; no core; hard. *Surface (Interior):* as paste. *(Exterior):* as paste.
5.	Pilgrim flask	G69, VI.NE24.133, No. 1 L. 24049P	(No description)
6.	Jar	G70, VI.NE34.82, No. 31 L. 34007	*Technique:* Wheelmade. *Paste:* 5YR ";reddish yellow" 6/6; few very small and large wadi gravel, very small to medium lime, small ceramic and very small crystal; no core; hard. *Surface (Interior):* as paste. *(Exterior):* as paste.
7.	Jar	G70, VI.NE34.72, No. 18 L. 34007	*Technique:* Wheelmade. *Paste:* 5YR "reddish yellow" 6/6; many very small and few small to large lime, few large wadi gravel, small and medium ceramic and organic and very small crystal; grey core; hard. *Surface (Interior):* as paste. *(Exterior):* as paste.
8.	Jar	G70, VI.NE34.80, No. 7 L. 34007	*Technique:* Wheelmade. *Paste:* 5YR "reddish yellow" 7/6; many very small lime, some very small crystal, few small wadi gravel and ceramic; core: 7.5YR "light brown" 6/4; hard. *Surface (Interior):* as paste. *(Exterior):* as paste.
9.	Jar	G70, VI.NE34.81, No. 3 L. 34007	*Technique:* Wheelmade. *Paste:* 5YR "reddish yellow" 6/6; few very small to large lime, medium ceramic and very small crystal; core: 7.5YR "light brown" 6/4; hard. *Surface (Interior):* as paste. *(Exterior):* as paste.
10.	Jar	G70, VI.NE34.71, No. 1 L. 34007	*Technique:* Wheelmade. *Paste:* 5YR "reddish yellow" 6'6; some very small and few large lime, some very small and few medium ceramic, some very small sand, and few large wadi gravel; grey core; hard. *Surface (Interior):* as paste. *(Exterior):* as paste.
11.	Base	G69, VI.NE34.16, No. 21 L. 34039	*Technique:* Wheelmade. *Paste:* inner: 10YR "grey" 5/1; outer: 5YR "reddish yellow" 6/6; some very small and few medium and large lime, some very small crystal, few large and medium ceramic, and small organic; no core; hard. *Surface (Interior):* as paste. *(Exterior):* as paste.
12.	Krater	G70, VI.NE34.55, No. 1 L. 34007	*Technique:* Wheelmade. *Paste:* 5YR "reddish yellow" 5/6; many small and few medium to large lime, few medium organic, medium and small ceramic and small and very small crystal; light grey core; hard. *Surface (Interior):* as paste. *(Exterior):* as paste.
13.	Krater	G70, VI.NE34.71, No. 2 L. 34007	*Technique:* Wheelmade. *Paste:* 5YR "reddish yellow" 7/6; some very small and few medium lime, some medium organic, few large iron, small ceramic and very small crystal; grey core; hard. *Surface (Interior):* as paste. *(Exterior):* as paste.
14.	Krater	G70, VI.NE34.82, No. 34 L. 34007	*Technique:* Wheelmade. *Paste:* 5YR "reddish yellow" 7/6; some very small and few small to large lime, few very small crystal and ceramic; grey core; hard. *Surface (Interior):* as paste. *(Exterior):* as paste.
15.	Krater	G70, VI.NE34.82, No. 16 L. 34007	*Technique:* Wheelmade. *Paste:* 5YR "reddish yellow" 6/6; many very small crystal and ceramic, few medium organic; grey core; hard. *Surface (Interior):* as paste; slip on rim as exterior. *(Exterior):* 10YR "white" 8/2; 10YR "red" 5/6 slip on rim, 5YR "reddish brown" 5/3, 2.5YR "reddish brown" 5/4 and 2.5YR "dusky red" 3/2 organic paint decoration.
16.	Krater	G70, VI.NE34.72, No. 1 L. 34007	*Technique:* Wheelmade. *Paste:* 7.5YR "light brown" 6/4; some very small lime and crystal and few very small ceramic, few large wadi gravel; grey core; hard. *Surface (Interior):* as paste; traces of reddish brown" 4/4 slip over slip on rim as exterior. *(Exterior):* 10YR "white" 8/2 slip 2.5YR "reddish brown" 4/4 and 2.5YR "very dusky red" 2.5/2 organic paint decoration.
17.	Bowl or cup	G70, VI.NE34.80, No. 11 L. 34007	*Technique:* Wheelmade. *Paste:* 5YR "reddish yellow" 6/6; some very small and few medium lime, few very small and small ceramic and very small crystal; no core; hard. *Surface (Interior):* as paste. *(Exterior):* as paste to 7.5YR "pink" 7/4.
18.	Bowl or cup	G70, VI.NE34.47, No. 3 L. 34007	*Technique:* Wheelmade. *Paste:* 5YR "reddish yellow" 5/6; few very small and small lime and ceramic and very small crystal; no core; hard. *Surface (Interior):* as paste; slip on rim as exterior. *(Exterior):* 10YR "white" 8/2 slip; 10YR "red" 4/6 organic paint decoration.
19.	Jug	G70, VI.NE34.71, No. 4 L. 34007	*Technique:* Wheelmade. *Paste:* 5YR "reddish yellow" 6/6; some very small and few medium lime and ceramic, few very small crystal; core: 7.5YR "light brown" 6/4; hard. *Surface (Interior):* as paste. *(Exterior):* as paste.
20.	Bowl	G70, VI.NE34.72, No. 21 L. 34007	*Technique:* Wheelmade. *Paste:* 5YR "reddish yellow" 7/6; some very small and few small to large lime, few large wadi gravel and iron, small organic and small and very small ceramic; grey core; hard. *Surface (Interior):* as paste; 10YR "red" 5/8 slip on rim. *(Exterior):* as paste; slip on rim as interior.

PLATE 33

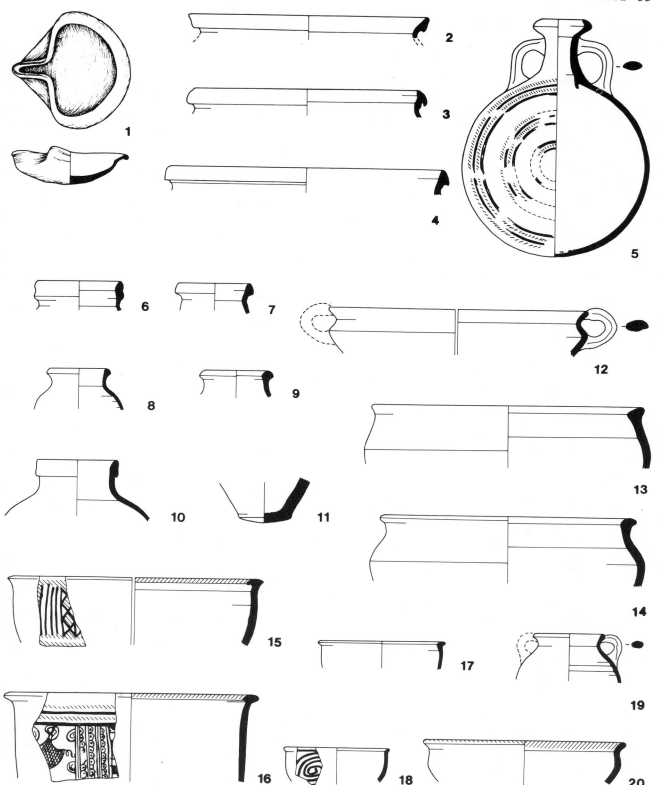

Plate Number	Pottery Type	Number and locus (see LOCUS INDEX)	Description (p. 277)
1.	Jug	G70, VI.NW5.156, No. 1 L. 5073	*Technique:* Wheelmade. *Paste:* 5YR "light reddish brown" 6/4; some very small and few small and large lime, few large wadi gravel, medium and small iron, very small to medium ceramic and very small crystal; grey core; hard. *Surface (Interior):* as paste to 5YR "dark grey" 4/1. *(Exterior):* 10YR "white" 8/2 slip; 10YR "dark reddish grey" 3/1 and 10YR "weak red" 4/4 organic paint decoration.
2.	Base	G70, VI.NW5.160, No. 12 L. 5073	*Technique:* Wheelmade. *Paste:* inner: 7.5YR "grey" N5/0; outer: 7.5YR "pink" 8/4; some very small wadi gravel, few large iron, very small and large crystal, small and medium ceramic and small to large lime; no core; hard. *Surface (Interior):* as inner paste to 7.5YR "pinkish white" 8/2. *(Exterior):* 5YR "reddish yellow" 7/6.
3.	Base	G70, VI.NW5.163, No. 1 L. 5073	*Technique:* Wheelmade. *Paste:* 5YR "light reddish brown" 6/4; some very small and few small to large lime, few medium and large iron, small and medium ceramic and very small crystal; grey core; hard. *Surface (Interior):* as paste. *(Exterior):* 7.5YR "pink" 7/4.
4.	Bowl	G70, VI.NW5.160, No. 16 L. 5073	*Technique:* Wheelmade. *Paste:* 5YR "reddish yellow" 6/6; few medium wadi gravel, very small to medium lime, very small and small ceramic and very small crystal; grey core; hard. *Surface (Interior):* as paste. *(Exterior):* as paste.
5.	Jug	G70, VI.NW5.160, No. 5 L. 5073	*Technique:* Wheelmade. *Paste:* 5YR "reddish yellow" 6/6; some very small and few small to large lime, few large iron, medium organic, small to medium ceramic and very small crystal; dark grey core; hard. *Surface (Interior):* as paste. *(Exterior):* 10YR "white" 8/2 slip; traces of 10YR "weak red" 4/4 slip.
6.	Bowl	G70, VI.NW5.163, No. 2 L. 5073	*Technique:* Wheelmade. *Paste:* 7.5YR "pink" 8/4; some very small and few small to large lime, few large iron, small and medium ceramic and very small crystal; light grey core; hard. *Surface (Interior):* 7.5YR "pinkish white" 8/2; 5YR "reddish brown" 5/4 slip on rim. *(Exterior):* as interior; slip on rim as interior.
7.	Bowl	G70, VI.NW5.160, No. 1 L. 5073	*Technique:* Wheelmade. *Paste:* 5YR "reddish yellow" 7/6; some very small and few small to large lime, few small to large iron, very small and medium wadi gravel and very small crystal; light grey core; hard. *Surface (Interior):* as paste; 2.5YR "red" 5/6 organic paint decoration. *(Exterior):* as paste to 7.5YR "pink" 8/4.
8.	Krater	G70, VI.NW5.154, No. 4 L. 5073	*Technique:* Wheelmade. *Paste:* 5YR "reddish yellow" 7/6; many very small wadi gravel, few very small to medium lime; no core; hard. *Surface (Interior):* as paste. *(Exterior):* as paste to 7.5YR "pink" 7/4.
9.	Cooking pot	G70, VI.NW5.160, No. 22 L. 5073	*Technique:* Wheelmade. *Paste:* 5YR "reddish brown" 4/3; some large and few very small to medium wadi gravel, few large organic; dark grey core; *Surface (Interior):* as paste. *(Exterior):* as paste.
10.	Cooking pot	G70, VI.NW5.124, No. 1 L. 5073	*Technique:* Wheelmade. *Paste:* 5YR "reddish brown" 5/3; few very small to large lime, large organic, small ceramic and very small crystal; dark grey core; hard. *Surface (Interior):* as core and paste. *(Exterior):* as paste.
11.	Base	G70, VI.NW5.160, No. 26 L. 5073	*Technique:* Wheelmade. *Paste:* 7.5YR "reddish yellow" 7/6; few to some large organic, few very small to large lime, very small and large wadi gravel and crystal and small ceramic; grey core; hard. *Surface (Interior):* as paste to 5YR "grey" 5/1. *(Exterior):* 7.5YR "pinkish white" 8/2 slip; 7.5YR "light brown" 6/4 organic paint decoration.
12.	Base	G70, VI.NW5.154, No. 1 L. 5073	*Technique:* Wheelmade. *Paste:* inner: 5YR "grey" 5/1; outer: 7.5YR "pink" 7/4; few very small to large lime, small to large organic, medium and large wadi gravel; no core; hard. *Surface (Interior):* as inner paste. *(Exterior):* as outer paste.
13.	Bowl	G70, VI.NW6.144, No. 10 L. 6063	*Technique:* Wheelmade. *Paste:* 7.5YR "reddish yellow" 7/6; many very small wadi gravel, few small organic and very small crystal; dark grey core; hard. *Surface (Interior):* 5YR "pink" 7/4. *(Exterior):* as interior.
14.	Bowl	G70, VI.NW6.133, No. 3 L. 6063	*Technique:* Wheelmade. *Paste:* 5YR "reddish yellow" 6/6; many very small wadi gravel, few small lime and organic, very small crystal; grey core; hard. *Surface (Interior):* as paste. *(Exterior):* as paste.
15.	Base	G70, VI.NE6.133, No. 19 L. 6063	*Technique:* Wheelmade. *Paste:* 7.5YR "light brown" 6/4; few small and medium lime and wadi gravel, very small and small crytal and small organic; grey core; hard. *Surface (Interior):* as paste. *(Exterior):* as paste.
16.	Jar	G70, VI.NW6.144, No. 15 L. 6063	*Technique:* Wheelmade. *Paste:* 5YR "reddish yellow" 7/6; few small ceramic and lime, very small wadi gravel and crystal; no core; hard. *Surface (Interior):* 7.5YR "pink" 8/4. *(Exterior):* as paste.
17.	Bowl	G70, VI.NW6.153, No. 4 L. 6068	*Technique:* Wheelmade. *Paste:* 5YR "reddish yellow" 6/6; some medium organic and very small wadi gravel, few small lime and very small crystal; light grey core; hard. *Surface (Interior):* 7.5YR "pink" 7/4. *(Exterior):* as interior.
18.	Jar	G70, VI.NW15.125, No. 9 L. 15051.1	*Technique:* Wheelmade. *Paste:* 5YR "pink" 7/4; very many very small wadi gravel, few medium ceramic, small organic and very small crystal and lime; no core; hard. *Surface (Interior):* 7.5YR "reddish yellow" 8/6. *(Exterior):* as interior.
19.	Bowl	G70, VI.NW15.125, No. 8 L. 15051.1	*Technique:* Wheelmade. *Paste:* 5YR "reddish yellow" 7/6; some very small and few large lime and crystal; grey core; hard. *Surface (Interior):* 7.5YR "pink" 7/4. *(Exterior):* as interior.
20.	Bowl	G70, VI.NW15.125, No. 4 L. 15051.1	*Technique:* Wheelmade. *Paste:* 5YR "pink" 7/4; some small organic, few very small or crystal and medium to large lime; grey core; hard. *Surface (Interior):* as paste. *(Exterior):* as paste.

PLATE 34

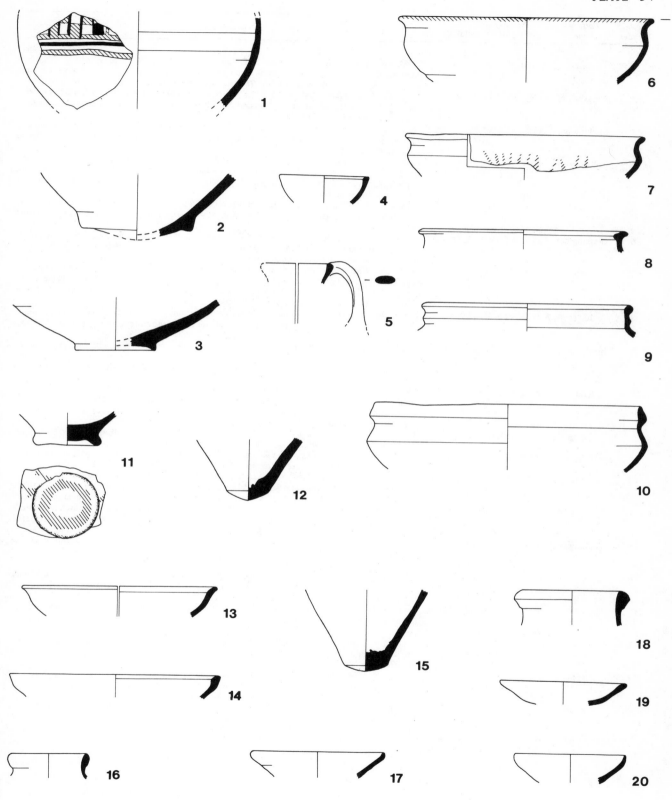

Plate Number	Pottery Type	Number and locus (see LOCUS INDEX)	Description (p. 277)
1.	Base	G70, VI.NW5.77, No. 1 L. 5037	*Technique:* Wheelmade. *Paste:* inner; 5YR "grey" 6/1; outer; 5YR "reddish yellow" 7/6;; very many small to very large organic, some small and few medium and large lime, few very crystal; core: 7.5YR "pink" 8/4; hard. *Surface (Interior):* as inner paste. *(Exterior):* as outer paste.
2.	Flask or jug	G69, VI.NW5.73, No. 31 L. 5037	*Technique:* Wheelmade. *Paste:* a7.5YR "pink" 7/4; some very small wadi gravel, few small to large lime, small ceramic, very small organic and crystal; no core; hard. *Surface (Interior):* as paste to as exterior. *(Exterior):* 7.5YR "pink" 8/4.
3.	Cooking pot	G69, VI.NW5.73, No. 22 L. 5037	*Technique:* Wheelmade. *Paste:* 5YR "light reddish brown" 6/4; some small and few medium and large lime, few small organic and very small crystal; dark grey core; hard. *Surface (Interior):* as paste. *(Exterior):* as paste.
4.	Krater	G69, VI.NW5.73, No. 14 L. 5037	*Technique:* Wheelmade. *Paste:* 5YR "reddish yellow" 7/6; some very small wadi gravel, few very small to large lime, very small ceramic and very small crystal; grey core; hard. *Surface (Interior):* as paste. *(Exterior):* 7.5YR "pinkish white" 8/2 slip; traces of burnish; 10YR "dark reddish grey" 3/1 organic paint decoration.
5.	Flask	G70, VI.NW5.135, No. 6 L. 5042.1	*Technique:* Wheelmade. *Paste:* 5YR "reddish yellow" 6/6; some very small wadi gravel, few very small organic and crystal; light grey core; hard. *Surface (Interior):* 7.5YR "pink" 7/4. *(Exterior):* as interior.
6.	Cooking pot	G70, VI.NW5.135, No. 7 L. 5042.1	*Technique:* Wheelmade. *Paste:* 5YR "reddish brown" 5/4; some large and few small to medium lime, few large and few small to medium lime, few large wadi gravel, medium and large ceramic and very small to medium crystal; grey core; hard. *Surface (Interior):* as paste. *(Exterior):* as paste.
7.	Krater	G69, VI.NW5.88, No. 3 L. 5042.1	*Technique:* Wheelmade. *Paste:* 5YR "reddish yellow" 7/6; few very large iron, some very small wadi gravel, few very small organic and crystal; grey core; hard. *Surface (Interior):* as paste; traces of slip as exterior on rim. *(Exterior):* 10YR "white" 8/2 slip; band of 10YR "dark red" 3/6 organic paint and 5YR "dark reddish brown" 3/2 organic paint decoration.
8.	Juglet	G71, VI.NW5.115, No. 1 L. 5042.1	*Technique:* Wheelmade. *Paste:* inner: 10YR "grey" 6/1; outer: 2.5YR "light red" 6/6; very many very small and few large lime, few large wadi gravel and medium to large ceramic and organic; grey core; hard. *Surface (Interior):* as inner paste to 10YR "white" 8/2.
9.	Bowl or cup	G70, VI.NW5.115, No. 7 L. 5042.1	*Technique:* Wheelmade. *Paste:* 5YR "pink" 7/4; many very small crystal and wadi gravel, some very small organic; no core; hard. *Surface (Interior):* as paste; traces of slip as exterior below rim. *(Exterior):* 2.5YR "white" 8/2 slip; bands of 5YR "red" 4/6 organic paint; 2.5YR "black" 2.5/0 organic paint decoration.
10.	Krater	G70, VI.NW5.138, No. 3 L. 5062	*Technique:* Wheelmade. *Paste:* striations: inner: 5YR "light reddish brown" 6/3; outer: 2/5YR "reddish brown" 5/4; some small to large lime and ceramic, few medium to large lime and ceramic, few medium to large wadi gravel, some large organic, few large crystal; light grey core; hard. *Surface (Interior):* 5YR "reddish yellow: 7/5. *(Exterior):* as interior.
11.	Lamp	G70, VI.NW5.142 L. 5062	*Technique:* Wheelmade. *Paste:* 7.5YR "light brown" 6/4; few small to medium lime and black grits; slight grey core; hard. *Surface (Interior):* as paste. *(Exterior):* as paste.
12.	Amphora	G70, VI.NW5.138, No. 2 L. 5062	*Technique:* Wheelmade. *Paste:* 2.5YR "red" 5.6; very many very small to few large lime, some wadi gravel; grey core; hard. *Surface (Interior):* 2.5YR "light red" 6/8. *(Exterior):* as interior.
13.	Bowl	G70, VI.NW5.144, No. 3 L. 5062	*Technique:* Wheelmade. *Paste:* 7.5YR "pink" 7/4; some very small and few small to large lime, few small and medium iron and very small crystal; light grey core; hard. *Surface (Interior):* 10YR "white" 8/2 slip; 10YR "weak red" 4/4 organic paint decoration. *(Exterior):* slip as interior.
14.	Bowl or cup	G70, VI.NW5.134, No. 2 L. 5063	*Technique:* Wheelmade. *Paste:* 7.5YR "light brown" 6/4; few medium iron, very small to medium iron, very small to medium lime, small organic and ceramic and very small wadi gravel and crystal; grey core; hard. *Surface (Interior):* 7.5YR "pinkish white" 8/2. *(Exterior):* as interior.
15.	Cooking pot	G70, VI.NW5.131, No. 1a L. 5063	*Technique:* Wheelmade. *Paste:* 5YR "reddish brown" 5/4; many small and few medium lime, few small organic and very small crystal; dark grey; hard. *Surface (Interior):* as paste. *(Exterior):* as paste.
16.	Bowl	G70, VI.NW5.151, No. 15 L. 5063	*Technique:* Wheelmade. *Paste:* 5YR "reddish yellow" 7/6; some very small lime and few very small crystal and ceramic; grey core; hard. *Surface (Interior):* as paste; 10YR "red" 5/6 slip on rim. *(Exterior):* as paste.
17.	Bowl	G70, VI.NW5.146, No. 3 L. 5063	*Technique:* Wheelmade. *Paste:* 7.5YR "pink" 7/4; some small organic and very small wadi gravel, few small lime and very small crystal; grey core; hard. *Surface (Interior):* as paste. *(Exterior):* as paste.
18.	Bowl	G70, VI.NE6.118, No. 1 L. 6023	*Technique:* Wheelmade. *Paste:* 5YR "light reddish brown" 64; many small to large organic, some small and medium lime, few medium wadi gravel and very small crystal; dark grey core; hard. *Surface (Interior):* as paste. *(Exterior):* as paste.
19.	Bowl	G70, VI.NW15.138, No. 8 L. 15039.1	*Technique:* Wheelmade. *Paste:* 5YR "reddish yellow" 6/6; some very small wadi gravel, few medium and large lime, very small ceramic and crystal; no core; hard. *Surface (Interior):* as paste. *(Exterior):* as paste.
20.	Chalice	G70, VI.NW15.134, No. 14, L. 15039.1	*Technique:* Wheelmade. *Paste:* 5YR "reddish yellow" 7/6; some very small wadi gravel and lime, few very small crystal; no core; hard. *Surface (Interior):* 7.5YR "pinkish white" 8/2 slip; 5YR "dusky red" 3/4 organic paint decoration. *(Exterior):* slip and organic paint on rim as interior.

PLATE 35

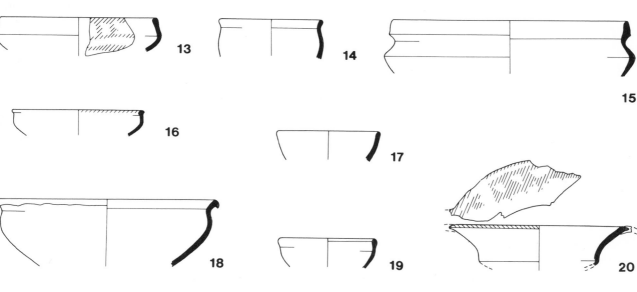

Plate Number	Pottery Type	Number and locus (see LOCUS INDEX)	Description (p. 277)
1.	Bowl	G70, VI.NW5.109, No. 1 L. 5052	*Technique:* Wheelmade. *Paste:* 7.5YR "pink" 7/4; very few fine lime and crystal; no core, hard. *Surface (Interior):* as paste. *(Exterior):* as paste; 2.5YR "red" 4/6 organic paint decoration.
2.	Bowl	G70, VI.NW5.109, No. 2 L. 5052	*Technique:* Wheelmade. *Paste:* 7.5YR "pink" 7/4; very few fine lime and crystal; no core; hard. *Surface (Interior):* as paste. *(Exterior):* as paste; 2/5YR "red" 4/6 organic paint decoration.
3.	Bowl or cup	G70, VI.NW5.109, No. 5 L. 5052	*Technique:* Wheelmade. *Paste:* 7.5YR "pink" 7/4; very few fine lime and crystal; grey core; hard. *Surface (Interior):* as paste; white slip. *(Exterior):* as paste; white slip.
4.	Bowl	G70, VI.NW5.109, No. 3 L. 5052	*Technique:* Wheelmade. *Paste:* 7.5YR "pink" 7/4; very few fine lime and crystal; no core; hard. *Surface (Interior):* as paste. *(Exterior):* as paste; 2.5YR "red" 4/6 organic paint decoration.
5.	Stirrup jar	G69, VI.NW5.80, No. 1 L. 5041.1	*Technique:* Wheelmade. *Paste:* 7.5YR "light brown" 6/4; few medium lime, few small to medium ceramic, few to some very small crystal; no core; hard. *Surface (Interior):* as paste. *(Exterior):* horizontal bands of 10YR "red" 4/6 organic paint and diagonal bands of 2.5YR "dusky red" 3/2 organic paint on 7.5YR "pinksih white" 8/2 organic painted background.
6.	Bowl	G69, VI.NW5.92, No. 7 L. 5046	*Technique:* Wheelmade. *Paste:* 2.5YR "red" 5/6; few very small to small wadi gravel, very small crystal and organic; grey core; hard. *Surface (Interior):* 5YR "pink" 8/3. *(Exterior):* as interior.
7.	Krater	G69, VI.NW5.61, No. 2 L. 5018	*Technique:* Wheelmade. *Paste:* 5YR "reddish yellow" 7/6; some very small and few medium and large wadi gravel and lime; grey core; hard. *Surface (Interior):* as paste. *(Exterior):* 10YR "white" 8/2 slip on rim and body; band of 2.5YR "red" 4/6 organic paint on rim; bands of 10YR "dusky red" 3/3 organic paint on 10YR "very dusky red" 2.5/2 organic paint decoration.
8.	Jug base	G69, VI.NW5.61, No. 9 L. 5018	*Technique:* Wheelmade. *Paste:* 5YR "reddish yellow" 6/6; some very small and few large lime, few medium and large iron, medium wadi gravel, small and medium ceramic and very small crystal; light grey core; hard. *Surface (Interior):* as paste. *(Exterior):* 7.5YR "pinkish white" 8/2 slip and 10YR "reddish black" 2.5/1 organic paint decoration.
9.	Cooking pot	G69, VI.NW5.61, No. 4 L. 5018	*Technique:* Wheelmade. *Paste:* 5YR "reddish brown" 5/4; some medium and large and few small lime and wadi gravel, few small ceramic; no core; hard. *Surface (Interior):* as paste. *(Exterior):* as paste.
10.	Krater	G69, VI.NW15.86, No. 2 L. 15024	*Technique:* Wheelmade. *Paste:* 7.5YR "brown" 4/4; many very small crystal, few small lime, wadi gravel and organic; dark grey core; hard. *Surface (Interior):* 2.5YR "white" 8/2; 10YR "red" 4/6 organic paint decoration.
11.	Bowl or cup	G70, VI.NW6.86, No. 2 L. 6035.1	*Technique:* Wheelmade. *Paste:* 2.5YR "light red" 6/6; many small wadi gravel, few very small organic and crystal; no core; hard. *Surface (Interior):* as paste. *(Exterior):* as paste.
12.	Bowl or krater	G70, VI.NW6.169, No. 3 L. 6049	*Technique:* Wheelmade. *Paste:* 10YR "very pale brown" 8/3; some very small crystal, few large lime and small organic; no core; hard. *Surface (Interior):* 2.5YR "white" 8/2; band of 10YR "dusky red" 3/3 slip on rim. *(Exterior):* as paste; slip on rim as interior.
13.	Bowl or cup	G70, VI.NW6.168, No. 4 L. 6045.1	*Technique:* Wheelmade. *Paste:* 5YR "reddish yellow" 6/6; some small wadi gravel, few small lime, very small organic and crystal; no core; hard. *Surface (Interior):* 5YR "white" 8/1 slip; band of 10YR "red" 5/6 organic paint on rim. *(Exterior):* slip as interior; 5YR "very dark grey" 3/1 organic paint decoration.
14.	Pyxis	G70, VI.NE6.169, No. 1 L. 6045.1	*Technique:* Wheelmade. *Paste:* 10YR "very pale brown" 7/3; few small lime, organic, and wadi gravel, very small crystal; dark grey core; hard. *Surface (Interior):* as paste. *(Exterior):* 10YR "white" 8/2 slip; bands of 10YR "weak red" 4/4 organic paint; 5YR "dark reddish brown" 3/2 organic paint decoration.
15.	Bowl or cup	G70, VI.NW6.169, No. 2 L. 6045.1	*Technique:* Wheelmade. *Paste:* 5YR "reddish yellow" 7/6; few small lime, organic, wadi gravel, very small crystal; no core; hard. *Surface (Interior):* as paste. *(Exterior):* as paste; bands of 10YR "red" 4/8 organic paint decoration.
16.	Bowl or cup	G70, VI.NE6.104, No. 8 L. 6048.1	*Technique:* Wheelmade. *Paste:* 7.5YR "pink" 7/4; some medium lime, few small organic and wadi gravel and very small crystal; light grey core; hard. *Surface (Interior):* as paste; band of 2.5YR "red" 5/6 organic paint on rim; decoration of 10YR "weak red" 5/4 organic paint. *(Exterior):* as paste.
17.	Jar	G70, VI.NW6.110, No. 6 L. 6049	*Technique:* Wheelmade. *Paste:* 5YR "reddish yellow" 7/6; many small organic, few small lime and very small crystal; grey core; hard. *Surface (Interior):* as paste. *(Exterior):* as paste.
18.	Krater	G70, VI.NW6.93, No. 1 L. 6049	*Technique:* Wheelmade. *Paste:* 5YR "pink" 7/4; many very small organic, some very small wadi gravel, few large lime and very small crystal; grey core; hard. *Surface (Interior):* as paste. *(Exterior):* 7.5YR "pinkish white" 8/2 slip; bands of 2.5YR "red" 5/6 organic paint, bands and decoration of 5YR "dark reddish brown" 3/2 to 5YR "light reddish brown" 6/4.

PLATE 36

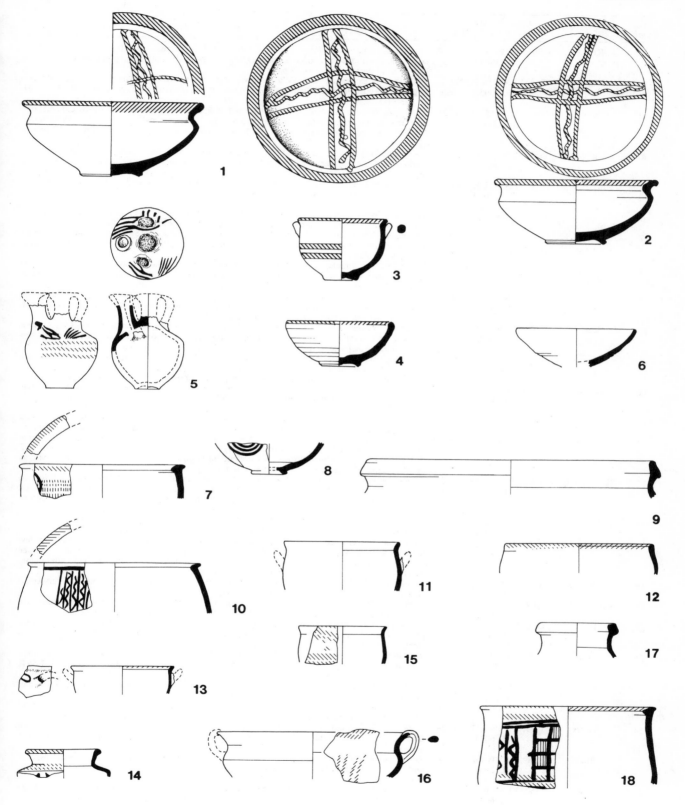

Plate Number	Pottery Type	Number and locus (see LOCUS INDEX)	Description (p. 277)
1.	Krater	G70, VI.NW15.109, No. 7 L. 15005A	*Technique:* Wheelmade. *Paste:* 5YR "reddish yellow" 6/6; some very small to few small lime, few large iron, small to large ceramic, small organic and very small crystal; dark grey core; hard. *Surface (Interior):* as paste. *(Exterior):* as paste
2.	Krater	G69, VI.NW15.37, No. 2 L. 15005A	*Technique:* Wheelmade. *Paste:* 5YR "yellowish red" 5/6; many very small and few large lime, few large and very small crystal; light grey core; hard. *Surface (Interior):* 7.5YR "pink" 7/4. *(Exterior):* as interior.
3.	Bowl	G69, VI.NW15.37, No. 21 L. 15005A	*Technique:* Wheelmade. *Paste:* 2.5YR "light red" 6/6; many very small and few medium and large lime, few large wadi gravel and ceramic, and medium and very small crystal; core: 7/5YR "pink" 7/4; hard. *Surface (Interior):* as paste; 10YR "weak red" 4/4 organic paint decoration. *(Exterior):* as paste.
4.	Jug base	G69, VI.NW15.41, No. 2 L. 15005A	*Technique:* Wheelmade. *Paste:* 7.5YR "pink" 7/4; many very small and few medium lime, few medium ceramic and very small crystal; no core; hard. *Surface (Interior):* as paste. *(Exterior):* as paste.
5.	Bowl or cup	G69, VI.NW15.37, No. 18 L. 15005A	*Technique:* Wheelmade. *Paste:* 7.5YR "light brown" 6/4; many small and few large crystal; no core; hard. *Surface (Interior):* as paste; slip on rim as exterior. *(Exterior):* as paste; bands of 2.5YR "reddish brown" 5/4 organic paint.
6.	Jar	G69, VI.NW15.37, No. 4 L. 15005A	*Technique:* Wheelmade. *Paste:* 5YR "reddish yellow" 6/6; some very small and small crystal, few very small lime; no core; hard. *Surface (Interior):* as paste. *(Exterior):* as paste.
7.	Jar	G70, VI.NW15.109, No. 8 L. 15005A	*Technique:* Wheelmade. *Paste:* 5YR "yellowish red" 5/6; some very small crystal and very small to medium lime, few very small to medium ceramic; grey core; hard. *Surface (Interior):* as paste. *(Exterior):* as paste.
8.	Chalice	G70, VI.NW15.109, No. 1 L. 15005A	*Technique:* Wheelmade. *Paste:* 5YR "reddish yellow" 6/6; few large wadi gravel and lime, small and large lime, very small to medium ceramic and very small and small wadi gravel; no core; hard. *Surface (Interior):* as paste; traces of 10YR "white" 8/1 organic paint. *(Exterior):* as paste.
9.	Jar	G70, VI.NW15.117, No. 2 L. 15047	*Technique:* Wheelmade. *Paste:* 5YR "reddish yellow" 6/6; some small to few medium and large ceramic, few large wadi gravel, very small to medium lime and very small crystal; grey core; hard. *Surface (Interior):* as paste. *(Exterior):* as paste.
10.	Krater	G70, VI.NW15.117, No. 7 L. 15047	*Technique:* Wheelmade. *Paste:* 5YR "reddish yellow" 7/6; some very small to small crystal, few medium lime, small and medium ceramic, small wadi gravel and organic; sporadic core; hard. *Surface (Interior):* as paste. *(Exterior):* as paste; 10YR "dark red" 3/6 organic paint on rim.
11.	Krater	G70, VI.NW15.117, No.12 L. 15047	*Technique:* Wheelmade. *Paste:* 5YR "yellowish red" 5/6; some small to large organic and very small crystal, few small to large ceramic and lime; grey core; hard. *Surface (Interior):* as paste; organic paint on rim as exterior. *(Exterior):* as paste; bands of 10YR "red" 4/6 organic paint.
12.	Cooking jug	G69, VI.NE5.54, No. 6 L. 5018	*Technique:* Wheelmade. *Paste:* 7.5YR "light brown" 6/4; some very small and few large lime, few large wadi gravel, medium ceramic and very small crystal; grey core; hard. *Surface (Interior):* 5YR "pink" 7/4 to 7.5YR "pink" 8/4. *(Exterior):* as paste to 5YR "very dark grey" 3/1.
13.	Jar	G69, VI.NW5.53, No. 1 L. 5018	*Technique:* Wheelmade. *Paste:* 7.5YR "light brown" 6/4; some very small and small crystal and small wadi gravel, few small lime; no core; hard. *Surface (Interior):* as paste. *(Exterior):* as paste.
14.	Bowl	G69, VI.NW5.74, No. 9 L. 5018	*Technique:* Wheelmade. *Paste:* inner: 7.5YR "pink" 8/4; outer: 5YR "reddish yellow" 7/6; some small and few medium and large lime; light grey core; hard. *Surface (Interior):* 10YR "white" 8/2 slip; band of 5YR "reddish brown" 5/4 organic paint on rim and decoration. *(Exterior):* slip as interior; band of organic paint on rim as interior.
15.	Bowl or cup	G69, VI.NW5.69, No. 3 L. 5018	*Technique:* Wheelmade. *Paste:* 5YR "pink" 7/4; many small wadi gravel, few medium lime and very small crystal; no core; hard. *Surface (Interior):* as paste; 10YR "white" 8/2 slip on rim; covered by band of 10YR "weak red" 5/4 organic paint. *(Exterior):* slip as interior, paint decoration as interior.
16.	Krater	G70, VI.NW5.147, No. 1 L. 5064	*Technique:* Wheelmade. *Paste:* 2.5YR "red" 5/6; some small to medium lime, few medium organic and very small crystal; grey core; hard. *Surface (Interior):* as paste. *(Exterior):* as paste.
17.	Pyxis	G69, VI.NE5.68, No. 1 L. 5029	*Technique:* Wheelmade. *Paste:* 5YR "reddish yellow" 7/6; many very small to small and few medium to large wadi gravel and crystal, few medium lime and ceramic; no core; hard. *Surface (Interior):* as paste; traces of 10YR "white" 8/2 slip. *(Exterior):* bands of 10YR "red" 4/6 organic paint on 10YR "white" 8/2 slip and traces of burnish.
18.	Cooking pot	G69, VI.NW5.53, No. 7 L. 5018	*Technique:* Wheelmade. *Paste:* 5YR "yellowish red" 5/6; few small to large lime, few very small crystal; grey core; hard. *Surface (Interior):* as paste. *(Exterior):* as paste.
19.	Cooking pot	G69, VI.NW5.56, No. 13 L. 5018	*Technique:* Wheelmade. *Paste:* 2.5YR "red" 5/6; many medium and large and few small lime, few very small crystal; dark grey core; hard. *Surface (Interior):* as paste. *(Exterior):* as paste.
20.	Bowl	G70, VI.NW6.27, No. 22 L. 6014	*Technique:* Wheelmade. *Paste:* 5YR "reddish yellow" 7/6; some small to large lime, small wadi grvel, few small organic and very small crystal; core: 7.5YR "pinkish grey" 7/2; hard. *Surface (Interior):* 7.5YR "pink" 8/4. *(Exterior):* as interior.
21.	Bowl	G70, VI.NW6.75, No. 8 L. 6025.1	*Technique:* Wheelmade. *Paste:* 5YR "reddish yellow" 7/6; some small wadi gravel, few small organic and very small crystal; grey core; hard. *Surface (Interior):* as paste. *(Exterior):* 7.5YR "pink" 8/4.
22.	Bowl	G70, VI.NW6.75, No. 15 L. 6025.1	*Technique:* Wheelmade. *Paste:* 7.5YR "pink" 7/4; many small wadi gravel, few very small crystal; no core; hard. *Surface (Interior):* as paste. *(Exterior):* as paste.
23.	Cooking pot	G70, VI.NW6.75, No. 19 L. 6025.1	*Technique:* Wheelmade. *Paste:* 7.5YR "brown" 4/4; many small to medium lime, few very small crystal; no core; hard. *Surface (Interior):* 5YR "reddish brown" 5/4. *(Exterior):* as interior.
24.	Krater	G69, VI.NW6.67, No. 26 L. 6031	*Technique:* Wheelmade. *Paste:* 5YR "reddish yellow" 7/6; few medium lime, small wadi gravel and organic, very small crystal; grey core; hard. *Surface (Interior):* as paste. *(Exterior):* 7.5YR "light brown" 6/4.
25.	Bowl	G69, VI.NW6.68, No. 9 L. 6031	*Technique:* Wheelmade. *Paste:* 7.5YR "light brown" 6/4; some small wadi gravel, few small organic and very small crystal; light grey core; hard. *Surface (Interior):* 10YR "very pale brown" 7/4. *(Exterior):* as interior.
26.	Jug	G69, VI.NW6.56, No. 14 L. 6031	*Technique:* Wheelmade. *Paste:* 5YR "reddish yellow" 7/6; very many small wadi gravel, few large lime and very small crystal; core: 10YR "very pale brown" 7/4; hard. *Surface (Interior):* as paste. *(Exterior):* as paste.

PLATE 37

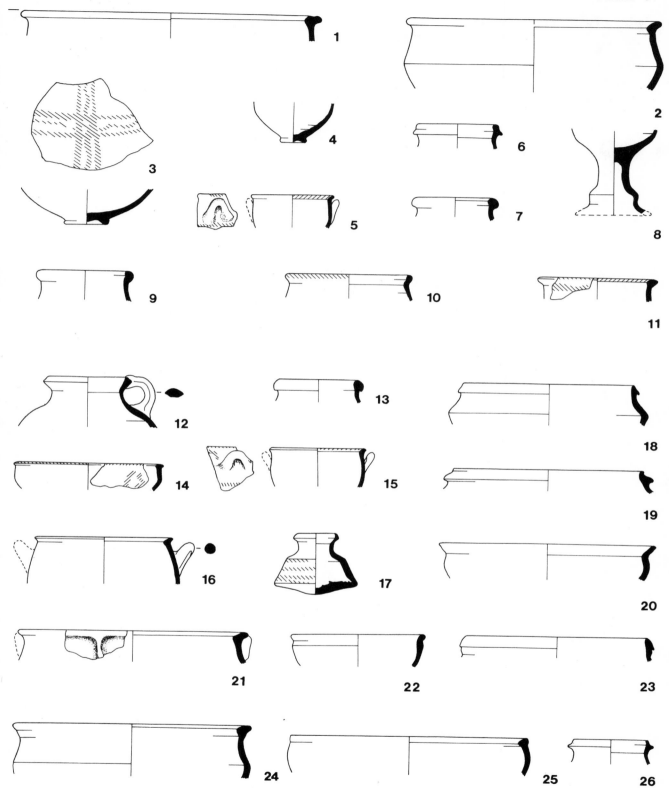

Plate Number	Pottery Type	Number and locus (see LOCUS INDEX)	Description (p. 277)
1.	Pilgrim flask	G70, VI.NE15.102, VI.NE15.106, Nos. 2–28 L. 15050.1	*Technique:* Wheelmade. *Paste:* 5YR "pink" 7/4; some small ceramic and calcite; light grey core; hard. *Surface (Interior):* as paste. *(Exterior):* 5YR "pinkish white" 8/2 slip; painted decoration.
2.	Jar	G70, VI.NE15.102, No. 8 L. 15050.1	*Technique:* Wheelmade. *Paste:* 5YR "light reddish brown" 6/4; many very small crystal, few large lime, small to large ceramic and small organic; grey core; hard. *Surface (Interior):* as paste. *(Exterior):* as paste.
3.	Base	G70, VI.NE16.153, No. 4 L. 16053	*Technique:* Wheelmade. *Paste:* 5YR "reddish brown" 5/3; some very small sand, few medium lime and small ceramic; no core; hard. *Surface* 2.5YR "light grey" 7/2. *(Exterior):* as interior.
4.	Bowl or cup	G70, VI.NE16.169, No. 2 L. 16053	*Technique:* Wheelmade. *Paste:* 7.5YR "light brown" 6/4; very many very small wadi gravel, some very small to medium organic, few very small crystal; grey core; hard. *Surface (Interior):* as paste; band of 5YR "weak red" 4/3 organic paint on rim. *(Exterior):* as paste; band of organic paint as interior on rim and body.
5.	Pyksis	G70, VI.NE26.166, L. 26060P	*Technique:* Wheelmade. *Paste:* 7.5YR "reddish yellow" 6/8; few small to medium limestone grits; no core; hard. *Surface (Interior):*
6.	Krater	G70, VI.NE35.50, L. 35025	*Technique:* Wheelmade. *Paste:* 5YR "pink" 7/4; many small crystal (quartz); no core; hard. *Surface (Interior):* as paste. *(Exterior):* as paste.
7.	Amphora	G70, VI.NE4, L. 4055	*Technique:* Wheelmade. *Paste:* 5YR "pink" 7/3; many small crystal; no core; hard. *Surface (Interior):* as paste. *(Exterior):* as paste.
8.	Bowl	G71, VI.NE36.54, No. 2 L. 36118	*Technique:* Wheelmade. *Paste:* 5YR "yellowish red" 5/6; some small organic, few very small to large lime and small ceramic; grey core; hard. *Surface (Interior):* as paste; 10YR "red" 4/6 slip on rim. *(Exterior):* as paste.
9.	Bowl	G71, VI.NE36.51, No. 2 L. 36018	*Technique:* Wheelmade. *Paste:* 5YR "reddish yellow" 6/8; few medium lime and some small lime, few very small crystal; no core; hard. *Surface (Interior):* 5YR "reddish yellow" 6/6; 2.5YR "red" 5/6 organic paint on rim and body. *(Exterior):* 5YR "reddish yellow" 6/6.
10.	Bowl	G71, VE.NE36.51, No. 1 L. 36018	*Technique:* Wheelmade. *Paste:* 5YR "pink" 7/3; some small to large lime, few large ceramic, few small crystal; no core; hard. *Surface (Interior):* as paste. *(Exterior):* as paste.
11.	Chalice	G71, VI.NE36.51, No. 3 L. 36018	*Technique:* Wheelmade. *Paste:* 2.5YR "light red" 6/8; very many very small crystal, few medium to large wadi gravel, lime and organic; dark grey core; hard. *Surface (Interior):* as paste; 10YR "red" 4/6 slip on rim. *(Exterior):* as paste to 10YR "very pale brown" 8/4.
12.	Lamp	G71, VI.NE36.51, No. 5 L. 36018	*Technique:* Wheelmade. *Paste:* 5YR "light reddish brown" 6/4; few large wadi gravel, few small to medium to large lime, very many small crystal; light grey core; hard. *Surface (Interior):* as paste. *(Exterior):* as paste.
13.	Lamp	G71, VI.NE36.51, No. 4 L. 36018	*Technique:* Wheelmade. *Paste:* 5YR "reddish yellow" 6/6; few small to medium wadi gravel, few large lime, many very small crystal, few small to large ceramic; light grey core; hard. *Surface (Interior):* as paste. *(Exterior):* as paste.

PLATE 38

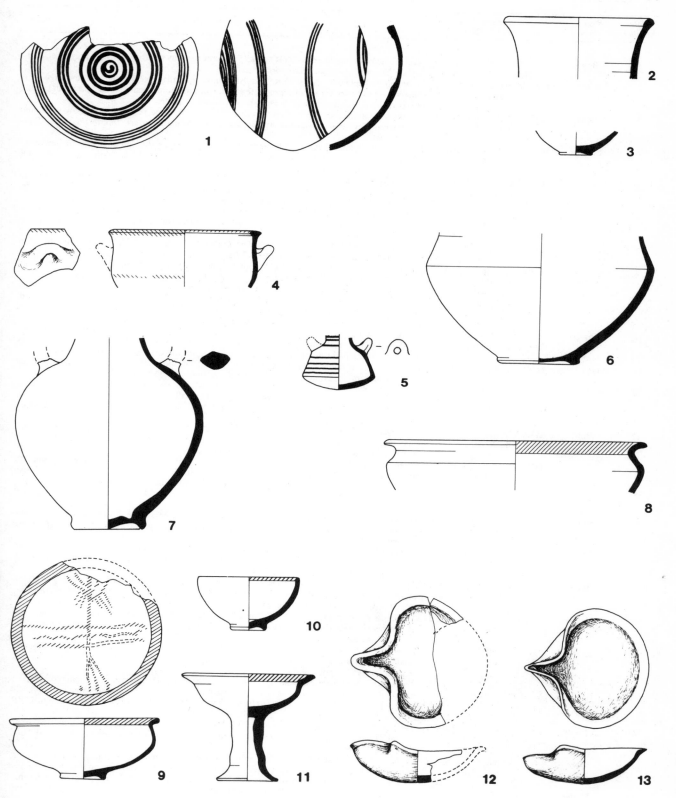

Plate Number	Pottery Type	Number and locus (see LOCUS INDEX)	Description (p. 277)
1.	Bowl	G69, VI.NE4.16A, Nos.1,4,5, L. 4018	*Technique:* Wheelmade. *Paste:* 5YR "pink" 7/3; some to many small crystal; light grey core; hard. *Surface (Interior):* as paste. *(Exterior):* as paste.
2.	Krater	G70, VI.NE26.161, No. 10 L. 26050.1	*Technique:* Wheelmade. *Paste:* 5YR "reddish yellow" 6/6; many very small and few large lime, some very small and few small ceramic, few small and medium organic, large and small crystal; grey core; hard. *Surface (Interior):* as paste. *(Exterior):* as paste.
3.	Bowl	G70, VI.NE26.161, No. 11 L. 26050.1	*Technique:* Wheelmade. *Paste:* 5YR "reddish yellow" 7/6; some very small and few small and medium lime, few small crystal and organic; dark grey core; hard. *Surface (Interior):* as paste. *(Exterior):* as paste.
4.	Chalice	G70, VI.NE26.145, No. 8 L. 26050.1	*Technique:* Wheelmade. *Paste:* 5YR "reddish yellow" 7/6; some small to large organic, few small to large lime, very small wadi gravel and crystal; dark grey core; hard. *Surface (Interior):* 5YR "pink" 8/3; *(Exterior):* as interior.
5.	Bowl	G70, VI.NE26.161, No. 3 L. 26050.1	*Technique:* Wheelmade. *Paste:* 7.5YR "pink" 8/4; many very small and few large wadi, few small and large lime, small organic and very small crystal; no core; hard. *Surface (Interior):* as paste; 10YR "weak red" 5/4 slip on rim. *(Exterior):* as paste; slip on rim as interior.
6.	Cooking pot	G70, VI.NE26.138, No. 8 L. 26050.1	*Technique:* Wheelmade. *Paste:* 7.5YR "light brown" 6/4; few very small and many small and medium crystal, some medium lime and small organic; grey core; hard. *Surface (Interior):* as paste. *(Exterior):* as paste.
7.	Cooking pot	G70, VI.NE16.152, No. 2 L. 26050.1	*Technique:* Wheelmade. *Paste:* 5YR "reddish brown" 5/4; some small and few medium lime, few very small crystal; grey core; hard. *Surface (Interior):* as paste. *(Exterior):* as paste.
8.	Cooking pot	G70, VI.NE26.146, No. 7 L. 26050.1	*Technique:* Wheelmade. *Paste:* 5YR "reddish brown" 5/4; few very small and very many small crystal, few small organic; no core; hard. *Surface (Interior):* as paste. *(Exterior):* as paste.
9.	Krater	G70, VI.NE26.146, L. 26060.1	*Technique:* Wheelmade. *Paste:* 5YR "reddish yellow" 7/6; some small organic and very small wadi gravel few small and medium lime and very small crystal; core: 7.5YR "light brown" 6/4; hard. *Surface (Interior):* as paste; 5YR "weak red" 4/4 organic paint on rim and decoration. *(Exterior):* 10YR "white" 8/1 slip; band of organic paint as interior below rim.
10.	Bowl	G70, VI.NE26.164, No. 3 L. 26050.1	*Technique:* Wheelmade. *Paste:* 5YR "reddish yellow" 6/6; any very small wadi gravel, some very small crystal, few small lime; grey core; hard. *Surface (Interior):* 7.5YR "pink" 8/4; 10YR "weak red" 5/4 organic paint decoration. *(Exterior):* as interior; decoration on rim as interior.
11.	Bowl or cup	G70, VI.NE26.161, No. 20 L. 26050.1	*Technique:* Wheelmade. *Paste:* 5YR "reddish yellow" 7/6; some very small wadi gravel, few small lime; no core; hard. *Surface (Interior):* as paste. *(Exterior):* 7.5YR "pink" 8/4.
12.	Bowl or cup	G70, VI.NE26.161, No. 9 L. 26050.1	*Technique:* Wheelmade. *Paste:* 5YR "reddish yellow" 6/6; very many very small organic, some very small wadi gravel, few very large lime and very small crystal; grey core; hard. *Surface (Interior):* as paste. *(Exterior):* as paste; bands of 10YR "red" 4/6 organic paint on edge of rim and on body.
13.	Bowl	G70, VI.NE26.161, No. 14 L. 26050.1	*Technique:* Wheelmade. *Paste:* 5YR "reddish yellow" 7/6; few large lime medium wadi gravel, small organic and very small crystal; dark grey core; hard. *Surface (Interior):* as paste; 10YR "weak red" 5/4 slip on rim. *(Exterior):* as paste; slip on rim as interior.
14.	Bowl	G70, VI.NE26.146, No. 31 L. 26050.1	*Technique:* Wheelmade. *Paste:* 5YR "reddish yellow" 7/6; some very small wadi gravel, small to large lime, few small ceramic and organic and very small crystal; core: 10YR "light yellowish brown" hard. *Surface (Interior):* as paste; bands of 10YR "dark red" 3/6 organic paint on rim, 10YR "red" 5/8 organic paint decoration. *(Exterior):* 7.5YR "pink" 7/4; band of organic paint on rim as interior.
15.	Krater	G70, VI.NE26.134, No. 1 L. 26050	*Technique:* Wheelmade. *Paste:* 5YR "yellowish red" 5/6; very many small and few large lime, some large organic, few large iron, medium ceramic and small crystal; grey core; hard. *Surface (Interior):* as paste. *(Exterior):* as paste to 10YR "very pale brown" 7/3.
16.	Jar	G70, VI.NE26.138, No. 7 L. 26050	*Technique:* Wheelmade. *Paste:* 7.5YR "light brown" 6/4; some very small and few small crystal, few medium and large lime, large wadi gravel and small and medium ceramic; grey core; hard. *Surface (Interior):* as paste. *(Exterior):* as paste to 7.5YR "pinkish white" 8/2.
17.	Bowl	G70, VI.NE26.138, No. 4 L. 26050	*Technique:* Wheelmade. *Paste:* 5YR "reddish yellow" 7/8; very many very small wadi gravel, few small lime and organic and very small crystal; core: 5YR "pink" 7/4; hard. *Surface (Interior):* 5YR "pink" 7/4. *(Exterior):* as interior.
18.	Krater	G70, VI.NE26.138, No. 5 L. 26050	*Technique:* Wheelmade. *Paste:* 5YR "pink" 7/4; many very small wadi gravel, few medium and large lime, small ceramic and very small crystal; light grey core; hard. *Surface (Interior):* as paste. *(Exterior):* as paste.
19.	Krater	G70, VI.NE16.144, No. 4 L. 16044	*Technique:* Wheelmade. *Paste:* 2.5YR "red" 5/6; some very small and few large crystal, few very small to large lime and very small and small ceramic; grey core; hard. *Surface (Interior):* as paste. *(Exterior):* 7.5YR "pink" 8/4.
20.	Jar	G70, VI.NE26.141, No. 6 L. 26050	*Technique:* Wheelmade. *Paste:* inner: 5YR "reddish yellow" 7/6; outer: 2.5YR "light red" 6/6; few medium and large wadi gravel, very small to medium lime, small organic, very small ceramic and crystal; light grey core; hard. *Surface (Interior):* as inner paste. *(Exterior):* as outer paste to 10YR "white" 8/2.
21.	Juglet	G70, VI.NE26.138, No. 6 L. 26050	*Technique:* Wheelmade. *Paste:* 5YR "pink" 7/4; many very small wadi gravel, some very small crystal, few small organic; light grey core; hard. *Surface (Interior):* as paste to 7.5YR "pink" 8/4. *(Exterior):* as paste.
22.	Bowl	G70, VI.NE16.144, No. 16 L. 16044	*Technique:* Wheelmade. *Paste:* 7.5YR "pink" 7/4; some very small and few medium and large lime, few very small and medium wadi gravel and crystal and very small ceramic; no core; hard. *Surface (Interior):* as paste; slip on rim as exterior. *(Exterior):* as paste; bands of 2.5YR "light red" 6/6 slip.
23.	Krater	G70, VI.NE16.164, No. 1 L. 16044	*Technique:* Wheelmade. *Paste:* 2.5YR "light red" 6/6; some very small to large wadi gravel and lime, few very small crystal; core: 7.5YR "pink" 8/4; hard. *Surface (Interior):* as paste. *(Exterior):* 7.5YR "pinkish white" 8/2.

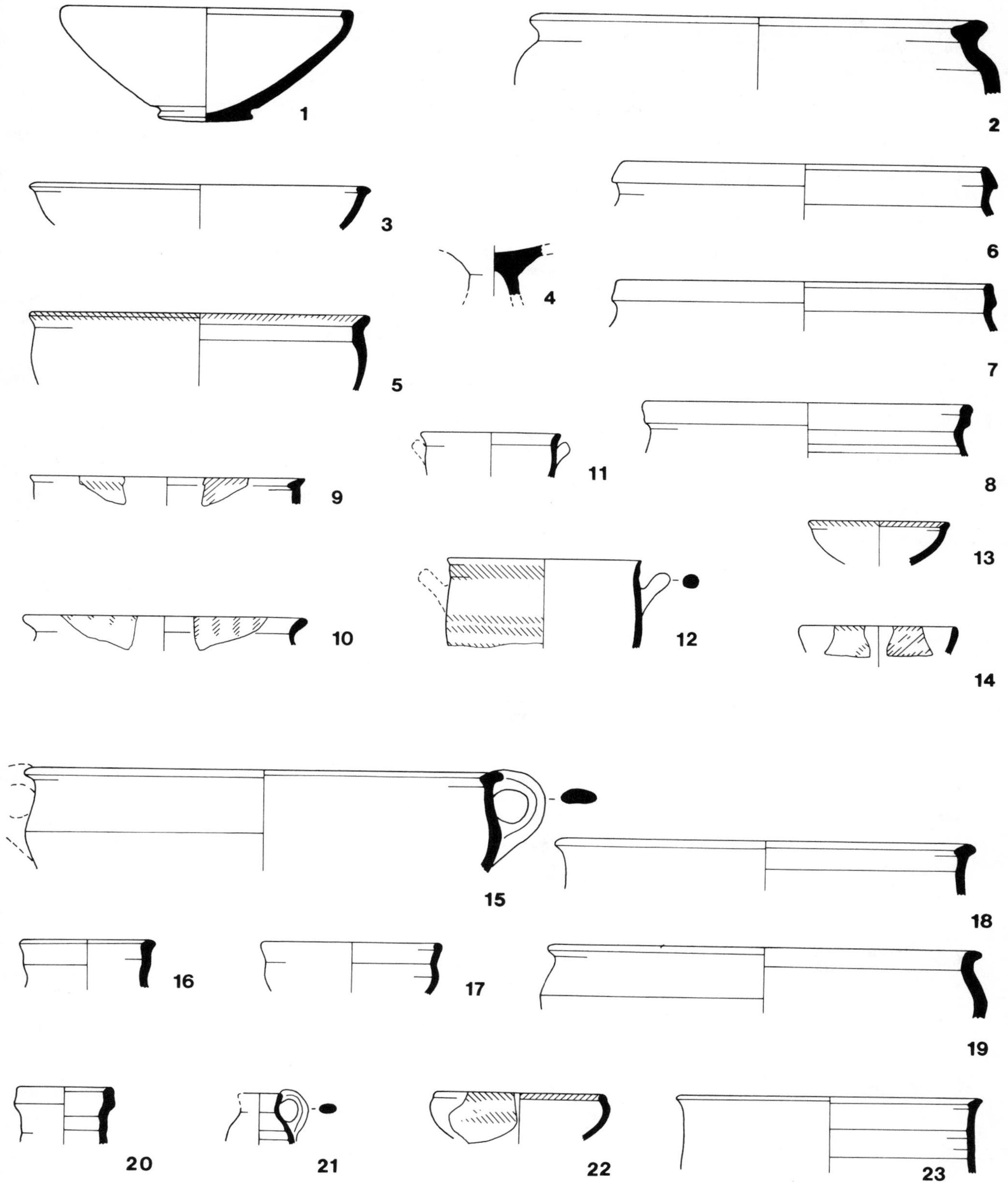
1
2
3
4
5
6
7
8
9
10
11
12
13
14
15
16
17
18
19
20
21
22
23

Plate Number	Pottery Type	Number and locus (see LOCUS INDEX)	Description (p. 277)
1.	Jar	G71, VI.NE5.125, No. 14 L. 5072	*Technique:* Wheelmade. *Paste:* 7.5YR "light brown" 6/4; some very small lime, few very small and large wadi gravel, medium ceramic and very small crystal; no core; hard. *Surface (Interior):* as paste. *(Exterior):* as paste.
2.	Jar	G71, VI.NE5.127, No. 15 L. 5072	*Technique:* Wheelmade. *Paste:* 5YR "yellowish red" 5/6; few very small to medium lime and ceramic and very small wadi gravel and crystal; no core; hard. *Surface (Interior):* 7.5YR "pink" 7/4. *(Exterior):* as paste.
3.	Bowl or cup	G71, VI.NE6.177, No. 2 L. 6984	*Technique:* Wheelmade. *Paste:* 5YR "reddish hellow" 7/6; some small organic and very small crystal, few very small to small wadi gravel and small lime; light grey core; hard. *Surface (Interior):* 7.5YR "pink" 8/4; 10YR "weak red" 5/4 slip onrim. *(Exterior):* as interior; band of slip below rim as interior.
4.	Bowl	G71, VI.NE5.114, No. 12 L. 5072	*Technique:* Wheelmade. *Paste:* 5YR "pink" 7/4; few to some very small and few small to medium lime, few small ceramic and very small crystal; grey core; hard. *Surface (Interior):* as paste. *(Exterior):* as paste.
5.	Bowl	G71, VI.NE5.126, No. 34 L. 5072	*Technique:* Wheelmade. *Paste:* 5YR "light reddish brown" 6/4; some very small wadi gravel, few very small to medium lime, small ceramic and very small crystal; no core; hard. *Surface (Interior):* as paste; 10YR "red" 4/6 slip on rim; traces of wheel burnish. *(Exterior):* as paste.
6.	Bowl	G71, I.NE6.177, No. 8 L. 6084	*Technique:* Wheelmade. *Paste:* 5YR "reddish yellow" 6/6; very many very small wadi gravel, few very small lime and crystal; core: 5YR "light reddish brown" 6/4; hard. *Surface (Interior):* as paste; 10YR "red" 4/6 slip on rim. *(Exterior):* as paste; slip on rim as interior.
7.	Bowl	G71, VI.NE15.138, No. 30 L. 15045	*Technique:* Wheelmade. *Paste:* 5YR "reddish yellow" 7/6; many very small and few large lime, few small and medium ceramic and large organic; grey core; hard. *Surface (Interior):* as paste; band of 2.5YR "red" 4/6 slip on rim and decoration. *(Exterior):* as paste; slip on rim as interior.
8.	Bowl	G70, VI.NE18.114, No. 3 L. 18086.1	*Technique:* Wheelmade. *Paste:* 5YR "reddish yellow" 6/6; some very small and few medium wadi gravel, few large iron and organic, small and large ceramic, very small to large lime, and very small crystal; light grey core; hard. *Surface (Interior):* as paste. *(Exterior):* as paste.
9.	Krater	G70, VI.NE16.116, No. 15 L. 16030	*Technique:* Wheelmade. *Paste:* inner: 5YR "light reddish brown" 6/4; outer: 5YR "pink" 7/4; some very small and few medium lime, few large iron, medium and large wadi gravel, very small and small ceramic and very small crystal; grey core; hard. *Surface (Interior):* 7.5YR "light brown" 6/4. *(Exterior):* as inner paste.
10.	Jar	G70, VI.NE18.105, No. 6 L. 18086.1	*Technique:* Wheelmade. *Paste:* 5YR "reddish yellow" 6/6; some very small and few small lime, some small wadi gravel and few small to large ceramic; light grey core; hard. *Surface (Interior):* as paste. *(Exterior):* as paste.
11.	Cooking pot	G70, I.NE18.126, No. 3 L. 18095.1	*Technique:* Wheelmade. *Paste:* 2.5YR "light red" 6/6; very many small to large lime, some medium wadi gravel, few small ceramic, and very small organic and crystal; no core; hard. *Surface (Interior):* as paste. *(Exterior):* as paste.
12.	Cooking pot	G70, VI.NE18.126, No. 1 L. 18095.1	*Technique:* Wheelmade. *Paste:* 5YR "reddish yellow" 6/6; very many medium lime, few small to medium wadi gravel, small organic, very small crystal; dark grey core; hard. *Surface (Interior):* as paste. *(Exterior):* as paste.
13.	Krater	G70, VI.NE18.138, No. 15 L. 18095.1	*Technique:* Wheelmade. *Paste:* 5YR "reddish yellow" 6/6; many very small wadi gravel, few small lime, organic and very small crystal; core: 7.5YR "pink" 7/4; hard. *Surface (Interior):* as paste; organic paint on rim as exterior. *(Exterior):* 7.5YR "pinkish white" 8/2 slip; 2.5YR "dark reddish brown" 3/4 organic paint on rim and decoration; traces of wheel burnish.
14.	Base	G70, VI.NE18.138, No. 23 L. 18095.1	*Technique:* Wheelmade. *Paste:* 5YR "pink" 7/4; many small crystal (quartz); grey core; hard. *Surface (Interior):* as paste. *(Exterior):* as paste.
15.	Krater	G70, VI.NE26.110, No. 4 L. 26035.1	*Technique:* Wheelmade. *Paste:* 5YR "reddish brown" 4/4; some small and few large wadi gravel, some very small and few small crystal, few small lime, organic and very small ceramic; no core; hard. *Surface (Interior):* as paste. *(Exterior):* 2.5YR "grey" 6/0 to 5YR "white" 8/1 slip; horizontal lines of burnish; bands of 2.5YR "dark red" 3/6 organic paint on and below rim; 5YR "dark reddish brown" 3/2 organic paint decoration.
16.	Krater	G70, VI.NE26.111, No. 11 L. 26035.1	*Technique:* Wheelmade. *Paste:* 5YR "reddish yellow" 7/6; some very small wadi gravel, few medium organic, small lime, very small crystal and ceramic; light grey core; hard. *Surface (Interior):* as paste. *(Exterior):* 10YR "white" 8/2.
17.	Krater	G70, VI.NE26.111, No. 16 L. 26035.1	*Technique:* Wheelmade. *Paste:* 5YR "yellowish red" 5/6; few small lime, ceramic, organic and very small crystal; grey core; hard. *Surface (Interior):* as paste. *(Exterior):* 5YR "pink" 7/4.
18.	Cooking pot	G70, VI.NE26.111, No. 12 L. 26035.1	*Technique:* Wheelmade. *Paste:* 5YR "yellowish red" 5/6; some very small and few small to large lime, few very small and medium crystal; no core; hard. *Surface (Interior):* as paste. *(Exterior):* as paste.
19.	Cooking pot	G70, VI.NE26.114, No. 7 L. 26035.1	*Technique:* Wheelmade. *Paste:* 5YR "light reddish brown" 6/4; some medium wadi gravel, lime, organic and small crystal; core: 7.5YR "light brown" 6/4; hard. *Surface (Interior):* as paste. *(Exterior):* as paste.
20.	Cooking pot	G70, VI.NE26.110, No. 13 L. 26035.1	*Technique:* Wheelmade. *Paste:* 7.5YR "pink" 7/4; very many very small crystal, few medium and very large lime and small iron; grey core; hard. *Surface (Interior):* 10YR "white" 8/2 slip? *(Exterior):* as interior.

PLATE 40

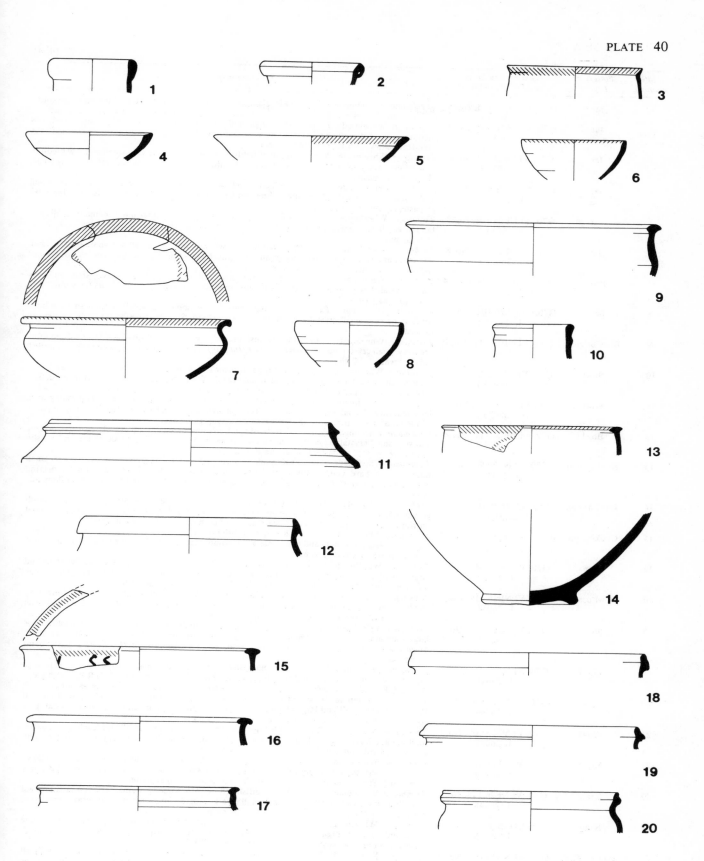

Plate Number	Pottery Type	Number and locus (see LOCUS INDEX)	Description (p. 277)
1.	Jar	G70, VI.NE26.105, No. 5 L. 26035.1	*Technique:* Wheelmade. *Paste:* 2.5YR "light red" 6/6; few very small to large lime, small ceramic and very small crystal; light grey core; hard. *Surface (Interior):* as paste. *(Exterior):* as paste.
2.	Jar	G70, VI.NE26.100, No. 3 L. 26035.1	*Technique:* Wheelmade. *Paste:* 2.5YR "light red" 6/6; very many very small wadi gravel, few medium lime and very small crystal; no core; hard. *Surface (Interior):* as paste. *(Exterior):* 5YR "reddish yellow" 7/6 to 5YR "white" 8/1.
3.	Jar	G70, VI.NE26.99, No. 4 L. 26035.1	*Technique:* Wheelmade. *Paste:* 5YR "light reddish brown" 6/4; some very small and few medium lime, some very small crystal, few very small ceramic; no core; hard. *Surface (Interior):* as paste. *(Exterior):* as paste.
4.	Jar	G70, VI.NE26.111, No. 5 L. 26035.1	*Technique:* Wheelmade. *Paste:* 5YR "reddish yellow" 7/6; few small to very large iron, very small and small crystal, small and medium lime and small organic; grey core; hard. *Surface (Interior):* as paste. *(Exterior):* as paste.
5.	Jar	G70, VI.NE26.108, No. 3 L. 26035.1	*Technique:* Wheelmade. *Paste:* 7.5YR "pinkish grey" 6/2; few very small and very many small crystal, few small wadi gravel and organic; no core; hard. *Surface (Interior):* 7.5YR "pink" 7/4. (Exterior): as paste.
6.	Jar	G70, VI.NE26.111, No. 8 L. 26035.1	*Technique:* Wheelmade. *Paste:* 5YR "reddish yellow" 6/6; few very small and some small crystal, few small and large lime, some very small wadi gravel, few small organic; grey core; hard. *Surface (Interior):* as paste. *(Exterior):* as paste.
7.	Bowl	G70, VI.NE26.104, No. 14 L. 26035.1	*Technique:* Wheelmade. *Paste:* 7.5YR "light brown" 6/4; some small wadi gravel, small and very small crystal, few small lime and organic; no core; hard. *Surface (Interior):* 10YR "white" 8/2. *(Exterior):* as paste.
8.	Bowl	G70, VI.NE26.104, No. 12 L. 26035.1	*Technique:* Wheelmade. *Paste:* 7.5YR "light brown" 6/4; some very small and few small to large lime, some very small crystal and ceramic; no core; hard. *Surface (Interior):* as paste. *(Exterior):* as paste.
9.	Bowl or cup	G70, VI.NE26.111, No. 7 L. 26035.1	*Technique:* Wheelmade. *Paste:* 5YR "reddish yellow" 7/6; some very small and few medium lime, few very small crystal; no core; hard. *Surface (Interior):* as paste; slip on rim as exterior. *(Exterior):* 7.5YR "white" 7/0 slip.
10.	Bowl	G70, VI.NE26.104, No. 4 L. 26035.1	*Technique:* Wheelmade. *Paste:* 5YR "reddish brown" 5/4; many very small and few large lime, some small to few large ceramic and medium organic, few very small crystal; grey core; hard. *Surface (Interior):* as paste; 2.5YR "light red" 6/8 slip on rim. *(Exterior):* as paste.
11.	Bowl	G70, VI.NE26.111, No. 15 L. 26035.1	*Technique:* Wheelmade. *Paste:* 5YR "reddish brown" 6/6; some small and very small wadi gravel, few medium and small lime and very small crystal; light grey core; hard. *Surface (Interior):* as paste; 10YR "red" 4/6 slip on rim. *(Exterior):* as paste; slip as interior.
12.	Bowl	G70, VI.NE26.111, No. 24 L. 26035.1	*Technique:* Wheelmade. *Paste:* 7.5YR "pink" 7/4; many very small wadi gravel, few small organic and very small crystal; no core; hard. *Surface (Interior):* as paste; 2.5YR "reddish brown" 5/4 slip on rim. *(Exterior):* as paste; slip on rim as interior.
13.	Bowl or cup	G70, VI.NE26.94, No. 2 L. 26035.1	*Technique:* Wheelmade. *Paste:* 5YR "pinkish white" 8/2; some very small ceramic, few very small lime; no core; hard. *Surface (Interior):* 7.5YR "pinkish white" 8/2; 10YR "red" 4/6 slip on rim. *(Exterior):* as interior; slip on rim as interior; traces of bands of 5YR "reddish brown" 4/3 organic paint.
14.	Bowl or cup	G70, VI.NE26.104, No. 2 L. 26035.1	*Technique:* Wheelmade. *Paste:* 7.5YR "pink" 7/4; many small and few large lime, few large wadi gravel, few medium organic, few small ceramic; no core; hard. *Surface (Interior):* as paste; paint on rim as exterior. *(Exterior):* as paste; bands of 10YR "red" 4/6" organic paint.
15.	Cooking pot	G70, VI.NE26.110, No. 17 L. 26035.1	*Technique:* Wheelmade. *Paste:* 5YR "light reddish brown" 6/3; few very small and many small and medium crystal, few small and large lime and medium organic; dark grey core; hard. *Surface (Interior):* as paste. *(Exterior):* as paste.
16.	Jar	G70, VI.NE26.148, No. 1 L. 26048	*Technique:* Wheelmade. *Paste:* 5YR "reddish yellow" 6/6; very many very small and few small and large lime, few large wadi gravel and organic, small and medium ceramic and very small crystal; grey core; hard. *Surface (Interior):* 7.5YR "pink" 7/4. *(Exterior):* as paste.
17.	Bowl or cup	G70, VI.NE26.119, No. 6 L. 26048	*Technique:* Wheelmade. *Paste:* 5YR "reddish yellow" 6/6; few very small to medium lime, very small ceramic and crystal; no core; hard. *Surface (Interior):* as paste; 2.5YR "red" 5/6 slip on rim and drip. *(Exterior):* as paste; slip on rim as interior.
18.	Bowl	G70, VI.NE26.123, No. 1 L. 26048	*Technique:* Wheelmade. *Paste:* 5YR "pink" 7/4; some small organic, few very small, medium and large wadi gravel, small to large lime, very large iron, and very small crystal; sporadic core; hard. *Surface (Interior):* as paste; bands of 10YR "weak red" 5/4 organic paint. *(Exterior):* as paste; paint on rim as interior.
19.	Bowl	G70, VI.NE26.96, No. 13 L. 26048	*Technique:* Wheelmade. *Paste:* 5YR "yellowish red" 5/6; few very small to large lime, small to large organic, very small ceramic and crystal; grey core; hard. *Surface (Interior):* 7.5YR "pinkish grey" 7/2; 2.5YR "reddish brown" 4/4 slip on rim. *(Exterior):* as interior; slip on rim as interior.
20.	Bowl	G70, VI.NE26.106, No. 2 L. 26048	*Technique:* Wheelmade. *Paste:* 5YR "brown" 5/4; some very small to small and few medium and large lime, few small and large ceramic, small and medium organic and very small crystal; grey core; hard. *Surface (Interior):* as paste. *(Exterior):* as paste.
21.	Bowl	G70, VI.NE26.109, No. 1 L. 26048	*Technique:* Wheelmade. *Paste:* 7.5YR "light brown" 6/4; some very small and few large lime, few medium and large organic, large wadi gravel, medium and small ceramic and very small crystal; grey core; hard. *Surface (Interior):* as paste. *(Exterior):* as paste.
22.	Krater	G70, VI.NE26.123, No. 6 L. 26048	*Technique:* Wheelmade. *Paste:* inner: 7.5YR "pinkish white" 8/2; outer: 5YR "reddish yellow" 7/6; many very small wadi gravel, few medium lime, small organic, very small crystal; light grey core; hard. *Surface (Interior):* as outer paste. *(Exterior):* as inner paste.
23.	Krater	G70, VI.NE26.118, No. 7 L. 26048	*Technique:* Wheelmade. *Paste:* 5YR "reddish yellow" 6/6; some very small and few medium and large lime, some very small crystal, few small to large organic, large iron and wadi gravel; grey core; hard. *Surface (Interior):* as paste. *(Exterior):* as paste.
24.	Krater	G70, VI.NE26.118, No. 10 L. 26048	*Technique:* Wheelmade. *Paste:* 7.5YR "pink" 7/4; some very small and few medium lime, some small and few large organic, some very small crystal and few large wadi gravel; grey core; hard. *Surface (Interior):* as paste. *(Exterior):* 10YR "white" 8/2.
25.	Krater (Philistine ware)	G70, VI.NE26.120, No. 19 L. 26048	*Technique:* Wheelmade. *Paste:* 7.5YR "reddish yellow" 7/6; some very small wadi gravel, few small and large lime, large iron, small organic, very small crystal; grey core; hard. *Surface (Interior):* as paste. *(Exterior):* 10YR "white" 8/1 slip; 7.5YR "dark brown" 3/2 organic paint decoration.
26.	Krater (Philistine ware)	G70, VI.NE26.124, No. 2 L. 26048	*Technique:* Wheelmade. *Paste:* 5YR "light reddish brown" 6/4; some very small to large lime, few small and medium organic and ceramic and medium and large wadi gravel; grey core; hard. *Surface (Interior):* color: traces of 7.5YR "pinkish white" slip 8/2. *(Exterior):* slip as interior; 5YR "reddish brown" 5/4 organic paint decoration and traces on rim.
27.	Cooking Pot	G70, VI.NE26.109, No. 1A L. 26048	*Technique:* Wheelmade. *Paste:* 5YR "reddish brown" 5/4; many medium and large lime, few very small crystal; no core; hard. *Surface (Interior):* as paste. *(Exterior):* as paste.

PLATE 41

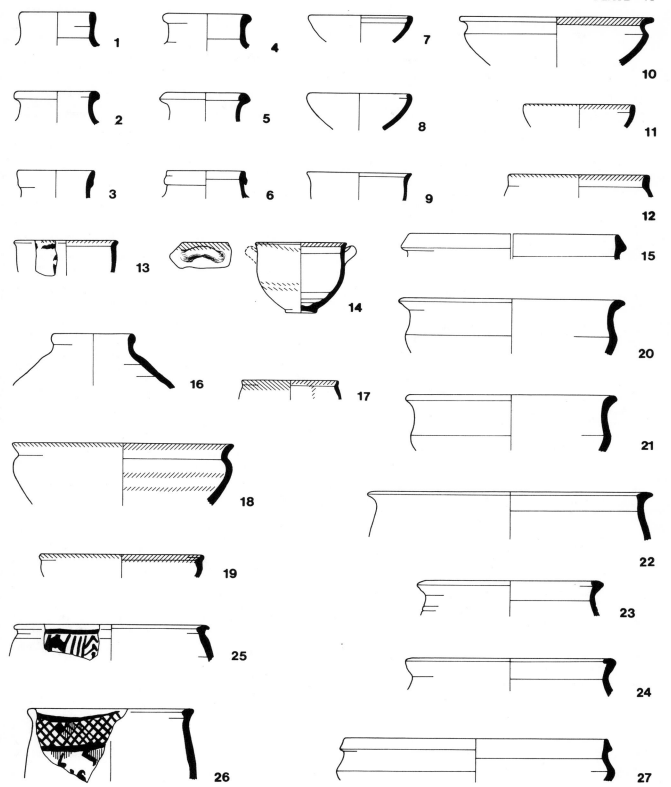

Plate Number	Pottery Type	Number and locus (see LOCUS INDEX)	Description (p. 277)
1.	Bowl	G70, VI.NE74, No. 1 L. 5027	*Technique:* Wheelmade. *Paste:* 5YR "reddish yellow" 7/6; few small to large lime, many very small crystal, few small ceramic; light grey core; hard. *Surface (Interior):* as paste. *(Exterior):* as paste.
2.	Bowl	G70, VI.NE16.126, No. 2 L. 16031	*Technique:* Wheelmade. *Paste:* 5YR "reddish yellow" 7/6; some small organic, few medium and large lime, very small wadi gravel and crystal; grey core; hard. *Surface (Interior):* as passte; 5YR "weak red" 4/4 slip on rim. *(Exterior):* as paste; slip on rim as interior.
3.	Jar	G69, VI.NE14.35, No. 1 L. 14016	*Technique:* Wheelmade. *Paste:* 5YR "yellowish red" 5/6; some very small and few medium and large lime, some very small to small and few medium ceramic, some very small sand; grey core; hard. *Surface (Interior):* as paste. *(Exterior):* as paste.
4.	Krater	G70, VI.NE16.131, No. 6 L. 16039.1	*Technique:* Wheelmade. *Paste:* 5YR "reddish brown" 6/4; some very small sand, few very small to large lime, large wadi gravel and very small to medium ceramic; grey core; hard. *Surface (Interior):* as paste. *(Exterior):* 10YR "white;; 7/1 slip; 10YR "red" 4/4 organic paint decoration on rim and body.
5.	Krater	G70, VI.NE16.129, No. 10 L. 16039.1	*Technique:* Wheelmade. *Paste:* 5YR "reddish yellow" 7/6; some very small and few small to medium lime, few large organic, very small and medium ceramic, and very small crystal; grey core; hard. *Surface (Interior):* as paste. *(Exterior):* as paste.
6.	Krater	G70, VI.NE26.84, No. 5 L. 26035.1	*Technique:* Wheelmade. *Paste:* 5YR "yellowish red" 5/6; some very small and few medium and large lime, some very small crystal, few small to large ceramic and small organic; grey core; hard. *Surface (Interior):* as paste. *(Exterior):* as paste.
7.	Jar	G70, VI.NE26.110, No. 9 L. 26035.1	*Technique:* Wheelmade. *Paste:* 7.5YR "light brown" 6/4; some very small wadi gravel, few small and large iron, small lime, very small crystal; sporadic dark grey core; hard. *Surface (Interior):* as paste. *(Exterior):* as paste.
8.	Jar	G70, VI.NE26.85, No. 25 L. 26035.1	*Technique:* Wheelmade. *Paste:* 7.5YR "light brown" 6/4; some very small and few medium lime, few small and very small ceramic and very small crystal; no core; hard. *Surface (Interior):* as paste. *(Exterior):* as paste; 10YR "red" 5/6 organic paint on rim.
9.	Jar	G70, VI.NE26.123, No. 3 L. 26048	*Technique:* Wheelmade. *Paste:* 5YR "reddish brown" 5/3; some very small and few small to large lime, few large organic, small and medium ceramic and very small crystal; grey core; hard. *Surface (Interior):* as paste. *(Exterior):* as paste.
10.	Jar	G70, VI.NE26.109, No. 2 L. 26048	*Technique:* Wheelmade. *Paste:* inner: 10YR "very pale brown" 7/4; outer: 5YR "reddish yellow" 6/4; some very small and few medium and large lime, few very small and medium crystal and small ceramic; no core; hard. *Surface (Interior):* as paste. *(Exterior):* as paste.
11.	Jar	G70, VI.NE26.85, No. 6 L. 26035.1	*Technique:* Wheelmade. *Paste:* 5YR "reddish yellow" 6/6; many very small and few small and medium lime, few medium wadi gravel, small and medium ceramic and very small crystal; light grey core; hard. *Surface (Interior):* 7.5YR "pink" 8/4. *(Exterior):* as paste.
12.	Jar	G70, VI.NE120, No. 15 L. 26035.1	*Technique:* Wheelmade. *Paste:* 7.5YR "pink" 7/4 to 5YR "pink" 7/4; very many very small wadi gravel, few small to medium lime, medium iron, small organic and very small crystal; no core; hard. *Surface (Interior):* as paste. *(Exterior):* as paste.
13.	Jar	G70, VI.NE26.96, No. 7 L. 26048	*Technique:* Wheelmade. *Paste:* 5YR "reddish yellow" 6/6; many very small and few small and medium lime, few vey small ceramic and crystal; grey core; hard. *Surface (Interior):* as paste. *(Exterior):* as paste.
14.	Jar	G70, VI.NE26.109, No. 16 L. 26048	*Technique:* Wheelmade. *Paste:* 5YR "reddish yellow" 7/6; some very small and few large lime, some very small wadi gravel, few medium ceramic and very small crystal; no core; hard. *Surface (Interior):* as paste. *(Exterior):* as paste; bands of 10YR "red" 4/4 organic paint.
15.	Jar	G70, VI.NE26.85, No. 12 L. 26035.1	*Technique:* Wheelmade. *Paste:* 7.5YR "light brown" 6/4; some very small and few large lime, some very small ceramic and crystal; no core; hard. *Surface (Interior):* as paste. *(Exterior):* as paste.
16.	Bowl	G70, VI.NE26.85, No. 15 L. 26035.1	*Technique:* Wheelmade. *Paste:* 5YR "reddish yellow" 6/6; few large wadi gravel, very small and small lime, very small crystal; no core; hard. *Surface (Interior):* as paste. *(Exterior):* as paste.
17.	Base	G70, VI.NE26.85, No. 7 L. 26035.1	*Technique:* Wheelmade. *Paste:* 5YR "reddish yellow" 6/6; some very small to small and large ceramic and few very small crystal; light grey core; hard. *Surface (Interior):* as paste. *(Exterior):* as paste; bands of 7.5YR "white" 8/2 organic paint and traces of 2.5YR "red" 4/6.
18.	Jar	G70, VI.NE35.101, L. 35043	*Technique:* Wheelmade. *Paste:* 5YR "pink" 7/4; many small crystals (quartz); no core; hard. *Surface (Interior):* as paste. *(Exterior):* as paste.
19.	Bowl	G70, VI.NE26.120, No. 8 L. 26048	*Technique:* Wheelmade. *Paste:* 5YR "reddish yellow" 7/6; some very small lime, few very small and small ceramic and crystal; grey core; hard. *Surface (Interior):* as paste. *(Exterior):* as paste; 2.5YR "red" 4/6 slip on rim.
20.	Bowl	G70, VI.NE35.82, Nos. 1, 4, 7, 9, 11, 13, 17, 18, 21, 22 L. 35013	*Technique:* Wheelmade. *Paste:* 5YR "pink" 7/4; many small quartz; no core; hard. *Surface (Interior):* 10YR "weak red" 4/4 slip on rim. *(Exterior):* as paste.
21.	Jar	G70, VI.NE35.101, No. L. 35013.1	*Technique:* Wheelmade. *Paste:* 5YR "pink" 7/4; many small crystal (quartz); light grey core; hard. *Surface (Interior):* as paste. *(Exterior):* as paste.

PLATE 42

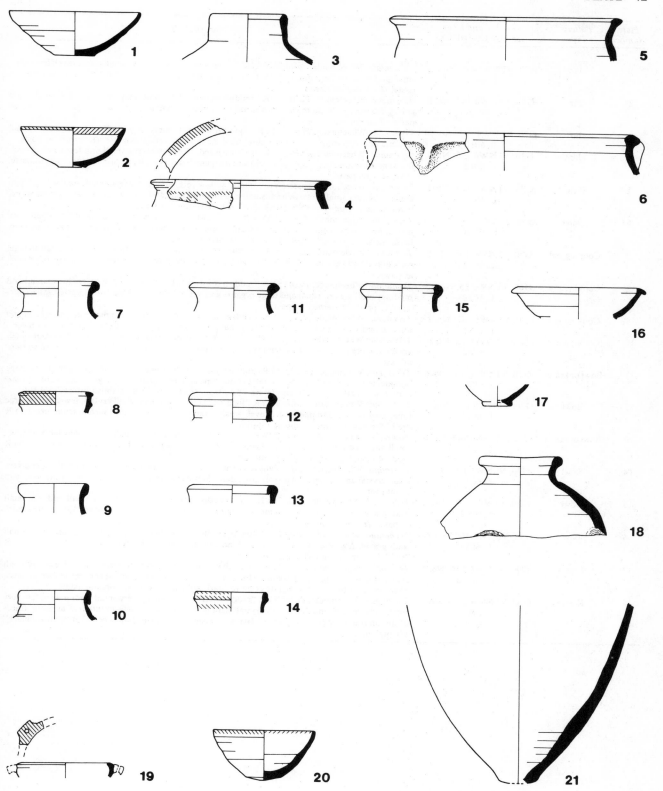

Plate Number	Pottery Type	Number and locus (see LOCUS INDEX)	Description (p. 277)
1.	Jar	G70, VI.NW6.107, No. 12 L. 6012	*Technique:* Wheelmade. *Paste:* 5YR "reddish yellow" 7/6; some very small wadi gravel, few very small and medium lime and very small ceramic and crystal; grey core; hard. *Surface (Interior):* as paste. *(Exterior):* as paste.
2.	Jar	G70, VI.NW6.147, No. 8 L. 6012C	*Technique:* Wheelmade. *Paste:* 5YR "reddish yellow" 7/6; some very small and few small wadi gravel, few very small to medium lime and very small crystal; no core; hard. *Surface (Interior):* as paste. *(Exterior):* as paste.
3.	Jar	G70, VI.NW6.107, No. 14 L. 6012	*Technique:* Wheelmade. *Paste:* 7.5YR "light brown" 6/4; many very small wadi gravel, few small ceramic and very small crystal; no core; hard. *Surface (Interior):* as paste. *(Exterior):* as paste.
4.	Jar	G70, VI.NW6.113, No. 9 L. 6012	*Technique:* Wheelmade. *Paste:* 5YR "yellowish red" 5/6; some very small and few small crystal, few very small to large wadi gravel and small organic; grey core; hard. *Surface (Interior):* as paste. *(Exterior):* as paste.
5.	Base	G70, VI.NW6.107, No. 1 L. 6012	*Technique:* Wheelmade. *Paste:* 5YR "reddish yellow" 6/6; very many very small and few large wadi gravel, few very small to large iron, small and medium lime and very small crystal; light grey core; hard. *Surface (Interior):* 5YR "dark grey" 4/1. *(Exterior):* as paste.
6.	Krater	G70, VI.NW6.147, No. 24 L. 60120	*Technique:* Wheelmade. *Paste:* 7.5YR "light brown" 6/4; many very small and few small wadi gravel, few medium shell, small and medium lime, small organic and very small crystal; no core; hard. *Surface (Interior):* 5YR "grey" 5/1. *(Exterior):* as paste.
7.	Cooking pot	G70, VI.NW6.107, No. 5 L. 6012	*Technique:* Wheelmade. *Paste:* 5YR "reddish brown" 5/4; some small organic, few small to large wadi gravel and very small and small crystal; grey core; hard. *Surface (Interior):* as paste. *(Exterior):* as paste.
8.	Cooking pot	G69, VI.NW6.25, No. 13 L. 6012	*Technique:* Wheelmade. *Paste:* 5YR "reddish brown" 5/3; few medium and large lime, small and medium wadi gravel, small and large organic and very small crystal; no core; hard. *Surface (Interior):* as paste. *(Exterior):* as paste.
9.	Cooking pot	G70, VI.NW6.147, No. 13 L. 6012	*Technique:* Wheelmade. *Paste:* 5YR "reddish brown" 5/4; few small and medium wadi gravel and organic and very small crystal; grey core; hard. *Surface (Interior):* as paste. *(Exterior):* as paste.
10.	Cooking pot	G69, VI.NW6.25, No. 5 L. 6012	*Technique:* Wheelmade. *Paste:* 2.5YR "red" 5/6; few small to large lime, small and medium wadi gravel and organic and very small crystal; grey core; hard. *Surface (Interior):* as paste. *(Exterior):* as paste.
11.	Bowl or krater	G70, VI.NW6.107, No. 6 L. 6012	*Technique:* Wheelmade. *Paste:* 5YR "reddish yellow" 7/6; some very small wadi gravel, few large organic, few small ceramic, very small to large lime and very small crystal; grey core; hard. *Surface (Interior):* 10YR "red" 4/6 slip; traces of burnish. *(Exterior):* 5YR "reddish brown" 5/4 slip.
12.	Bowl	G70, VI.NW6.107, No. 12 L. 6012	*Technique:* Wheelmade. *Paste:* 2.5YR "light red" 6/6; many very small crystal, few small to large lime, very small and small wadi gravel, small organic; grey core; hard. *Surface (Interior):* 2.5YR "red" 5/6 slip. *(Exterior):* slip as interior.
13.	Bowl or krater	G70, VI.NW6.145, No. 5 L. 6012	*Technique:* Wheelmade. *Paste:* 2.5YR "light red" 6/6; many very small crystal, few large organic, small and medium lime, very small ceramic and crystal; grey core hard. *Surface (Interior):* 10YR "red" 4/6 slip. *(Exterior):* slip as interior.
14.	Bowl	G70, VI.NW6.107, No. 9 L. 6012	*Technique:* Wheelmade. *Paste:* many very small wadi gravel, few small and medium lime, and very small crystal and ceramic; light grey core; hard. *Surface (Interior):* 10YR "red" 4/6. *(Exterior):* slip as interior.
15.	Bowl	G70, VI.NW6.107, No. 4 L. 6012	*Technique:* Wheelmade. *Paste:* 5YR "light reddish brown" 6/4; many very small and few small wadi gravel, few small to large lime, very small ceramic crystal; no core; hard. *Surface (Interior):* as paste. *(Exterior):* as paste.
16.	Base	G70, VI.NW6.107, No. 6A L. 6012	*Technique:* Wheelmade. *Paste:* 5YR "reddish yellow" 6/6; many very small sand, some very small wadi gravel, few small to large lime and large organic; grey core; hard. *Surface (Interior):* 10YR "red" 4/6 slip. *(Exterior):* slip as interior.
17.	Krater	G70, VI.NW6.134, No. 2 L. 6012B	*Technique:* Wheelmade. *Paste:* 5YR "reddish yellow" 7/6; many very small lime and few very small crystal; light grey core; hard. *Surface (Interior):* as paste; slip as exterior at rim. *(Exterior):* as paste; 5YR "reddish brown" 5/4; bands of 5YR "dark reddish brown" 3/2 organic paint.
18.	Krater	G70, VI.NW6.1213, No. 1 L. 6012	*Technique:* Wheelmade. *Paste:* 5YR "reddish yellow" 7/6; many very small wadi gravel, few small to large lime and very small crystal; light grey core; hard. *Surface (Interior):* as paste; traces of slip on rim as exterior. *(Exterior):* 10YR " "weak red" 4/4 slip; bands of 10YR "reddish black" 5/1 organic paint.

PLATE 43

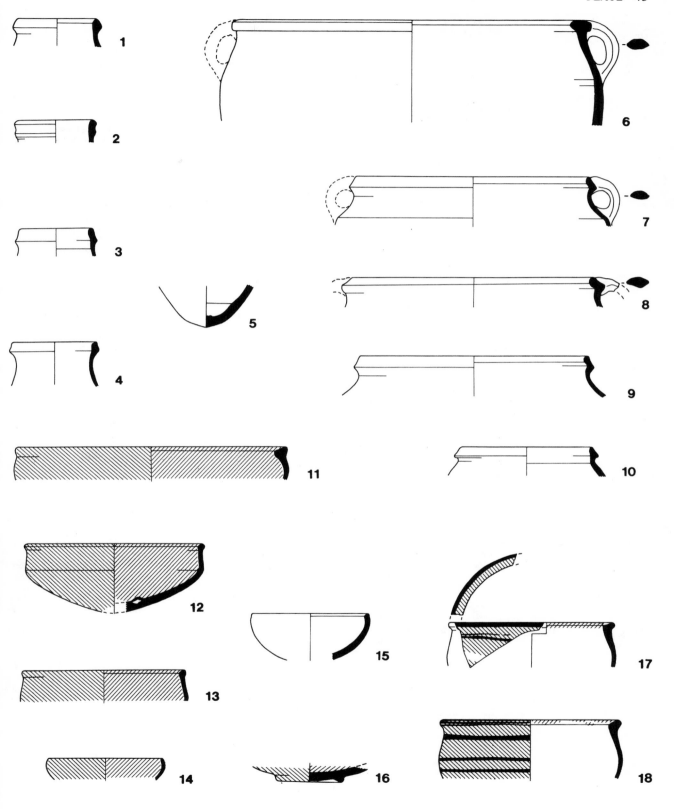

Plate Number	Pottery Type	Number and locus (see LOCUS INDEX)	Description (p. 277)
1.	Krater	G70, VI.NE6.87, No. 3 L. 6011.1	*Technique:* Wheelmade. *Paste:* 5YR "reddish yellow" 7/6; many very small and few large wadi gravel, few large organic, small and medium lime, very small and small ceramic and very small crystal; grey core; hard. *Surface (Interior):* as paste. *(Exterior):* as paste.
2.	Krater	G69, VI.NE6.61, No. 12 L. 6011.1	*Technique:* Wheelmade. *Paste:* 5YR "reddish yellow" 6/6; very many very small and few medium wadi gravel, few very small to medium iron, small lime and very small ceramic and crystal; grey core; hard. *Surface (Interior):* 7.5YR "pink" 7/4. *(Exterior):* as paste.
3.	Krater	G70, VI.NE6.82, No. 20 L. 6011.1	*Technique:* Wheelmade. *Paste:* 5YR "reddish yellow" 6/6; many very small and few small wadi gravel, few very small and large organic, very small to large lime and very small crystal; grey core; hard. *Surface (Interior):* as paste. *(Exterior):* as paste to 7.5YR "pinkish white" 8/2.
4.	Cooking pot	G70, VI.NE6.86, No. 4 L. 6011.1	*Technique:* Wheelmade. *Paste:* 5YR "reddish brown" 5/3; some small and few medium and large lime, few small to large wadi gravel, medium organic and very small crystal; grey core; hard. *Surface (Interior):* as paste. *(Exterior):* as paste.
5.	Cooking pot	G70, VI.NE6.87, No. 13 L. 6011.1	*Technique:* Wheelmade. *Paste:* 5YR "reddish yellow" 6/6; some small and few medium wadi gravel and some very small crystal; no core; hard. *Surface (Interior):* as paste. *(Exterior):* as paste.
6.	Bowl	G69, VI.NE62, No. 8 L. 6011.1	*Technique:* Wheelmade. *Paste:* 5YR "reddish yellow" 6/6; many very small wadi gravel, few medium lime, very small and medium crystal; no core; hard. *Surface (Interior):* as paste. *(Exterior):* as paste; 10YR "weak red" 4/3 slip on rim.
7.	Bowl	G69, VI.NE6.57, No. 3 L. 6011.1	*Technique:* Wheelmade. *Paste:* 5YR "reddish yellow" 6/6; many very small wadi gravel, few very small, small and large lime and very small crystal; no core; hard. *Surface (Interior):* as paste. *(Exterior):* as paste; 10YR "weak red" 4/3 slip on rim.
8.	Spouted juglet	G70, VI.NE6.86, No. 15 L. 6011.1	*Technique:* Wheelmade. *Paste:* 2.5YR "light red" 6/6; some very small and few small to medium lime, some very small wadi gravel, few small ceramic and very small crystal; no core; hard. *Surface (Interior):* as paste. *(Exterior):* as paste.
9.	Bowl	G70, VI.NE6.82, No. 14 L. 6011.1	*Technique:* Wheelmade. *Paste:* 7.5YR "pink" 7.4; some very small and few small ceramic, some very small, few small and medium lime, few very small wadi gravel and crystal; no core; hard. *Surface (Interior):* as paste; slip on rim and traces as exterior. *(Exterior):* 10YR "red" 4/6 slip.
10.	Jar	G70, VI.NE6.82, No. 12 L. 6011.1	*Technique:* Wheelmade. *Paste:* 5YR "reddish yellow" 6/6; few very small to large lime and wadi gravel, medium and small iron, small organic, very small and small ceramic and very small crystal; grey core; hard. *Surface (Interior):* as paste. *(Exterior):* as paste.
11.	Jar	G70, VI.NE6.86, No. 10 L. 6011.1	*Technique:* Wheelmade. *Paste:* 7.5YR "pink" 7/4; many very small wadi gravel, few medium iron, very small to medium lime, very small and small ceramic; light grey core; hard. *Surface (Interior):* 7.5YR "pinkish white" 8/2. *(Exterior):* as paste.
12.	Bowl	G70, VI.NE18.101, No. 1 L. 18084.1	*Technique:* Wheelmade. *Paste:* 5YR "reddish yellow" 6/6; some very small crystal, small ceramic and small and few medium lime, few large iron; grey core; hard. *Surface (Interior):* as paste. *(Exterior):* as paste to 7.5YR "pink" 8/4; traces of 10YR "red" 5/6 slip on rim.
13.	Krater	G70, VI.NE18.88, No. 2 L. 18084.1	*Technique:* Wheelmade. *Paste:* 5YR "reddish yellow" 7/6; many very small and few large wadi gravel, few large organic, very small and small ceramic and lime and very small crystal; grey core; hard. *Surface (Interior):* as paste. *(Exterior):* as paste.
14.	Krater	G70, VI.NE18.132, No. 2 L. 18084.1	*Technique:* Wheelmade. *Paste:* 5YR "reddish yellow" 6/6; some very small and few large wadi gravel, few large organic, small to large lime, small iron and very small crystal; grey core; hard. *Surface (Interior):* as paste. *(Exterior):* as paste.
15.	Cooking pot	G70, VI.NE18.79, No. 4 L. 18084.1	*Technique:* Wheelmade. *Paste:* 5YR "reddish yellow" 7/6; some very small crystal and wadi gravel, few large iron, very small to medium organic and lime, grey core; hard. *Surface (Interior):* as paste. *(Exterior):* as paste.
16.	Jar	G70, VI.NE18.93, No. 15 L. 18084.1	*Technique:* Wheelmade. *Paste:* 7.5YR "light brown" 6/4; some very small and few large lime, few very small crystal; no core; hard. *Surface (Interior):* as paste. *(Exterior):* as paste.
17.	Bowl	G70, VI.NE18.94, No. 10 L. 18085.1	*Technique:* Wheelmade. *Paste:* 5YR "reddish yellow" 7/6; some very small wadi gravel, few very small and small lime, and very small ceramic and crystal; no core; hard. *Surface (Interior):* 10YR "white" 8/2; bands of 10YR "weak red" 4/4 slip. *(Exterior):* as interior; slip on rim as interior.
18.	Krater	G70, VI.NE18.105, No. 1 L. 18086	*Technique:* Wheelmade. *Paste:* 7.5YR "pink" 7/4; many very small wadi gravel, few very small to large lime, few small iron and very small crystal; grey core; hard. *Surface (Interior):* 7.5YR "pinkish white" 8/2. *(Exterior):* as interior.
19.	Cooking pot	G70, VI.NE18.114, No. 4 L. 18086.1	*Technique:* Wheelmade. *Paste:* 5YR "reddish brown" 5/4; many small to large lime and very small crystal, some small wadi gravel; dark grey core; hard. *Surface (Interior):* 5YR "pinkish grey" 7/2. *(Exterior):* as paste.
20.	Cooking pot	G70, VI.NE18.105, No. 3, L. 18086.1	*Technique:* Wheelmade. *Paste:* 5YR "reddish brown" 5/4; few small to medium lime and wadi gravel, small ceramic and very small crystal; grey core; hard. *Surface (Interior):* as paste. *(Exterior):* as paste.
21.	Cooking pot	G69, VI.NE18.110, No. 3 L. 18086.1	*Technique:* Wheelmade. *Paste:* 5YR "reddish brown" 5/4; some small lime, few small wadi gravel and very small to small crystal; grey core; hard. *Surface (Interior):* as paste. *(Exterior):* as paste.

PLATE 44

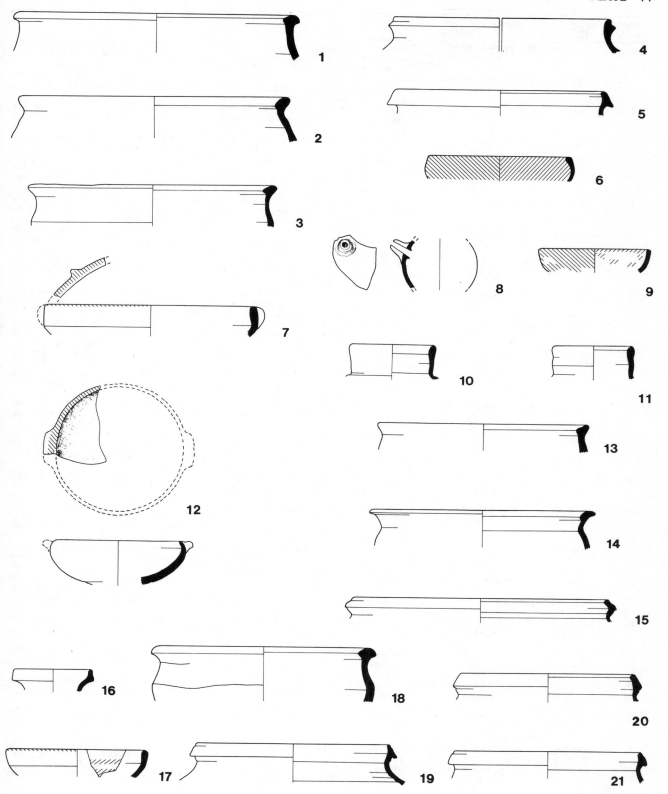

Plate Number	Pottery Type	Number and locus (see LOCUS INDEX)	Description (p. 277)
1.	Jar	G70, VI.NE6.108, No. 13 L. 6026	*Technique:* Wheelmade. *Paste:* inner: 7.5YR "pink" 7/4; outer: 5YR "light red" 6/8; few large iron, small to large organic, very small to medium lime and ceramic, very small wadi gravel and crystal; grey core; hard. *Surface (Interior):* as paste, inner and outer. *(Exterior):* as outer paste.
2.	Jar	G70, VI.NE6.89, No. 1 L. 6026	*Technique:* Wheelmade. *Paste:* 5YR "reddish yellow" 6/6; some very small and small and few medium wadi gravel, few very small and medium crystal; grey core; hard. *Surface (Interior):* 7.5YR "pink" 8/4. *(Exterior):* as interior.
3.	Jar	G69, VI.NE6.66, No. 18 L. 6026	*Technique:* Wheelmade. *Paste:* 7.5YR "light brown" 6/4; some small to medium wadi gravel, few medium lime and very small crystal; no core; hard. *Surface (Interior):* as paste. *(Exterior):* 7.5YR "pink" 8/4.
4.	Jar	G70, VI.NE6.93, No. 9 L. 6026	*Technique:* Wheelmade. *Paste:* inner: 7.5YR "pink" 8/4; outer: 5YR "reddish yellow" 7/6; few very small to large lime, few very small ceramic and wadi gravel; no core; hard. *Surface (Interior):* as inner paste. *(Exterior):* as outer paste.
5.	Jar	G70, VI.NE6.105, No. 25 L. 6026	*Technique:* Wheelmade. *Paste:* 5YR "reddish yellow" 7/6; some very small and small lime, few small and medium wadi gravel and very small ceramic and crystal; grey core; hard. *Surface (Interior):* as paste. *(Exterior):* as paste.
6.	Jug	G70, VI.NE6.104, No. 1 L. 6026	*Technique:* Wheelmade. *Paste:* 5YR "reddish yellow" 7/6; some very small and few small and medium lime, few very small, medium and large ceramic, very small wadi gravel and crystal; no core; hard. *Surface (Interior):* as paste. *(Exterior):* 10YR "white" 8/2.
7.	Cooking jug	G70, VI.NE6.103, No. 7 L. 6026	*Technique:* Wheelmade. *Paste:* 5YR "reddish yellow" 6/6; some very small crystal, few large organic, very small and medium ceramic and small and medium lime; grey core; hard. *Surface (Interior):* as paste. *(Exterior):* as paste.
8.	Cooking jug	G70, VI.NE6.100, No. 19 L. 6026	*Technique:* Wheelmade. *Paste:* 7.5YR "light brown" 6/4; some very small and few medium and large lime, some very small wadi gravel, few very small crystal; core: 7.5YR "pink" 8/4; hard. *Surface (Interior):* as paste. *(Exterior):* 10YR "white" 8/2.
9.	Krater	G70, VI.NE6.120, No. 12 L. 6026	*Technique:* Wheelmade. *Paste:* 2.5YR "light red" 6/6; some very small crystal, few medium and large wadi gravel and iron, very small to large lime; grey core; hard. *Surface (Interior):* 7.5YR "pinkish white" 8/2. *(Exterior):* as paste and interior.
10.	Krater	G70, VI.NE6.97, No. 1 L. 6026	*Technique:* Wheelmade. *Paste:* 7.5YR "light brown" 6/4; some very small and few medium lime, few very small ceramic and crystal; no core; hard. *Surface (Interior):* as paste; traces of slip on rim as exterior. *(Exterior):* 10YR "white" 8/2 slip; band of slip as paste; wheel burnish on rim.
11.	Krater	G70, VI.NE6.76, No. 2 L. 6026	*Technique:* Wheelmade. *Paste:* 7.5YR "light brown" 6/4; some very small wadi gravel, few large iron, small and medium ceramic, and very small and small lime; grey core; hard. *Surface (Interior):* as paste. *(Exterior):* 10YR "white" 8/2 slip on body and rim; band of 10YR "red" 4/6 slip on rim; band of 7.5YR "light brown" 6/4 slip below rim; 5YR "reddish brown" 4/3 organic paint decoration; wheel burnish on rim and body.
12.	Krater	G70, VI.NE6.103, No. 1 L. 6026	*Technique:* Wheelmade. *Paste:* 5YR "light reddish brown" 7/6; some very small lime, few very small and small ceramic and very small crystal; grey core; hard. *Surface (Interior):* as paste. *(Exterior):* as paste.
13.	Bowl	G70, VI.NE6.114, No. 5 L. 6026	*Technique:* Wheelmade. *Paste:* 2.5YR "light red" 6/6; few medium iron, very small and small lime, very small wadi gravel, ceramic and crystal; no core; hard. *Surface (Interior):* 10YR "white" 8/2 slip; 10YR "red" 4/8 slip on rim; hand burnish. *(Exterior):* slip on rim and body as interior; hand burnish as interior.
14.	Bowl or cup	G70, VI.NE6.93, No. 4 L. 6026	*Technique:* Wheelmade. *Paste:* 7.5YR "light brown" 6/4; some very small lime, crystal and wadi gravel, few small ceramic; no core; hard. *Surface (Interior):* 10YR "white" 8/2 slip. *(Exterior):* as paste; 2.5YR "red" 5/6 slip on rim.
15.	Bowl or cup	G70, VI.NE6.107, No. 6 L. 6026	*Technique:* Wheelmade. *Paste:* 5YR "reddish yellow" 7/6; some very small and few medium lime, few very small and small ceramic and very small crystal; light grey core; hard. *Surface (Interior):* as paste; slip and paint on rim as exterior. *(Exterior):* 10YR "white" 8/2 slip; bands of 2.5YR "reddish brown" 5/4 organic paint on rim and body.
16.	Bowl	G70, VI.NE6.105, No. 18 L. 6026	*Technique:* Wheelmade. *Paste:* 5YR "light reddish brown" 6/4; few very small to large lime, small organic, very small and small ceramic and crystal and very small wadi gravel; grey core; hard. *Surface (Interior):* as paste. *(Exterior):* as paste to 10YR "very pale brown" 7/4.
17.	Bowl	G69, VI.NE24.92, No. 1 L. 24018	*Technique:* Wheelmade. *Paste:* 7.,5YR "light brown" 6/4; some very small and few medium and large lime, some very small crystal, few small wadi gravel and small to large ceramic; light grey core; 10YR "white" 8/2 slip. 10YR "red" 4/6 slip on rim; wheelburnish. *(Exterior):* slip and burnish as interior.
18.	Bowl or cup	G70, VI.NE6.100, No. 18 L. 6026	*Technique:* Wheelmade. *Paste:* 5YR "reddish yellow" 6/6; few very small to medium lime and very small ceramic, wadi gravel and crystal; no core; hard. *Surface (Interior):* as paste. *(Exterior):* as paste.
19.	Bowl	G69, VI.NE26.68, No. 3 L. 26015	*Technique:* Wheelmade. *Paste:* 5YR "reddish yellow" 7/6; very many very small and few small to large wadi gravel, few small and large lime and very small crystal; light grey core; hard. *Surface (Interior):* as paste. *(Exterior):* as paste.
20.	Cooking pot	G69, VI.NE6.97, No. 15 L. 6026	*Technique:* Wheelmade. *Paste:* 5YR "reddish yellow" 6/6; some very small and few small to medium and large lime and wadi gravel; grey core; hard. *Surface (Interior):* as paste. *(Exterior):* as paste.
21.	Cooking pot	G70, VI.NE6.103, No. 15 L. 6026	*Technique:* Wheelmade. *Paste:* 2.5YR "red" 5/6; some medium and few small and large lime, few small wadi gravel and very small crystal; grey core; hard. *Surface (Interior):* as paste. *(Exterior):* as paste.
22.	Cooking pot	G70, VI.NE6.114, No. 13 L. 6026	*Technique:* Wheelmade. *Paste:* 5YR "reddish brown" 5/4; few small to large wadi gravel, small organic and very small crystal; grey core; hard. *Surface (Interior):* as paste. *(Exterior):* as paste.
23.	Cooking pot	G69, VI.NE6.66, No. 37 L. 6016	*Technique:* Wheelmade. *Paste:* 5YR "light reddish brown" 6/4; some large wadi gravel, few medium and large lime, small organic, ceramic and crystal; light grey core; hard. *Surface (Interior):* as paste. *(Exterior):* as paste.

PLATE 45

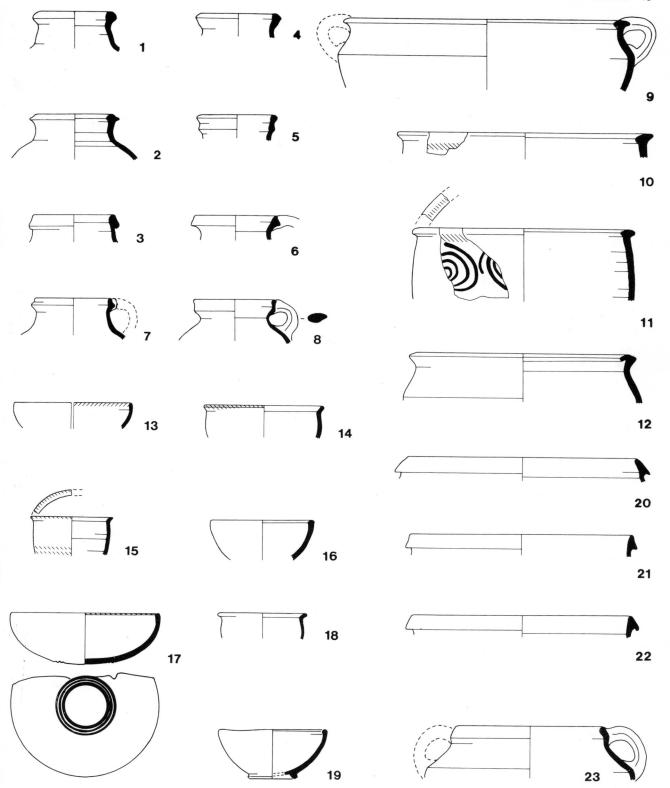

Plate Number	Pottery Type	Number and locus (see LOCUS INDEX)	Description (p. 277)
1.	Cooking pot	G70. VI.NE16.112, No. 1 L. 16038.1	*Technique:* Wheelmade. *Paste:* 5YR "reddish yellow" 6/6; many small calcite; no core; hard. *Surface (Interior):* as paste. *(Exterior):* as paste
2.	Bowl or cup	G70, VI.NE16.116, No. 29 L. 16030	*Technique:* Wheelmade. *Paste:* 7.5YR "pink" 7/4; some very small and few medium ceramic and lime, few very small wadi gravel; no core; hard. *Surface (Interior):* as paste; slip on rim as exterior. *(Exterior):* as paste; bands of 10YR "red" 4/6 slip on rim and body.
3.	Cooking pot	G70, VI.NE18.51, No. 13 L. 18038.1	*Technique:* Wheelmade. *Paste:* 5YR "reddish brown" 5/4; some medium and few very small and small lime, few small and medium wadi gravel and very small crystal; grey core; hard. *Surface (Interior):* as paste. *(Exterior):* as paste.
4.	Jug	G80, VI.NE18.55, No. 16 L. 18038.1	*Technique:* Wheelmade. *Paste:* 5YR "reddish yellow" 6/6; very many very small and few large wadi gravel, few large iron and very small crystal; core: 7.5YR "light brown" 6/4; hard. *Surface (Interior):* as paste. *(Exterior):* as paste.
5.	Jar	G70, VI.NE16.110, No. 7 L. 16030	*Technique:* Wheelmade. *Paste:* 7.5YR "pink" 7/4; some very small wadi gravel, few small organic and very small crystal and ceramic; light grey core; hard. *Surface (Interior):* 5YR "pink" 7/4. *(Exterior):* as interior.
6.	Jar	G70, VI.NE16.116, No. 19 L. 16030	*Technique:* Wheelmade. *Paste:* 5YR "reddish yellow" 6/6; few very small to large ceramic, very small and medium lime and crystal and very small wadi gravel; grey core; hard. *Surface (Interior):* 7.5YR "light brown" 6/4. *(Exterior):* as interior to 5YR "dark grey" 4/1.
7.	Jar	G70, VI.NE16.112, No. 3 L. 16030	*Technique:* Wheelmade. *Paste:* 7.5YR "light brown" 6/4; some very small and few medium lime, few medium organic, small to large iron (?) and very small crystal; dark grey core; hard. *Surface (Interior):* 7.5YR "pinkish grey" 6/2. *(Exterior):* as interior.
8.	Bowl	G70, VI.NE16.159, No. 4 L. 16030	*Technique:* Wheelmade. *Paste:* 5YR "light reddish brown" 6/4; very many very small and wadi gravel, some very small crystal, few small organic; light grey core; hard. *Surface (Interior):* 7.5YR "pink" 8/4. *(Exterior):* as interior to 5YR "white" 8/1.
9.	Bowl	G70, VI.NE16.110, No. 3 L. 16030	*Technique:* Wheelmade. *Paste:* 5YR "reddish yellow" 7/6; many very small and few medium lime, few medium iron, very small ceramic, wadi gravel and crystal; no core; hard. *Surface (Interior):* as paste. *(Exterior):* as paste.
10.	Bowl	G70, VI.NE16.113, No. 2 L. 16030	*Technique:* Wheelmade. *Paste:* 5YR "reddish yellow" 7/6; many very small wadi gravel, some medium lime, few small organic and lime and very small crystal; light grey core; hard. *Surface (Interior):* as paste; 10YR "red" 4/6 organic paint on rim and decoration. *(Exterior):* as paste; organic paint on rim as interior.
11.	Base	G70, VI.NE16.125, No. 28 L. 16030	*Technique:* Wheelmade. *Paste:* 5YR "reddish yellow" 7/6; some very small and few small to medium lime, few small and very small ceramic and crystal and very small wadi gravel; grey core; hard. *Surface (Interior):* as paste. *(Exterior):* as paste to 5YR "reddish brown" 5/3.
12.	Base	G70, VI.NE16.113, No. 1 L. 16030	*Technique:* Wheelmade. *Paste:* 2.5YR "red" 5/6; some small to few medium lime, few small organic and very small crystal and wadi gravel; core: 7.5YR "light brown" 6/4; hard. *Surface (Interior):* 10YR "white" 8/2 to 5YR "pink" 7/4. *(Exterior):* as interior.
13.	Lamp	G70, VI.NE16.125, No. 22 L. 16030	*Technique:* Wheelmade. *Paste:* 2.5YR "light red" 6/8; many very small crystal, few large lime, few medium organic, few very small wadi gravel, few small and large ceramic; grey core; hard. *Surface (Interior):* as paste. *(Exterior):* as paste to 10YR "very pale brown" 7/3.
14.	Krater	G70, VI.NE6.73, No. 4 L. 6008	*Technique:* Wheelmade. *Paste:* 5YR "light reddish brown" 6/4; some very small wadi gravel, few large and small iron, small organic, very small and small ceramic and lime and very small crystal; grey core; hard. *Surface (Interior):* as paste. *(Exterior):* as paste.
15.	Bowl	G69, VI.NE6.25, No. 7 L. 6008	*Technique:* Wheelmade. *Paste:* 5YR "reddish yellow" 7/6; many very small wadi gravel, few small lime and ceramic and very small crystal; light grey core; hard. *Surface (Interior):* 10YR "red" 4/6 slip. *(Exterior):* slip as interior.
16.	Bowl	G69, VI.NE6.50, No. 37 L. 6008	*Technique:* Wheelmade. *Paste:* 5YR "reddish yellow" 7/6; some to many very small wadi gravel, few small and large lime, very small ceramic and crystal; no core; hard. *Surface (Interior):* 7.5YR "very dark grey" N3/0. *(Exterior):* 7.5YR "pinkish grey" 6/2; wet-smoothed.
17.	Bowl	G69, VI.NE6.50, No. 2 L. 6008	*Technique:* Wheelmade. *Paste:* 5YR "reddish yellow" 7/6; many very small wadi gravel, few organic, and very small and small ceramic and crystal; grey core; hard. *Surface (Interior):* 10YR "red" 4/6 slip. *(Exterior):* slip as interior.
18.	Jar	G70, VI.NE6.69, No. 6 L. 6008	*Technique:* Wheelmade. *Paste:* 2.5YR "light red" 6/6; some very small wadi gravel, few very small to large lime and very small crystal; no core; hard. *Surface (Interior):* as paste. *(Exterior):* 7.5YR "pinkish white" 8/2.
19.	Base	G69, VI.NE6.35, No. 1 L. 6008	*Technique:* Wheelmade. *Paste:* inner: 7.5YR "pinkish grey" 7/2; outer: 7.5YR "pink" 7/4; very many very small and few small wadi gravel, few very small small to large lime; no core; hard. *Surface (Interior):* as inner paste. *(Exterior):* as outer paste.
20.	Bowl	G69, VI.NE26.68, No. 26 L. 26015	*Technique:* Wheelmade. *Paste:* 5YR "reddishyellow" 7/6; many very small wadi gravel, few large organic and iron, very small to medium lime, small ceramic and very small crystal; grey core; hard. *Surface (Interior):* 7.5YR "light brown" 6/4; 2.5YR "red" 4/6 slip on rim. *(Exterior):* as paste; slip on rim as interior.
21.	Chalice with strainer	G69, VI.NE26.68, No. 15 L. 26015	*Technique:* Wheelmade. *Paste:* 5YR "reddish dark yellow" 7/6; many very small and few small wadi gravel, few very small and medium lime and very small crystal; no core; hard. *Surface (Interior):* as paste; 10YR "red" 4/6 slip on rim. *(Exterior):* as paste to 7.5YR "pink" 8/4.
22.	Krater	G70, VI.NE18.40, Nos. 1–7 L. 18038P	*Technique:* Wheelmade. *Paste:* 5YR "pink" 7/4; many small wadi gravel, mostly quartz; no core; hard. *Surface (Interior):* as paste; 10YR "red" slip on rim. *(Exterior):* as paste.

PLATE 46

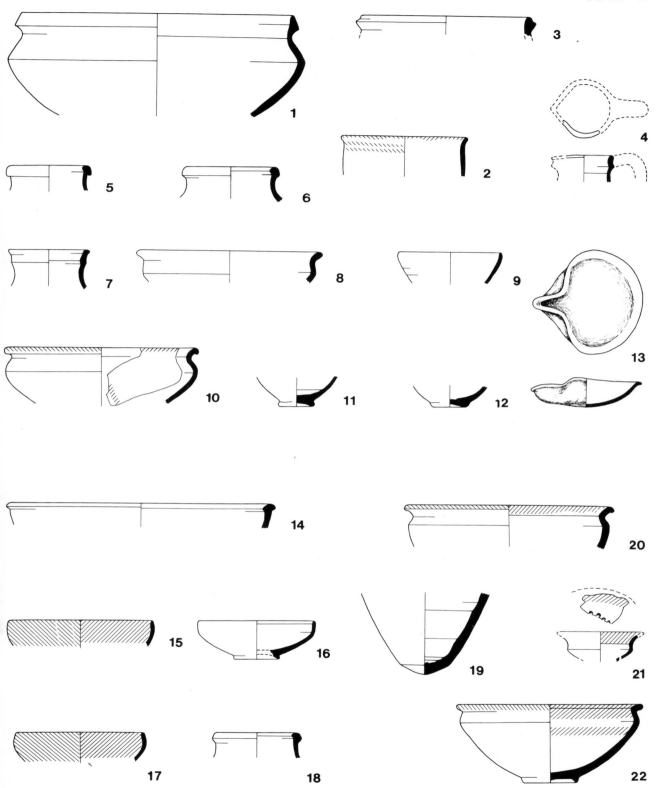

Plate Number	Pottery Type	Number and locus (see LOCUS INDEX)	Description (p. 277)
1.	Jar base	G69, VI.NE17.106, L. 17032	*Technique:* Wheelmade. *Paste:* 5YR "pink" 7/3; some small crystal; light grey core; hard. *Surface (Interior):* as paste. *(Exterior):* pattern (5YR "reddish brown" 5/4); 10YR "dark reddish grey" 3/7.
2.	Jug	G70, VI.NE17.106 L. 17032	*Technique:* Wheelmade. *Paste:* 5YR "pink" 7/4–8/4; some to many small crystal, few small lime; no core; hard. *Surface (Interior):* as paste. *(Exterior):* as paste.
3.	Krater	G69, VI.NE17.150, 198, 141, Nos.,2–5 L. 17050	*Technique:* Wheelmade. *Paste:* 5YR "pink" 7/4; many small wadi gravel, mostly quarz; no core; hard. *Surface (Interior):* as paste. *(Exterior):* 2.5YR "red" 5/6 slip; lines (5YR "pink" 8/3); (2.5YR "dusky red" 3/2).
4.	Bowl	G69, VI.NE17.89, 93, Nos.2–8, L. 17032	*Technique:* Wheelmade. *Paste:* 2.5YR "red" 5/8; many small to medium quartz; light brown core; hard. *Surface (Interior):* as paste. *(Exterior):* as paste.
5.	Cooking pot	G69, VI.NE17.150, No. 1 L. 17050	*Technique:* Wheelmade. *Paste:* 5YR "reddish yellow" 6/6; some small to medium wadi gravel and medium lime, few small organic and very small crystal; dark grey core; hard. *Surface (Interior):* as paste. *(Exterior):* as paste.
6.	Bowl	G69, VI.NE17.89, No. 5 L. 17032	*Technique:* Wheelmade. *Paste:* 7.5YR "reddish yellow" 7/4; many small to medium lime, some small organic, few medium wadi gravel; no core; hard. *Surface (Interior):* 2.5YR "red" 5/6 slip. *(Exterior):* 5YR "light reddish brown" 6/6 slip with patches of slip near rim as interior.
7.	Cooking pot	G69, VI.NE17.89, No. 8 L. 17032	*Technique:* Wheelmade. *Paste:* 7.5YR "brown" 5/4; some very small to medium crystal, few medium lime and organic, and very small wadi gravel; no core; hard. *Surface (Interior):* as paste. *(Exterior):* as paste

PLATE 47

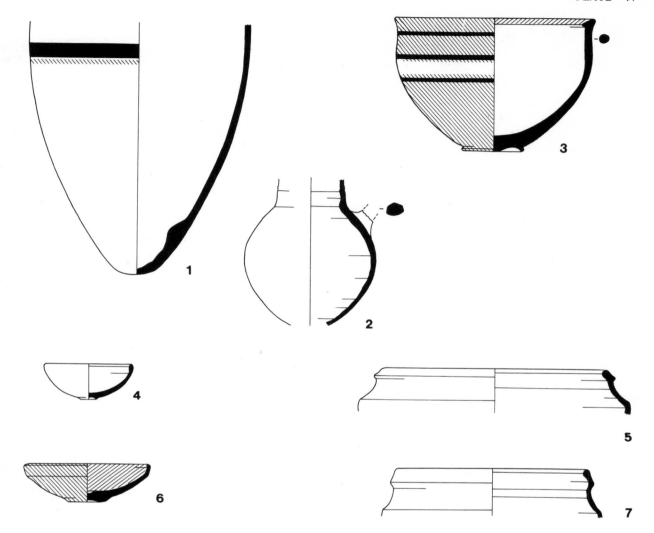

Plate Number	Pottery Type	Number and locus (see LOCUS INDEX)	Description (p. 277)
1.	Jar	G69, VI.NW16.40, No. 4 L. 16007	*Technique:* Wheelmade. *Paste:* 5YR "reddish yellow" 7/6; some very small wadi gravel, few very small and small organic, small iron and lime and very small crystal; no core; hard. *Surface (Interior):* as paste. *(Exterior):* as paste.
2.	Jar	G69, VI.NW16.40, No. 5 L. 16007	*Technique:* Wheelmade. *Paste:* 5YR "light reddish brown" 6/4; very many very small and few small lime, few very small to medium ceramic; grey core; hare. *Surface (Interior):* as paste. *(Exterior):* as paste.
3.	Jar	G69, VI.NW16.45, No. 9 L. 16007	*Technique:* Wheelmade. *Paste:* 2.5YR "light red" 6/6; many very small lime, few large ceramic and very small crystal; no core; hard. *Surface (Interior):* as paste. *(Exterior):* 10YR "white' 8/2.
4.	Jar	G69, VI.NW16.40, No. 7 L. 16007	*Technique:* Wheelmade. *Paste:* 7.5YR "light brown" 6/4; some very small and few small wadi gravel, few very small and small lime and crystal and small iron; no core; hard. *Surface* as paste and exterior. *(Exterior):* 7.5YR "pinkish white" 8/2.
5.	Jug	G69, VI.NW16.45, No. 18 L. 16007	*Technique:* Wheelmade. *Paste:* 5YR "grey" 5/1; some very small wadi gravel, few small lime and very small crystal and organic; core; 7.5YR "light brown" 6/4; hard. *Surface (Interior):* as paste to 7.5YR "pinkish grey" 6/2. *(Exterior):* 7.5YR "pinkish white" 8/2 to 7.5YR "dark brown" 4/2.
6.	Base	G69, VI.NW15.45, No. 5 L. 16007	*Technique:* Wheelmade. *Paste:* 5YR "pink" 8/4; some vry small sand, few small ceramic and very small wadi gravel and crystal; core: 7.5YR "pink" 8/4; hard. *Surface (Interior):* 2.5YR "reddish brown" 4/4 slip. *(Exterior):* as paste and core.
7.	Krater	G69, VI.NW16.45, No. 15 L. 16007	*Technique:* Wheelmade. *Paste:* 5YR "light reddish brown" 6/4; some very small and few small wadi gravel, few very small and small lime, and ceramic; core: 5YR "pink" 7/4; hard. *Surface (Interior):* as core. *(Exterior):* 7.5YR "pinkish white" 8/2.
8.	Fish plate	G69, VI.NW16.40, No. 9 L. 16007	*Technique:* Wheelmade. *Paste:* 7.5YR "pink" 8/4; many very small sand, few very small and medium wadi gravel and few medium lime. *Surface (Interior):* 2.5YR "red" 4/6 and 2/5YR "black" N2.5/0 slip, mottled. *(Exterior):* as paste; slip as interior.
9.	Fish plate	G69, VI.NW16.40, No. 1 L. 16007	*Technique:* Wheelmade. *Paste:* 2.5YR "red" 5/8; some very small and few small crystal, few very small and small lime and very small wadi gravel, well-levigated; grey core; metallic. *Surface (Interior):* 10YR "red" 4/6 slip. *(Exterior):* as interior.
10.	Bowl	G69, VI.NW16.45, No. 17 L. 16007	*Technique:* Wheelmade. *Paste:* 2.5YR "red" 5/6; many very small and few very small wadi gravel, few very small to medium lime, small ceramic and very small crystal; no core; hard. *Surface (Interior):* as paste. *(Exterior):* as paste to 10YR "white" 8/1.
11.	Juglet	G69, VI.NW16.40, No. 3 L. 16007	*Technique:* Wheelmade. *Paste:* 7.5YR "brown" 5/4; many very small crystal, few very small to large lime; no core; hard. *Surface (Interior):* 2.5YR "light red" 6/6; *(Exterior):* 7.5YR "pinkish white" 8/2.
12.	Jar	G70, VI.NW16.87, No. 8 L. 16015	*Technique:* Wheelmade. *Paste:* inner: 7.5YR "pinkish grey" 6/2; outer: 7.5YR "brown" 5/2; many very small and few small to medium lime, few small organic and very small and small ceramic; grey core; hard. *Surface (Interior):* as inner paste. *(Exterior):* 7.5YR "pink" 7/4.
13.	Jar	G70, VI.NW16.87, No. 11 L. 16015	*Technique:* Wheelmade. *Paste:* 10YR "very pale brown" 7/3; some very small wadi gravel, few large organic and very small crystal; no core; hard. *Surface (Interior):* as paste. *(Exterior):* as paste.
14.	Jar	G70, VI.NW16.87, No. 17 L. 16015	*Technique:* Wheelmade. *Paste:* 2.5YR "light red" 6/8; some very small and few small lime, few very small crystal and organic; core: 2.5YR "reddish brown" 4/4; hard. *Surface (Interior):* 7.5YR "pinkish grey" 6/2 to 10YR "light grey" 7/2. *(Exterior):* as interior.
15.	Jar	G70, VI.NW16.87, No. 13 l. 16015	*Technique:* Wheelmade. *Paste:* inner: 7.5YR "pink" 7/4; outer: 2.5YR "light red" 6/6; some small crystal, few medium lime, small ceramic and organic and very small wadi gravel; no core; hard. *Surface (Interior):* as inner paste. *(Exterior):* as outer paste to 5YR "white" 8/1.
16.	Jug	G70, VI.NW16.87, No. 15 L. 16015	*Technique:* Wheelmade. *Paste:* 7.5YR "pink" 7/4; many very small wadi gravel, few medium lime, small organic and very small crystal; no core; hard. *Surface (Interior):* 7.5YR "pikish white" 8/2. *(Exterior):* as interior.
17.	Jar	G70, VI.NW16.87, No. 7 L. 16015	*Technique:* Wheelmade. *Paste:* 7.6YR "pink" 8/4; some very small wadi gravel, few small iron and very small crystal; no core; hard. *Surface (Interior):* as paste. *(Exterior):* as paste.
18.	Krater	G70, VI.NW16.87, No. 6 L. 16015	*Technique:* Wheelmade. *Paste:* 7.5YR "pink" 7/4; some very small wadi gravel, few very small and small lime; no core; hard. *Surface (Interior):* as paste. *(Exterior):* as paste.
19.	Mortarium	G70, VI.NW16.87, No. 10 L. 16015	*Technique:* Wheelmade. *Paste:* 5YR "reddish yellow" 6/6; some very small crystal, few small lime, very small and medium wadi gravel; core: 10YR "pale brown" 6/3; hard. *Surface (Interior):* as paste; wet-smoothed. *(Exterior):* as paste; wet-smoothed; incised line.
20.	Bowl	G70, VI.NW16.87, No. 22 L. 16015	*Technique:* Wheelmade. *Paste:* 2.5YR "light red" 6/6; few very small lime and crystal; well-levigated; no core; hard. *Surface (Interior):* 2.5YR "red" 4/6 glaze. *(Exterior):* glaze as interior.
21.	Cooking pot	G70, VI.NW16.87, No. 1 L. 16015	*Technique:* Wheelmade. *Paste:* 2.5YR "red" 5/6; some very small crystal, few small lime and very small wadi gravel; core: 5YR "reddish brown" 5/3 hard. *Surface (Interior):* as paste. *(Exterior):* as paste; two incised lines on neck.
22.	Krater	G70, VI.NW16.87, No. 5 L. 16015	*Technique:* Wheelmade. *Paste:* 5YR "pink" 7/4; few very small and small wadi gravel and lime and very small ceramic and crystal; light grey core; hard. *Surface (Interior):* as paste. *(Exterior):* 10YR "white" 8/2; bands of 2.5YR "reddish brown" 4/4 slip on rim and body.
23.	Bowl	G70, VI.NE16.87, No. 3 L. 16015	*Technique:* Wheelmade. *Paste:* 7.5YR "pink" 7/4; many very small and few small wadi gravel, few small and medium lime, small ceramic and very small crystal; no core; hard. *Surface (Interior):* 10YR "dark reddish grey" 3/1 slip. *(Exterior):* slip as interior to 10YR "red" 4/6; mottled.
24.	Bowl	G70, VI.NW16.87, No. 16 L. 16015	*Technique:* Wheelmade. *Paste:* 2.5YR "red" 5/6; some small and few medium and large lime, few very small wadi gravel and crystal; core: 7.5YR "brown" 5/4; hard. *Surface (Interior):* 10YR "red" 4/6 slip. *(Exterior):* as paste; slip as interior.
25.	Bowl	G70, VI.NW16.87, No. 23 L. 16015	*Technique:* Wheelmade. *Paste:* 2.5YR "red" 5/6; few very small and small lime and very small crystal, well-levigated; no core; metallic. *Surface (Interior):* 10YR "red" 5/8 slip. *(Exterior):* band of sloppily applied 10YR "white" 8/2 organic paint; slip as interior.
26.	Fish plate	G70, VI.NW16.87, No. 21 L. 16015	*Technique:* Wheelmade. *Paste:* 7.5YR "pink" 8/4; few medium iron, some very small and few small lime, few very small wadi gravel and crystal; light grey core; hard. *Surface (Interior):* 5YR "reddish brown" 4/3, 2.5YR "red" 4/6 and 2.5YR "very dusky red" 2.5/2 slip; mottled. *(Exterior):* slip as interior.
27.	Cooking pot	G70, VI.NW16.87, No. 11a L. 16015	*Technique:* Wheelmade. *Paste:* inner: 2.5YR "weak red" 4/2; outer: 2.5YR "red" 4/6; some very small crystal, few large organic, small to medium lime and very small and small wadi gravel; core: as outer paste; hard. *Surface (Interior):* as outer paste. *(Exterior):* as outer paste.
28.	Juglet	G70, VI.NW16.87, No. 12 L. 16015	*Technique:* Wheelmade. *Paste:* 2.5YR "red" 5/6; many very small wadi gravel, few very small and small lime; grey paste; hard. *Surface (Interior):* 10YR "weak red" 4/4 slip on rim. *(Exterior):* slip as interior to 10YR "reddish black" 2.5/1.
29.	Juglet (Unguentarium)	G70, VI.NW16.87, No. 2	*Technique:* Wheelmade. *Paste:* 2.5YR "light red" 6/8; many very small and few small to large lime; no core; hard. *Surface (Interior):* as paste. *(Exterior):* 7.5YR "pink" 8/4.

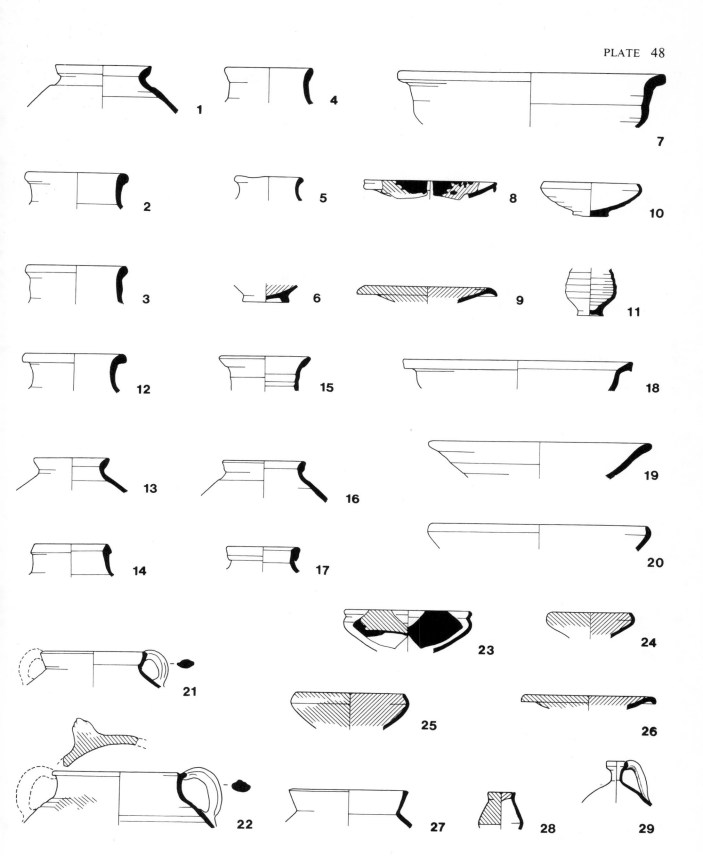

PLATE 48

Plate number	Object (Refs. in parenthesis)	Registry No., Basket, Locus (see LOCUS INDEX)	Str.	Description (p. 277); Israel Department of Antiquities number
1.	Basalt Loom Weight	No. 1384, VI.NE13.256, L. 13116.1	12?	Basalt; drilled through from both sides
2.	Toggle Pin	No. 1393, VI.NE14.370, L. 14146	12?	Copper/bronze
3.	Funnel (or *Tuyère?*)	No. 1394, VI.NE14.373, L. 14147	12?	Chalk; surface pared; holes drilled from both sides (DA 74–76)
4.	Eye fragment from zoomorphic vessel	No. 1383, VI.NE24.432, L. 24048	12	Ceramic; wheelmade; surface 10YR "brownish yellow" 6/6; finely burnished, punctate holes chalk-filled (Tell el-Yehudiyeh ware)
5.	Wire fragment	No. 1397, VI.NE24.452, L. 24148	12	Copper/bronze
6.	Earrings	No. 1381, VI.NE24.386, L. 24181	12	Silver
7	*Kernos* head	No. 1339, VI.NE24.384, L. 24183P	12	Ceramic; handmade; surface 5YR "light reddish yellow-brown" 6/5; metallic ware with few medium white inclusions
8.	Chariot Wheel	No. 1392, VI.NE24.420, L. 24187	12	Ceramic; wheelmade; surface 5YR "reddish-yellow" 7/6; soft fired ware with many sand grits; hub is string-cut
9.	Weight?	No. 1329, VI.NE14. L. 14132	11	Goethite nodule
10.	Bead	No. 1347, VI.NE14.349, L. 14132	11	Bone; surface highly polished, 10YR "very pale brown" 8/3; hole drilled from one side
11.	Bar fragments	No. 1314, VI.NE23.290, L. 23102	11	Copper/bronze
12.	Vessel	No. 1373, VI.NE23.315, L. 23111	11	Limestone
13.	Amulet or Celt	No. 1357, VI.NE23.315, L. 23111	11	Stone; green with traces of gold on both broad sides (DA 74–72)
14.	Stopper	No. 1082A, VI.NE33.158, L. 33067	12/11	Ceramic; top surface 2.5YR "light red" 6/7; few small to large white and buff inclusions; well fired; edges ground smooth
15.	Stopper	No. 1082B, VI.NE33.158, L. 33067	12/11	Ceramic; top surface 10YR "very pale brown" 7/3; some small to medium brown and black inclusions; well fired, edges unevenly ground

PLATE 49

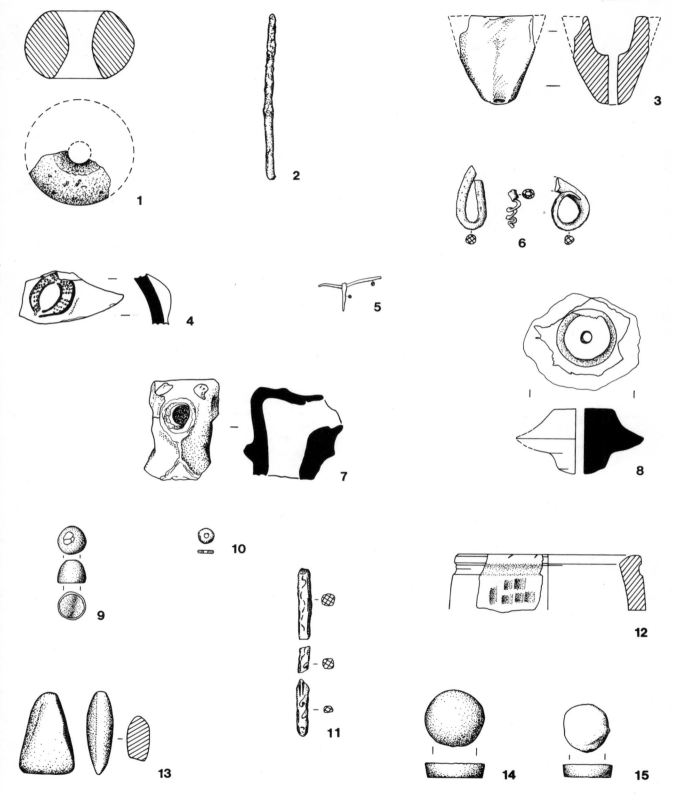

Pl. 50

Plate number	Object (Refs. in parenthesis)	Registry No., Basket, Locus (see LOCUS INDEX)	Str.	Description (p. 277); Israel Department of Antiquities number
1.	Loom weight	No. 1312, VI.NE14.324, L. 14122	10A	Ceramic;
2.	*Kernos* ring fragment	No. 1385, VI.NE14.356, L. 14142	11/10B	Ceramic; handmade; surface 10YR "very pale brown" 8/3; paste well levigated.
3.	Worked stone	No. 1375B, VI.NE23.331, L. 23122	10B	Specular haematite
4.	Spatula	No. 1299, VI.NE24.341, L. 24160	11–10	Copper/bronze
5.	Foil fragments	No. 1326, VI.NE36.343 L. 34103.1	11/10	Lead; folded over
6.	Needle	No. 900, VI.NE33.133, L. 33057.1	11/10	Copper/bronze
7.	Stamp impression	No. 1230, VI.NE23.226, L. 23075	10/9	Ceramic; surface 5YR "reddish yellow" 6/6; some medium to large, few medium white inclusions; well fired (DA 74–75)
8.	Projectile Point	No. 1260, VI.NE24.310, L. 23134	9	Copper/bronze
9.	*Tuyère*	No. 1257, VI.NE24.310, L. 24134	9	Steatite; surface polished, "very dark gray" 3/?; drill marks visible inside
10.	Pendant, inlay, gaming piece?	No. 1395, VI.NE23.144, L. 23058	8B–A	Lapis lazuli
11.	Beads	No. 1268, VI.NE24.301, L. 24144	9	Glass
12.	Beads	No. 1259, VI.NE24.301, L. 23144	9	Frit; "white" 8/
13.	Bead	No. 1348, VI.NE24.333 L. 23144	9	Glass
14.	Bead	No. 1182, VI.NE24.293, L. 24144	9	Frit; surface glazed, 10YR "red" 4/6; eyelet made separately
15.	Bead	No. 1263, VI.NE24.301, L. 24144	9	Glass
16.	Beads	No. 1220, VI.NE24.319, L. 24144	9	Pale blue faience (first and last in group) and frit, YR "white" 8/

PLATE 50

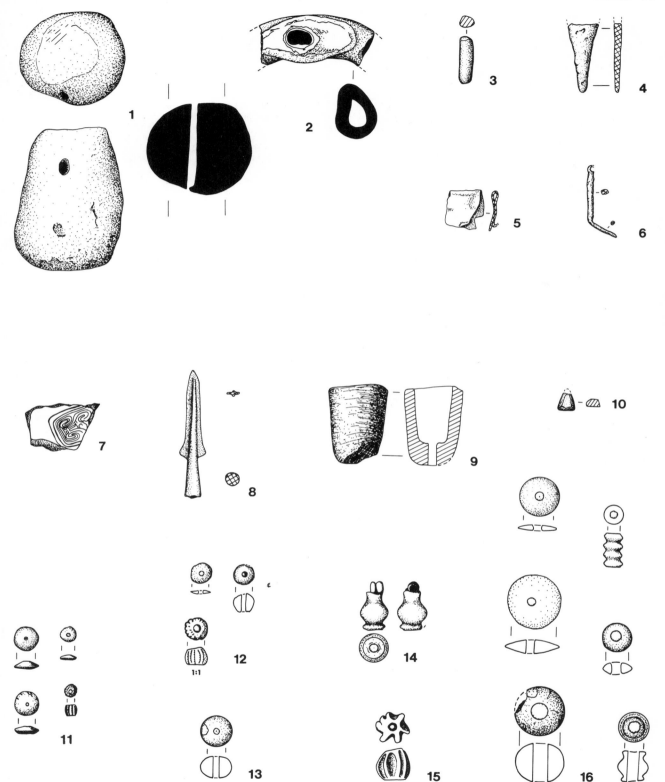

Pl. 51

Plate number	Object (Refs. in parenthesis)	Registry No., Basket, Locus (see LOCUS INDEX)	Str.	Description (p. 277); Israel Department of Antiquities number
1.	Crucible	No. 1371, VI.NE24.301, L. 24144	9	Ceramic; handmade; ware and surface 5YR "reddish yellow" 7/6; well fired, very light gray core; few medium to large white and buff inclusions; dark bluish-green oxidized copper slag adhering to inside, YR "gray" 5/
2.	Serpent	No. 1229, VI.NE24.301, L. 24144	9	Copper/bronze (DA 74–67)
3.	Bowl fragment	No. 1254, VI.NE24.301, L. 24144	9	Faience; paste YR "white" 8/; outer surface pale blue; inner surface 10YR "white 8/2
4.	Inlay fragment	No. 1190, VI.NE24.293, L. 24144	9	Bone; incised and drilled
5.	Zoomorphic figurine	No. 1211, VI.NE34.280, L. 34088	9A	Ceramic; handmade; surface 5YR "reddish yellow" 6/6; well fired, thick gray core; some black, red, and white medium inclusions, many sand inclusions
6.	Gaming piece	No. 1320, VI.NE24.328, L. 24150	9	Frit; YR "white" 8/
7.	Vessel fragment	No. 1217, VI.NE24.324, L. 24150	9	Faience; paste YR "white" 8/; surface glaze decoration N "very dark gray" 3/
8.	Earring	No. 1376, VI.NE24 (no locus, sieving)	9?	Silver; well preserved (DA 74–70)
9.	Bowl fragment	No. 1151, VI.NE24 (no locus, sieving)	9?	Faience; paste YR "white" 8/; surface pale blue; decorating YR "very dark gray" 3/
10.	Inlay fragment	No. 1218, VI.NE24.323, L. 24129	11–9	Bone; drilled
11.	Ring	No. 1308, VI.NE24.342, L. 24129	11–9	Silver
12.	Inlay fragment	No. 1226, VI.NE24.323, L. 24129	11–9	Bone; incised
13.	Dagger Pommel	No. 1228, VI.NE24.323, L. 24129	11–9	Limestone; unfinished

PLATE 51

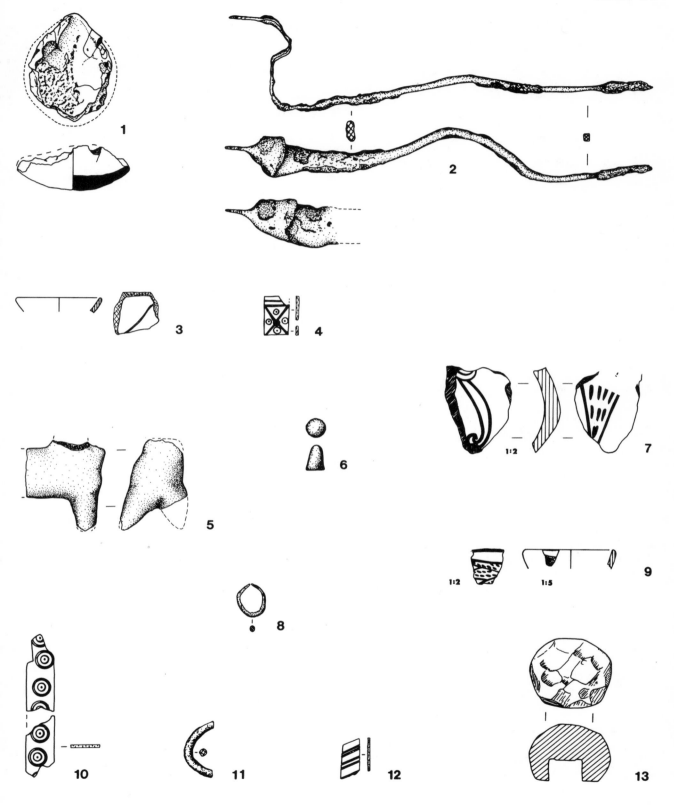

Pl. 52

Plate number	Object (Refs. in parenthesis)	Registry No., Basket, Locus (see LOCUS INDEX)	Str.	Description (p. 277); Israel Department of Antiquities number
1.	Stopper	No. 1216, VI.NE14.301, L. 14144	9/8	Ceramic; wheelmade, surface 7.5YR "light brown" 6/4; incised before firing (DA 74–73)
2.	Scaraboid	No. 1099, VI.NE23.172, L. 23056	9/9	Steatite; crudely incised; perhaps unfinished (DA 74–94)
3.	Cylinder	No. 995, VI.NE23.129, L. 23056	9/8	Chalk; YR "white" 8/; sides knife-pared
4.	Spike or awl	No. 1088, VI.NE23.168, L. 23056	9/8	Copper/bronze
5.	Chisel	No. 1123, VI.NE23.189, L. 23056	9/8	Copper/bronze
6.	Bead	No. 1164, VI.NE24.287, L. 24131	9/8	Ceramic; surface and paste 10YR "pale brown" 6/3
7.	Pike	No. 1142, VI.NE14.253, L. 14100P	8	Copper/bronze
8.	Arrow or lance head	No. 1102, VI.NE23.176, L. 23049	8	Copper/bronze
9.	Miniature Vessel	No. 1361, VI.NE24.330, L. 24132	8	Ceramic; handmade; surface 10YR "very pale brown" 7/3; many very small sand inclusions
10.	Needle fragments	No. 1276, VI.NE24.330, L. 24132	8	Copper/bronze
11.	Vessel fragments	No. 1366, VI.NE25.267, L. 25112	8/7	Alabaster
12.	Vessel fragment	No. 1364, VI.NE25.283, L. 25112	8/7	Alabaster
13.	Zoomorphic figurine	No. 1108, VI.NE3.140, L. 3059	7	Ceramic; handmade; surface 5YR "reddish yellow" 6/8; many medium black, few medium brown inclusions; thick light grey core; two sideparts broken off.
14.	Toggle pin	No. 1107, VI.NE4.230, L. 4069	7	Copper/bronze
15.	Bead	No. 1119, VI.NE4.226, L. 4069	7	Cobalt blue
16.	Inlay fragment	No. 1353, VI.NE5.251, L. 5090	7	Bone; sawn on three sides; perhaps a blank for incised inlay
17.	Spindle whorl	No. 1240, VI.NE5.166, L. 5093	7	Limestone; surface 5YR "white" 8/1; surfaces ground smooth; hole drilled from both sides (DA 74–82)
18.	Harpoon?	No. 1328, VI.NE5.240, L. 5093	7	Bone (DA 74–82)
19.	Spatula	No. 1273, VI.NE5.190, L. 5093	7	Copper/bronze

PLATE 52

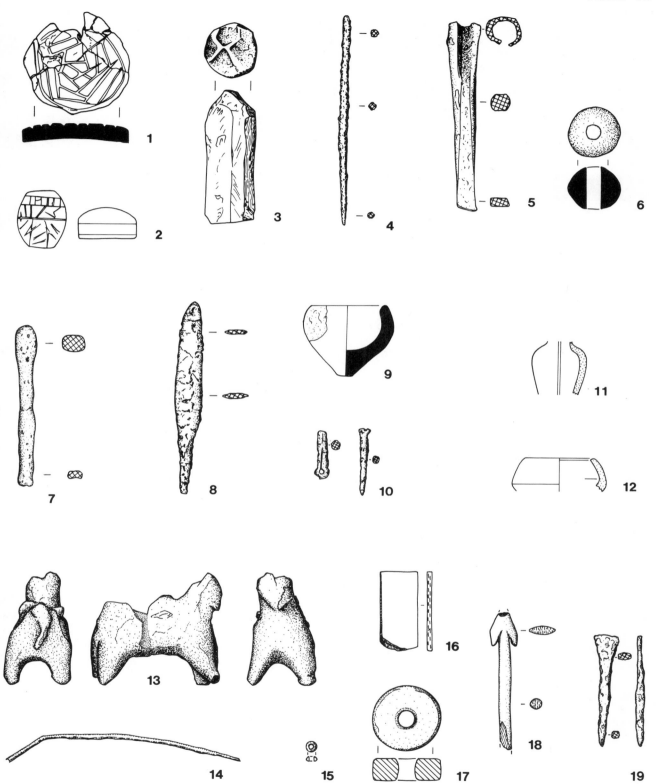

Pl. 53

Plate number	Object (Refs. in parenthesis)	Registry No., Basket, Locus (see LOCUS INDEX)	Str.	Description (p. 277); Israel Department of Antiquities number
1.	Needle	No. 1140, VI.NE14.255, L. 14083 D.A. 74–69	7	Copper/bronze
2.	Needle	No. 1246, VI.NE14.293, L. 14083	7	Copper/bronze
3.	Foil	No. 1174, VI.NE14.292, L. 14083	7	Crumpled gold foil (see also Nos. 1175, 1176, not illustrated)
4.	Incense Burner?	No. 1243, VI.NE14.289, L. 14083	7	Ceramic; handmade; surface 10YR "very pale brown" 7/3; same medium to large white and grey inclusions; surface cracked and burnt from heat
5.	Mortar	No. 1137, VI.NE14.232, L. 14090	7?	Basalt
6.	Vessel fragment	No. 1169, VI.NE23.198, L. 23074	7	Alabaster
7.	Scaraboid	No. 1236, VI.NE24.311, L. 24098	7	Carnelian; unfinished
8.	Gaming piece	No. 1258, VI.NE24.305, L. 24098	7	Chalk; YR "white" 8/ (DA 74–85)
9.	Tool blank	No. 1116, VI.NE24.257, L. 24098	7	Copper/bronze (DA 74–84)
10.	Amulet	No. 1237, VI.NE24.302 L. 24098	7	Faience; Bes figure; pale blue glaze; patina on back (DA 74–90)
11.	Bead	No. 1135, VI.NE24.268, L. 24098	7	Glass
12.	Vessel fragment	No. 1098, VI.NE24.253, L. 24098 D.A. 74–91	7	Glass (DA 74–91)
13.	Beads	No. 1171, VI.NE24.280, L. 24127	7	Frit and carnelian
14.	Ring	No. 1327, VI.NE24.311, L. 24098	7	Copper/bronze
15.	Kernos foot?	No. 1295, VI.NE24.308, L. 24135	7	Ceramic; entire surface fire-blackened; vertical burnish
16.	Inlay fragment	No. 1281, VI.NE25.253, L. 25097	7	Bone; incised
17.	Beads	No. 1252, VI.NE24.321, L. 24127	7	Frit and faience
18.	Button or pendant	No. 1167, VI.NE25.200, L. 25097	7	Bone; polished (DA 74–89)
19.	Vessel fragment	No. 1291, VI.NE25.247, L. 25097	7	Faience; paste and surface 5YR "white" 8/1; decoration 10YR "very dark grey" 3/1
20.	Weapon Mold	No. 892, VI.NE33.124, L. 33052	7	Chalk; YR "white" 8/; broad sides are shaved; inset molds on three sides; some traces of dark grey slag (mold for poker not illustrated; DA 74–65)

PLATE 53

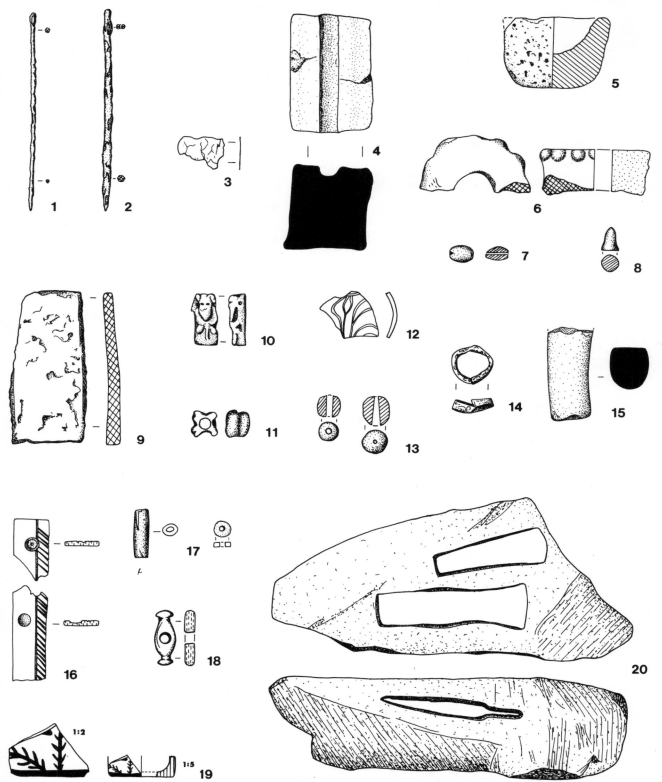

Pl. 54

Plate number	Object (Refs. in parenthesis)	Registry No., Basket, Locus (see LOCUS INDEX)	Str.	Description (p. 277); Israel Department of Antiquities number
1.	Stopper	No. 1094, VI.NE34.216, L. 34086	7	Ceramic; wheelmade; surface 5YR "reddish yellow" 6/6; few medium grey, black, brown inclusions; well fired; edges evenly ground
2.	Plaque	No. 1297, VI.NE34.314, L. 34086	10?	Ceramic; mold made; at Hathor figure; surface 7.5YR "light brown" 6/4; some small buff, brown, black inclusions; back smoothed
3.	Spindle whorl	No. 1067, VI.NE34.192, L. 34086	7	Ceramic; surface 10YR "very pale brown" 7/4; bottom roughly smoothed
4.	Plaque	No. 1262, VI.NE34.288, L. 34086	7	Ceramic; surface 10YR "very pale brown" 7/4; many fine red, grey, black inclusions, front hand-smoothed, indented
5.	Bead	No. 1084, VI.NE34.199, L. 34086	7	Faience; light blue; hole drilled from both ends.
6.	Fragment	No. 1180, VI.NE34.260, L. 34086	7	Iron; encrusted, surface 7.5YR "reddish yellow" 6/6
7.	Chariot wheel	No. 1287, VI.NE35.336, L. 35069	7	Ceramic; wheelmade; surface 5YR "light reddish yellow-brown" 5/7; few medium brown, grey, white inclusions; continuous burnish on surface
8.	Vessel fragment	No. 1368, VI.NE35.331, L. 35069	7	Alabaster (D.A. 74–81)
9.	Loomweight	No. 1369, VI.NE35.383, L. 35069	7	Ceramic; paste and surface 5YR "light reddish yellow-brown" 6/5; some large dark grey and small lime inclusions; hole drilled from both sides
10.	Bead	No. 1346, VI.NE26.331, L. 2600931	7/6C	Faience; paste 5YR "white 8/1; surface pale blue glaze
11.	Pendant	No. 1362, VI.NE26.339, L. 26099.1	7/6C	Stone
12.	Pin	No. 1013, VI.NE33.98 L. 33047	7/6C	Copper/bronze
13.	Bead	No. 988B, VI.NE34.158, L. 34058	7/6C	Frit
14.	Arrowhead	No. 1177, VI.NE35.333, L. 35060	7/6C	Copper/bronze
15.	Pin	No. 959, VI.NE34.158, L. 34058	7/6C	Copper/bronze
16.	Bowl Base	No. 1045, VI.NE34.159, L. 34058	7/6C	Ceramic; wheelmade; surface 10YR "very pale brown" 7/3; few medium buff and grey inclusions; thick grey core; well fired; pierced in center for reuse

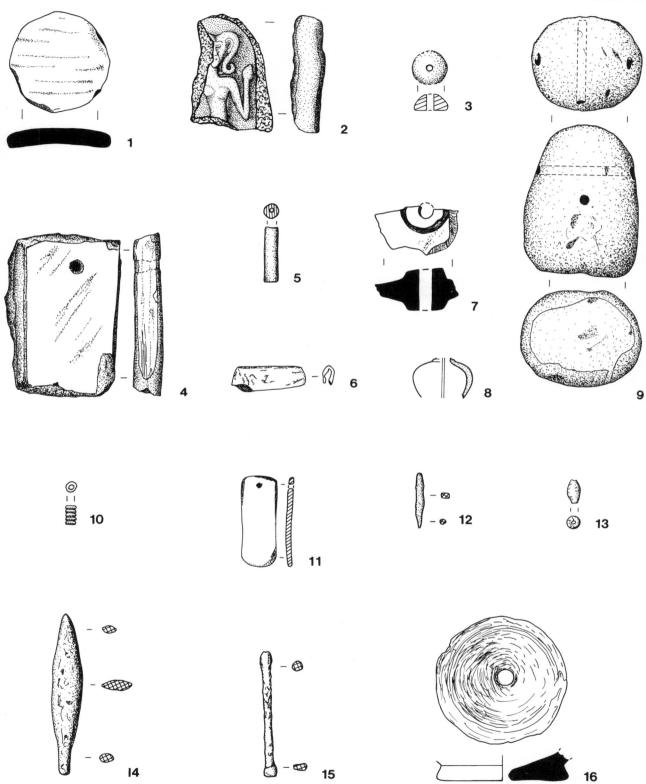

PLATE 54

Pl. 55

Plate number	Object (Refs. in parenthesis)	Registry No., Basket, Locus (see LOCUS INDEX)	Str.	Description (p. 277); Israel Department of Antiquities number
1.	Vessel fragment	No. 894, VI.NE4.157, L. 4057	6C	Alabaster
2.	Zoomorphic figurine	No. 1192, VI.NE6.188, L. 6102	6C	Ceramic; handmade; surface 10YR "white" 8/2; few medium brown and black inclusions; thick grey core; well fired
3.	Button	No. 905, VI.NE14.169, L. 14057	6C	Bone; polished
4.	Plaque	No. 1359, VI.NE26 (no pottery basket–6C Wall)	6C	Ceramic; modmade; "Astarte" figure; paste and surface 5YR "reddish yellow" 7/6; few medium white and grey inclusions; well fired; back knife-shaved and smoothed; surface 10YR "dark red" 3/6; polished
5.	Spindle whorl	No. 943, VI.NE34.137,	6C	Steatite; surface 10YR "dark red" 3/6; polished
6.	Bead	No. 898, VI.NE34.144, L. 34053.1	6C	Frit
7.	Pin	No. 1138, VI.NE5.169, L. 5068	6C–B	Copper/bronze; bent in middle
8.	Arrowhead	No. 1256, VI.NE5.169, L. 5068	6C–B	Copper/bronze
9.	Bead	No. 1242, VI.NE5.169, L. 5068	6C–B	Agate; highly polished brown and white surfaces; hole drilled from one end
10.	Antler	No. 1172, VI.NE6.185, L. 6096	6C–B	Worked, squared at tip
11.	Chisel	No. 976, VI.NE14.195, (no locus, Rm. 3 fill)	6C/B	Copper/bronze
12.	Kernos head	No. 1241, VI.NE16.212, L. 16082	6C–B	Ceramic; handmade; surface 10YR "very pale brown" 7/4; very marshy sand inclusions; no core; haphazard burnishing
13.	Arrowhead	No. 1296, VI.NE16.288, L. 16110	6C–B	Copper/bronze
14.	Bowl fragment	No. 909, VI.NE23.94, (no locus, Room 5, occupation fill between surfaces)	6C/B	Faience; paste 10YR "white" 7/1; pale blue surface glaze; decoration 10YR "very dark grey" 3/1
15.	Stamp seal impression	No. 1059A, VI.NE23.102, L. 23036	6C/B	Ceramic; paste and surface 10YR "very dark grey" 3/1; few medium clack and brown inclusions; well fired. finer impressions on back (DA 74–96)
16.	Bar	No. 926, VI.NE23.101, L. 23036	6C/B	Copper/bronze

PLATE 55

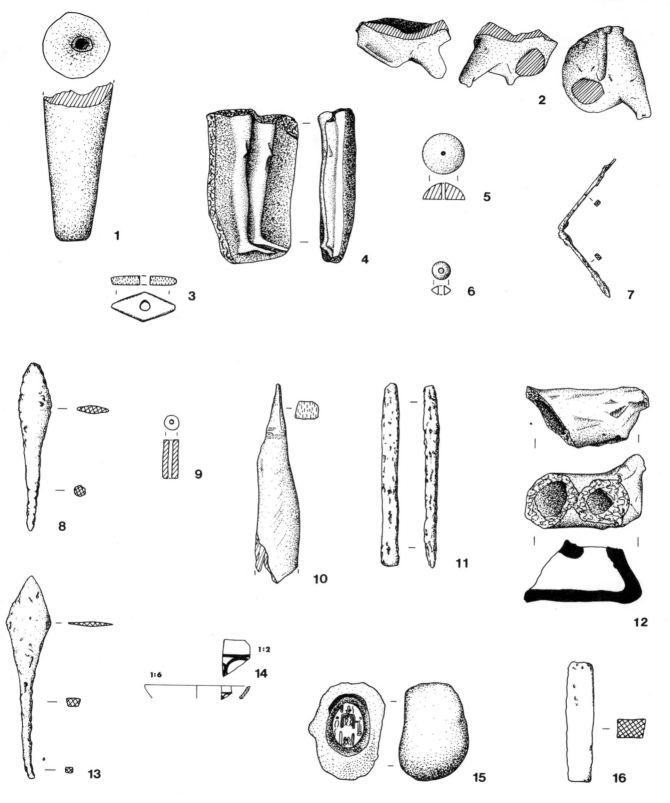

Pl. 56

Plate number	Object (Refs. in parenthesis)	Registry No., Basket, Locus (see LOCUS INDEX)	Str.	Description (p. 277); Israel Department of Antiquities number
1.	"Eye of Horus" fragment	No. 919, VI.NE23.97, L. 23036	6C/B	Faience; pale blue glaze
2.	Bracelet	No. 1097, VI.NE24.255, L. 24087	6C–B	Copper/bronze
3.	Inlay fragment	No. 1372, VI.NE25.212, L. 25084.1	6C/B	Bone; incised
4.	Spindle whorl	No. 884, VI.NE34.125, L. 34063A	6C–B	Bone; polished
5.	Bowl fragments	No. 1021, VI.NE33.84, L. 33042	6C/B	Copper/bronze
6.	Scaraboid seal	No. 936, VI.NE34.115, L. 34063A	6C–B	Frit; paste 2.5YR "yellow" 8/4; pale blue glaze; mold-made
7.	Arrowhead	No. 878, VI.NE14.113, L. 14055	6C/B	Copper/bronze
8.	Zoomorphic figurine	No. 921, VI.NE3.113, L. 3038	6B	Ceramic; wheelmade; surface 10YR "very pale brown" 8/3; many very small white inclusions; metallic firing; horizontal parallel burnishing
9.	Bowl fragment	No. 547, VI.NE4.88, L. 4017	6B	Basalt; broken, but perhaps a pedestal bowl
10.	Awl	No. 407, VI.NE4.53A, L. 4017	6B	Bone
11.	Arrowhead	No. 462, VI.NE4.86B, L. 4025P	6B	Copper/bronze
12.	Zoomorphic figurine head	No. 1212, VI.NE5.153B, L. 5057.1	6B	Ceramic; handmade; surface 2.5YR "light red" 6/7; some very small brown and grey inclusions; well fired, no core
13.	Bowl fragment	No. 1039, VI.NE14.152, L. 14011B (built into a wall)	6B	Basalt
14.	Bowl	No. 814, VI.NE14.115, L. 14035.1	6B	Alabaster
15.	Bead	No. 748, VI.NE24.145, L. 24068	6B	Faience, pale blue
16.	Fragment	No. 933, VI.NE34.106, L. 34022.1	6B	Alabaster; inscribed
17.	Mortar	No. 990, VI.NE33.79, L. 33040	6B	Basalt
18.	Projectile point	No. 840, VI.NE33.82, L. 33041	6B	Copper/bronze

PLATE 56

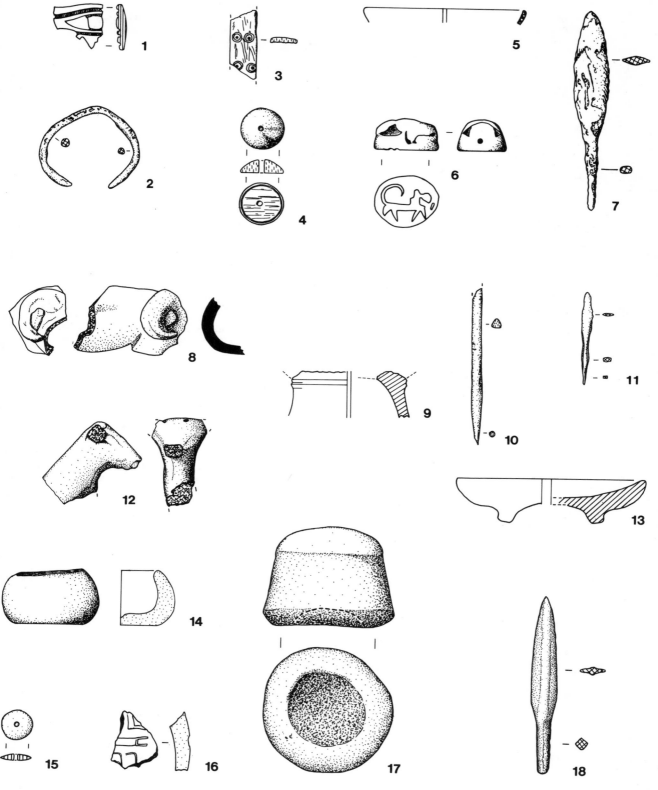

Pl. 57

Plate number	Object (Refs. in parenthesis)	Registry No., Basket, Locus (see LOCUS INDEX)	Str.	Description (p. 277); Israel Department of Antiquities number
1.	Awl	No. 798, VI.NE3.77, L. 3020	6B/A	Bone
2.	Bead	No. 790, VI.NE3.71,	6B/A	Glass
3.	Bead	No. 941, VI.NE4.100, L. 4035.1	6B/A	Carnelian
4.	Saddle quern	No. 1053, VI.NE13.190, L. 13038.1	6B.A	Basalt
5.	Loomweight	No. 1219, VI.NE16.235, L. 16088	6B/A	Terra cotta; pierced
6.	Ring	No. 928, VI.NE29.79, L. 23027	6B/A	Copper/bronze
7.	Pedestal bowl	No. 961, VI.NE23.83, L. 23027	6B/A	Vesicular basalt; reused as a rubbing stone
8.	Nail	o. 977, VI.NE24.104,	6B/A	Copper/bronze
9.	Spindle whorl	No. 574, VI.NE24.122, L. 24059	6B/A	Bone
10.	Blade fragments	No. 568, VI.NE24.121, L. 24059	6B/A	Copper/bronze
11.	Bead	No. 823, VI.NE34.85, L. 34032	6B/A	Frit; surface YR "gray" 5/; incised on surface; drilled from both sides
12.	Gaming piece?	No. 850, VI.NE34.94, L. 34032	6B/A	Ceramic; handmade; surface 7.5YR "light brown" 6/4; some small sand inclusions; hole partially drilled in top
13.	Chalice	No. 904, VI.NE35.196, L. 35057	6B/A	Alabaster; lathe-turned; top part of two-piece pedestal chalice
14.	Jug spout	No. 731, VI.NE3., L. 3004.1	6A	Ceramic; handmade; surface 10YR "white" 8/2; many very small sand inclusions; well fired; hole drilled before firing
15.	Bowl	No. 507, VI.NE13.68, L. 13030	6A	Basalt
16.	Sickle blade	No. 760, VI.NE13.124, L. 13037A–B	6A	Flint
17.	Toggle pin	No. 587, VI.NE13.151, L 13038P	6A	Ivory; pierced at top
18.	Kernos ring fragment	No. 464, VI.NE14.67, L. 14015	6A	Ceramic; handmade; surface 10YR "very pale brown" 8/3; paint 5YR "dark grey" 4/1; some very small to small brown and black inclusions; well fired; seam visible at top (DA 74–118)
19.	Blade or point	No. 551, VI.NE14.54, L. 14015	6A	Copper/bronze
20.	Button	No. 523, VI.NE23.18, L. 23010	6A	Ceramic; two holes, drilled from both sides; surface 5YR "pink" 7/4; some medium gray and white inclusions; well fired (DA 74–87)
21.	Bowl	No. 514, VI.NE23.21, L. 23012	6A	Basalt

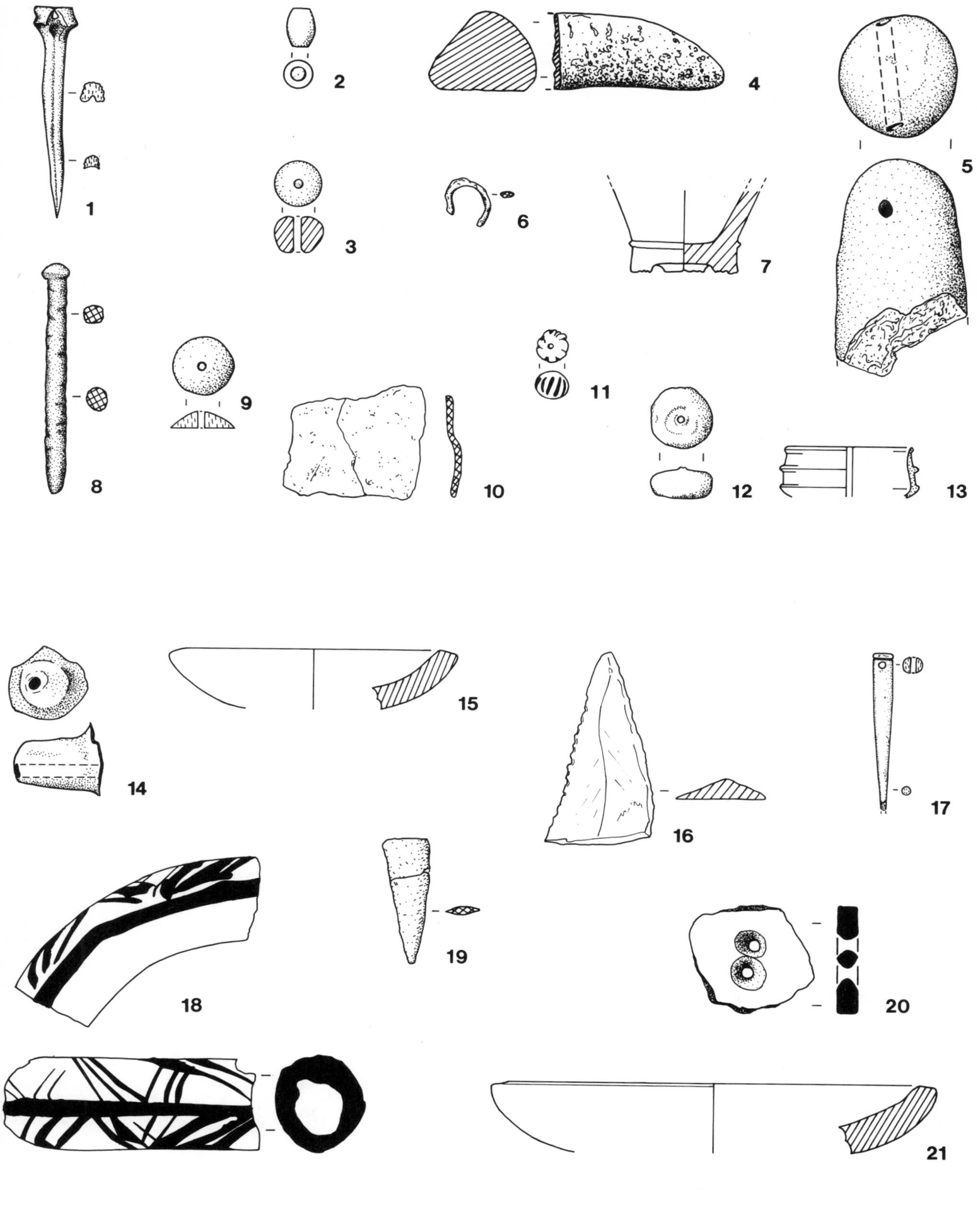
1
2
3
4
5
6
7
8
9
10
11
12
13
14
15
16
17
18
19
20
21

Pl. 58

Plate number	Object (Refs. in parenthesis)	Registry No., Basket, Locus (see LOCUS INDEX)	Str.	Description (p. 277); Israel Department of Antiquities number
1.	Spindle whorl	No. 1024, VI.NE23.86, L. 23014P	6A	Chalk
2.	Bangle	No. 522, VI.NE24.89, L. 24042	6A	Copper/bronze
3.	Zoomorphic figurine head	No. 455, VI.NE24.55, L. 24022	6A	Ceramic; handmade; surface 7.5YR "greyish pibnk" 7/4; few small brown, grey, and sand inclusions; well fired; large grey core
4.	Tripod bowl	No. 1059, VI.NE24.140, L. 24049P	6A	Granite monzonite
5.	Spindle whorl	No. 626D, VI.NE24.133, L. 24049P	6A	Ceramic; wheelmade; surface 10YR "very pale brown" 8/3; and white inclusions; well fired; drilled from both sides
6.	Horn fragment	No. 626H, VI.NE24.135, L. 24040P	6A	Sculptured, bored
7.	Bowl	No. 589, VI.NE24.140, L. 24049P	6A	Faience; paste YR "white 8/; thick pale blue glaze; decoration 2.5YR "black" N (DA 74–99)
8.	Plaque	No. 907, VI.NE25.100, L. 25047	6A	Ceramic; mold-made; Hathor figure; surface 7.5YR "greyish pink" 7/3; thick grey core; back hand-smoothed
9.	Javelin	No. 948, VI.NE25.92, L. 25044	6A	Copper/bronze
10.	Pin	No. 957, VI.NE25.105, L. 25044	6A	Copper/bronze; bent
11.	Arrowhead	No. 1193, VI.NE26.242, L. 26077	6A	Copper/bronze
12.	Arrowhead	No. 1189, VI.NE26 L. 26077	6A	Copper/bronze
13.	Bead	No. 1194, VI.NE26.235, L. 26077	6A	Frit
14.	Spindle whorl	No. 588, VI.NE34.41, L. 34007	6A	Steatite; polished
15.	Pin	No. 578, VI.NE34.39 L. 34007	6A	Copper/bronze
16.	Zoomorphic figurine	No. 576, VI.NE34.35, L. 34007	6A	Ceramic; handmade; surface 10YR "very pale brown" 7/3

PLATE 58

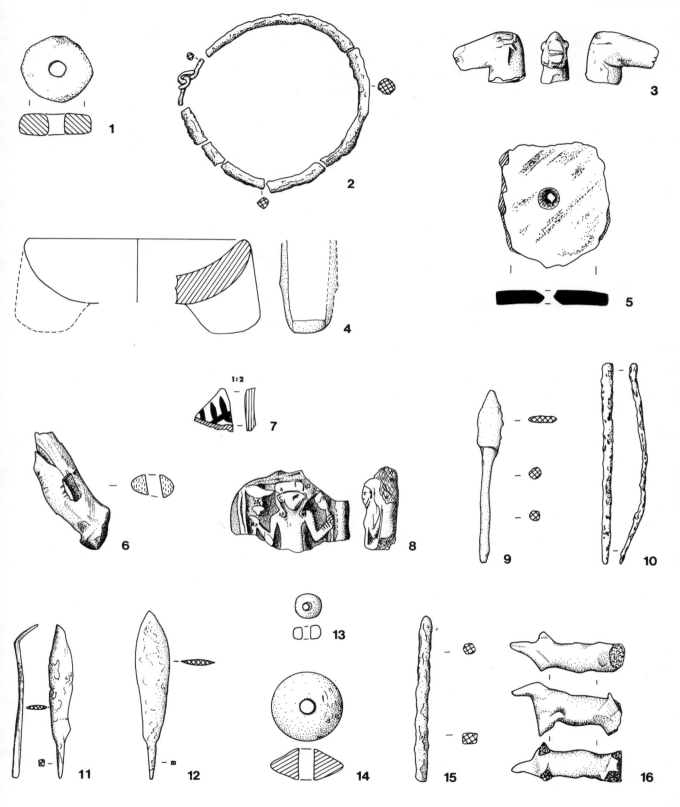

Pl. 59

Plate number	Object (Refs. in parenthesis)	Registry No., Basket, Locus (see LOCUS INDEX)	Str.	Description (p. 277); Israel Department of Antiquities number
1.	Rubbing stone	No. 782, VI.NE34.76, L. 34016	6A	Quartzolite
2.	Pommel or chariot fitting	No. 797, VI.NE34.63, L. 34024	6A	Alabaster; drilled
3.	Cylinder seal	No. 925, VI.NE35.153, L. 35035	6A	Faience
4.	Figurine	No. 1356, VI.NE13 L. 13040	6?	Chalk; crudely smoothed, perhaps unfinished (DA 74–101)
5.	Tuyère (?)	No. 1160, VI.NE23.201, L. 23054B	10–6	Ceramic; handmade; surface 5YR "reddish yellow" 6/4; few small black and organic inclusions; thick dark grey core; continuous burnish
6.	Lance point or goad	No. 1215, VI.NE23.251, L. 23054B	10–6	Copper/bronze
7.	Gaming piece	No. 960, VI.NE3.107, L. 3042	post-6	Frit; surface 10YR "white" 8/2
8.	Beads	No. 828, VI.NE3.69, L. 3054	post-6A?	Frit
9.	Spindle whorl	No. 1115A, VI.NE5.127, L. 5072S	6A/5C	Bone; polished
10.	Bead	No. 1197, VI.NE5.148, L. 5052	6A/5C	Faience; cobalt blue surface glaze
11.	Bowl fragment	No. 1106, VI.NE5.125, L. 5072S D.A. 74–98	6A/5C	Faience; paste 5YR "white 8/1; surface thick pale blue glaze; decoration 5YR "very dark grey" 3/1
12.	Spindle whorl	No. 1121, VI.NE26.200, L. 26061.1	6A/5C	Ceramic; wheelmade; surface 7.5YR "pink" 8/4; some medium to large red and white inclusions; thick grey core; edges roughly shaped
13.	Spindle whorl	No. 1114, VI.NE26.188, L. 26061.1	6A/5C	Bone; polished
14.	Bead	No. 467, VI.NE14.75, L. 14017	6A/5	Varicolored glass
15.	Tool?	No. 820, VI.NW5.119, L. 5077	5C	Bone; worked
16.	Pedestal bowl fragment	No. 871, VI.NW5.162, L. 5077	5C	Basalt

PLATE 59

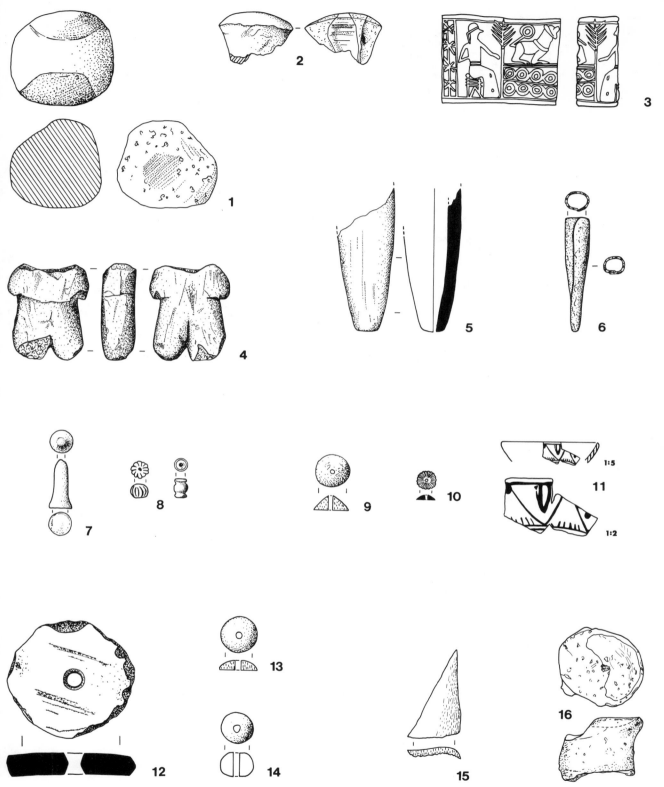

Pl. 60

Plate number	Object (Refs. in parenthesis)	Registry No., Basket, Locus (see LOCUS INDEX)	Str.	Description (p. 277); Israel Department of Antiquities number
1.	Chisel or spearbutt	No. 954, VI.NW5. 1. 50421	5C/B	Copper/bronze; exceptionally well preserved (DA 74–124)
2.	Blade	No. 955, VI.NW5. L. 5063	5C/B	Copper/bronze
3.	Armour scale (?)	No. 807, VI.NW5. L. 5063	5C/B	Copper/bronze
4.	Button/bead	No. 873, VI.NW15.138, L. 15039.1	5C/B	Faience; white paste, light greenish blue glaze; back uneven and rough
5.	Figurine	No. 1062, VI.NE6.159, L. 6041.1	5C/B	Chalk; crudely carved, perhaps unfinished (DA 74–88)
6.	Button	No. 1001, VI.NE26.149, L. 26050.1	5C/B	Ceramic; surface 10YR "very pale brown" 7/4; few medium red and black inclusions; well fired; edges roughly smoothed
7.	Bead	No. 896, VI.NE26.146, L. 26050.1	5C/B	Faience; blue glaze
8.	Cauldron handle	No. 951, VI.NW15.134, L. 15039.1	5C/B	Copper/bronze; exceptionally well preserved; both handles broken at rivet holes (DA 74–123)
9.	Arrowhead	No. 1055, VI.NE26.7, L. 26050	5B	Copper/bronze
10.	Vessel fragment	No. 443, VI.NW5.80, L. 5041.1	5B–4/B–3	Faience; paste 5YR "white" 8/1; glaze light blue; decoration YR "black" 2.5/
11.	Phallus (circumcised)	No. 459, VI.NW5.87, L. 4040.1	5B–4/B–3	Ceramic; handmade; surface 10YR "very pale brown" 8/3; some very small grey and brown inclusions; thick grey core; well fired (DA 74–106)
12.	Figurine or *Kernos* head	No. 537, VI.NE35.20, L. 35010	5B	Ceramic; handmade; surface 10YR "light grey" 7/2; paint 10YR "red" 5/6; few medium to large red, grey, white; well fired (DA 74–110)
13.	Pin	No. 1104, VI.NE36B.42, L. 36011.1	5C/A	Copper/bronze

PLATE 60

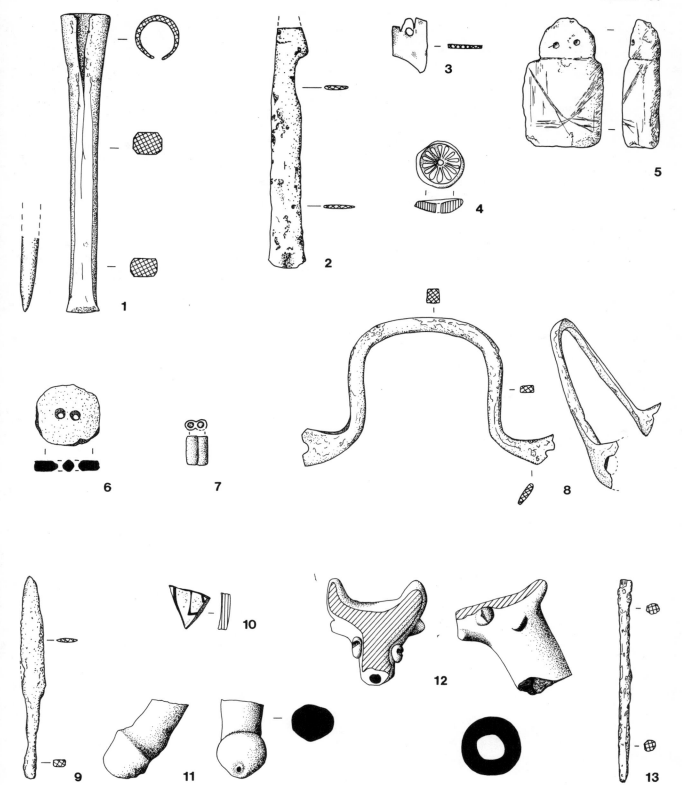

Pl. 61

Plate number	Object (Refs. in parenthesis)	Registry No., Basket, Locus (see LOCUS INDEX)	Str.	Description (p. 277); Israel Department of Antiquities number
1.	Chariot fitting	No 1081, VI.NE5.79, L. 5027	5B/A	Ivory, well polished (DA 74–74)
2.	Pommel or chariot fitting	No. 724, VI.NE5.79, L. 5027	5B/A	Alabaster
3.	Bowl	No. 811, VI.NE26.111, L. 26035.1	5B/A	Basalt
4.	Bead fragments	No. 789, VI.NW6.148, L. 6066	5B/A	Faience; blue glaze
5.	Bead	No. 831, VI.NE26.98, L. 26048	5B/A	Agate; translucent orange and white; hole drilled from one side
6.	Weight or gaming piece	No. 843, VI.NE16.122, L. 16038.1	5B/A	Haematite; polished
7.	Arrowhead	No. 847, VI.NE35.81, L. 35031	5B/A	Copper/bronze
8.	Arrowhead or spear point	No. 805, VI.NE35.87, L. 35022	5B/A	Copper/bronze
9.	Button	No. 484, VI.NW6.44, L. 6022	5A–2/A–1	Ceramic; surface 10YR "very pale brown" 8/3; some small to large black, grey, white inclusions; well fired; pedges chipped but not ground; partially drilled from both sides
10.	Swan's head	No. 417, VI.NW5.41, L. 5018	5A	Ceramic; handmade; paste 5YR "light reddish brown" 6/4; slip 10YR "very pale brown" 8/3; some very small brown and grey inclusions; well fired; eyes aplied secondarily (DA 74–119)
11.	Plate (armour scale?)	No. 498, VI.NE25.20, L. 25013	5A	Copper/bronze
12.	Tournette base	No. 423, VI.NW5.68, L. 5029	5A–4	Basalt; worn
13.	Basin	No. 832, VI.NE5.104,	5A	Basalt
14.	Scarab	No. 842, VI.NE15.102, L. 15045	5B/A	Schist
15.	Stand	No. 735, VI.NE25.45, L. 25024	5A–4	Terra cotta; handmade; surface 10YR "very pale brown" 7/4; paint 10YR "red" 5/6; many small brown, few medium large black inclusions; well fired; fragment of square fenestrated stand
16.	Base fragment	No. 425, VI.NE14.35,	5	Alabaster

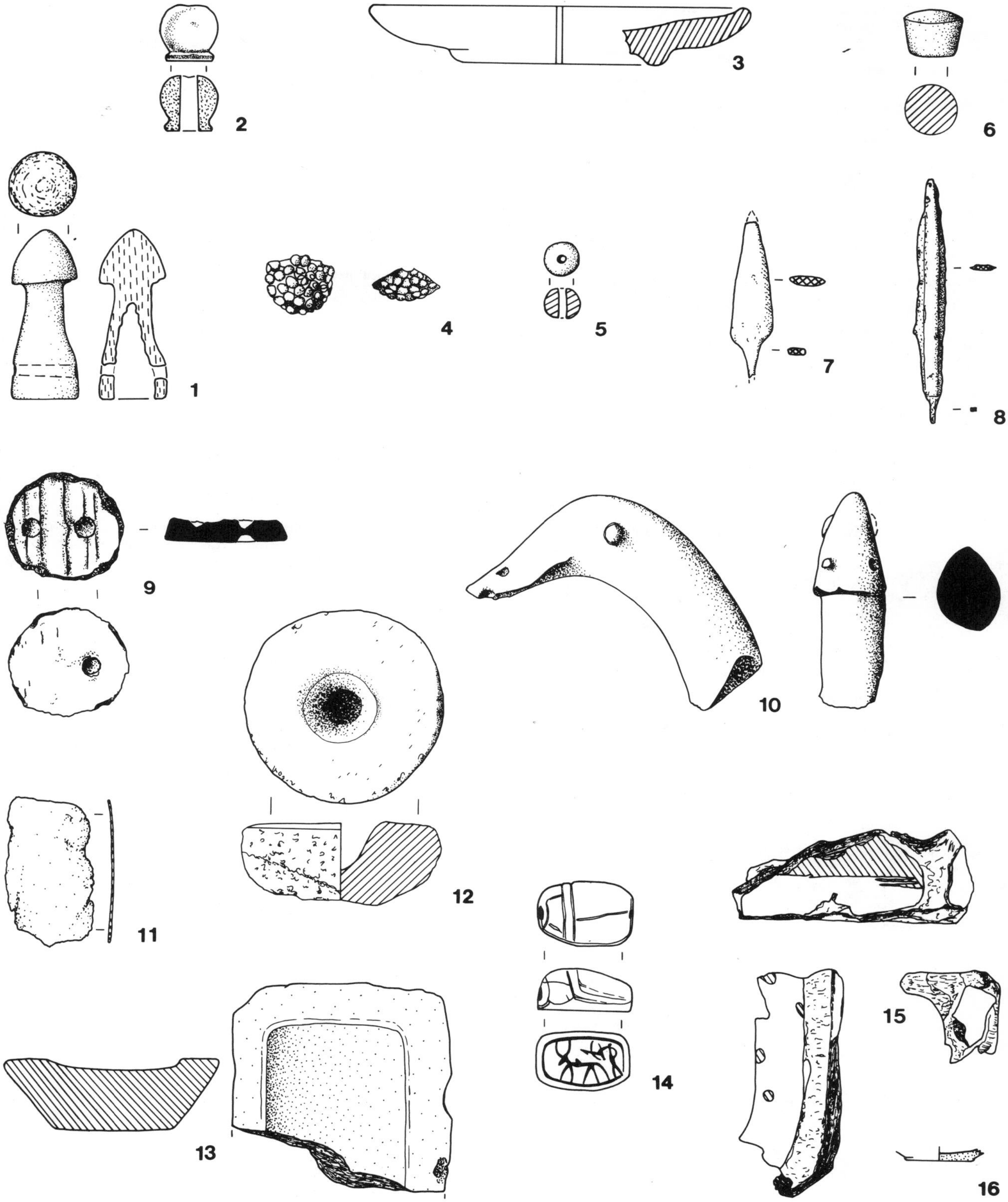

PLATE 61

Pl. 62

Plate number	Object (Refs. in parenthesis)	Registry No., Basket, Locus (see LOCUS INDEX)	Str.	Description (p.277; Israel Department of Antiquities number
1.	Bowl fragment	No. 741, VI.NE5.80, L. 5025	5A/4B	Basalt
2.	Amulet	No. 440, VI.NE16.45, L. 16008.1	5A/4	Faience; Isis figure; light greenish blue glaze (DA 74–100)
3.	Base fragment	No. 759, VI.NE25.58, L. 25024	5A–4	Alabaster
4.	Spear	No. 883, VI.NE18.99, L. 18086.1	5A/4B	Copper/bronze
5.	Pommel	No. 938, VI.NE6.108, L. 6026	4B/A	Alabaster
6.	Ring	No. 845, VI.NE18.61, L. 18030.1	4B.A	Copper/bronze
7.	Button/jar lid fragment	No. 515, VI.NE24.80, L. 24046	4?	Alabaster
8.	Platelet	No. 846, VI.NE18.53, L. 18038.1	5B/a	Copper/bronze
9.	Figurine head	No. 859, VI.NW7, L. 7020	5? 4?	Faience; light blue glaze
10.	Tripod bowl fragment	No. 546, VI.NE24.44, L. 24018	Post-5	Basalt
11.	Zoomorphic Figurine head	No. 504, VI.NE17.145, L. 17049	3	Ceramic; handmade; horse figure; surface 10YR "very pale brown" 7/3; some small sand, few medium to large brown and black inclusions; well fired; bride represented (DA 74–115).
12.	Gaming Piece	No. 456, VI.NE17.98, L. 17032	3	Ivory; polished, drilled; a die (DA 74–92)
13.	Ostracon	No. 770, VI.NW7.8,	2?	Ceramic; wheelmade; surface 5YR "reddish yellow" 7/6; few small to medium brown and gray inclusions; well fired; letters painted in 2.5YR "dark reddish brown" 3/4.
14.	Tripod Bowl	No. 506, VI.NE27.27, L. 27007	2	Basalt
15.	Scaraboid	No. 412, VI.NE17.10, L. 17000		Surface; striated limestone; 2.5YR "red-dark red" 5/6–5/8; hole drilled from both sides (DA 74–83)
16.	Swan's Head	No. 442, VI.NE13.53, L. 13000		Surface Ceramic; handmade; surface 10YR "very pale brown" 8/3; paint 5YR "reddish brown" 5/4; few medium white and gray inclusions; well fired
17.	Stamp Seal	No. 482, VI.NE36. L. 36000		Surface; fieldstone; 10YR "very dark grayish brown" 3/2; hole drilled from both sides (DA 74–116)
18.	"Couch" Figurine	No. 533, VI.NW15.95, L. 15000		Surface Ceramic; handmade; surface 7.5YR "light brown" 6/4; small brown and gray inclusions; well fired (DA 74–120)

PLATE 62

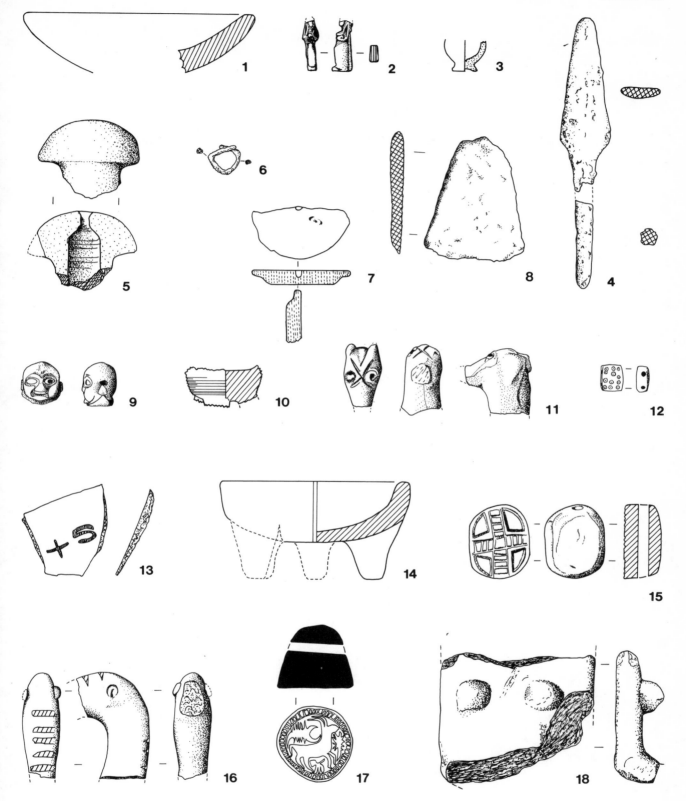

PHOTOGRAPHIC PLATES

PLATE 63

Pl. 63A. General view of Field VI.NE, looking north.

Pl. 63B. Core, Supervisory, and Assistant Staff, 1969 season (Core Staff designated*). Back row, left to right: John F. X. Mckeon, Dean L. Moe, B. Elmo Scoggin, Eric M. Meyers, Philip J. King, John E. Landgraf, Cearbhall O'Meadhra. Middle row, left to right: Abu Issa, Judith Lerner, Lawrence A. Stager, Karen Seger, Janet MacLennan, James F. Strange, John Worrell, Gerald B. Lindell, Lawrence T. Geraty, Edward B. Anderson. Front row, left to right: Frank J. Glassy, *Reuben G. Bullard, *Joe D. Seger, *Anita M. Walker, *H. Darrell Lance, *William G. Dever, *John S. Holladay, Jr., *Dan P. Cole, *Robert B. Wright, Hannah Scoggin, Carole Bohn. (*Norma E. Dever not shown.)

PLATE 64

Pl. 64A. Core, Supervisory, and Assistant Staff, 1970 season. (Core Staff designated*). Back row, left to right: Paul D. Hanson, Werner E. Lemke, John Matthers, Melvin K. Lyons, Christopher A. Carr. B. Elmo Scoggin, Harold Spivak, Seymour Gitin, John M. Salmon, Eugene L. Collins, Alberic R. Culhane. Middle row, left to right: Wendy Shattil, Miranda Marvin, Bruce K. Waltke, Hannah Scoggin, Gerald B. Lindell, Karen Seger, Janet MacLennan, John R. Osborne. Front row, left to right: *John S. Holladay, Jr., *Anita M. Walker, *Reuben G. Bullard, *H. Darrell Lance, *William G. Dever, *Norma E. Dever, *Joe D. Seger, *Robert B. Wright, *Dan P. Cole.

Pl. 64B. Core, Supervisory, and Assistant Staff, 1971 season. (Core Staff designated.*) Back row, left to right: Christopher A. Carr, Albert Leonard, Jr., John Matthers, a volunteer, Duane E. Smith, Mary Russell, Albert R. Culhane, Theodore A. Rosen, Benjamin Caplan, John R. Osborne, James M. Weinstein. Middle row, left to right: Karen Seger, Linda B. Ginsburg, Phyllis Holladay, Sonia Margolin, Pamela Gaber, Don Hobson, Mary Wright, Eugene L. Collins, Suzanne Richard, Wendy Shattil, Martha Anders, Janet MacLennan. Front row, left to right: *Joe D. Seger, *John S. Holladay, Jr., *Anita M. Walker, *William G. Dever, *H. Darrell Lance, *Dan P. Cole, *Robert B. Wright, *Reuben G. Bullard. (*Norma E. Dever not shown).

PLATE 65

Pl. 65A. Area 4, Str. Granary 24220, looking south. To left, Silo 24181; in center, Step 24211; at lower right are Silos 24174, 24215, Jarstand 24198; note fine plaster (L. 23210) on floor and sidewalls (pp. 11–16; Plan X).

Pl. 65B. Area 4, Str. 12, Granary 24220. Step 24211, looking northwest; note collapsed stones of L. 24206 (part of Debris 24179); to left is plastered Wall 24195; below is Surface 24218 (pp. 11–16; Plan X).

PLATE 66

Pl. 66A. **General view of Area 4 at Str. 11 level, looking east. To left center is Surface 4139; in center are Cobbles 4147, between Walls 4133 (L.) and 4148 (R.); below, Str. 7 Trench 4069; Str. 12 Burial 4121 is below Cobbles 4147, at left center of Wall 4148 (pp. 15, 22, 23; Plan XI).**

Pl. 66B. Area 4, partially cleared Str. 12 Jar Burial 4121. Biconical juglet is in large storejar (Pl. 1:1, 2), with infant bones at right (p. 15; Plan XI).

PLATE 67

Bl. 67A. Area 4, Str. 12 Jar Burial 4121. Above is Str. 11 Wall 4148; below the large storejar (Pl. 1:L) are a carinated bowl (Pl. 1:4) to the left, a dipper juglet (Pl. 1:3) to the right (p. 15; Pl. XI).

Pl. 67B. Area 23, Str. 12 Jar Burial 23110, looking west. Inside large storejar are infant bones to left and two juglets to right; at lower left is a smaller storejar (Pl. 1:5–7; p. 15; Plan X).

PLATE 68

Pl. 68A. Area 24, Str. 12 Debris 24148, looking west toward east balk. At left is Silo 24181, below is plastered Surface 24218, to right is plastered Wall 24168/23124 (pp. 11–16; Plan X).

Pl. 68B. Area 23, Str. 11(–10) looking north. Above is Surface 23111, with Jarstand 23102 to left, Str. 12 Rockfall 23086 at upper right. Below are Wall 23087, Surfaces 23117 and 23120, all cut by Str. 8 Trench 23060; at lower right is Str. 10 Wall 23069 (pp. 20, 28, 29; Plan XI).

PLATE 69

Pl. 69A. Area 23, Str. 11(–10), looking south. Below is Surface 23111; above are Wall 23087, Surfaces 23117 and 23120, cut by Str. 8 Trench 23060. Cistern at upper center (Shaft 23054C) belongs to Str. 10, as does Wall 23069 at upper left (pp. 20, 28, 29; Plan XI).

Pl. 69B. Area 13, Str. 11, looking east. At right is *Ṭabûn* 13118 and Wall 13111; to left is plaster Surface 13123. Wall 13098 in foreground belongs to Str. 10; at far left, in balk, is Str. 9 Wall 13080 (pp. 22, 28, 37; Plan XI).

PLATE 70

Pl. 70A. Area 13, Str. 11–10, looking north. At right center are Str. 11 Wall 13111, Ṭabûn 13118, Surface 13123 and 13100; in center (to left of long wall) are Wall 13135 and Surface 13116. Overriding the Str. 11 structures are Str. 10 Wall 13098 and corner Wall 13103 (Str. 11 Wall 13111 is reused with them). At upper left is Str. 8/7 Trench 13058 (pp. 22, 28; Plans XI, XII.)

Pl. 70B. Area 14, Str. 10B–A, looking south. In center is Wall 14110; to left is 10A Drain 14131, uncapped to show construction; to right is 10A Surface 14122 ((pp. 30–32; Plan XII).

PLATE 71

Pl. 71A. Area 34, Str. 12–10, looking south. At top right is Str. 12 Granary Wall 34128/34132 in deep probe; at center left are Str. 11 Wall 34112 and Surface 34123, at lower left Cobbles 34127; breakthrough to Macalister Tunnel 34084 is seen at very top ((pp. 11–16, 23, 41; Plans X, XI).

Pl. 71B. Area 34, Str. 11–10 Street 35093, looking east. To left is massive Str. 11–10 Wall 35088; above is Str. 10 Wall 35082; to left are Str. 11–10 mudbrick Walls 35095/35095A; at upper right are Str. 7 Trenches 35069 and 35091 (pp. 24, 25, 32; Plans XI, XII).

PLATE 72

Pl. 72A. Area 13, Str. 10B–A, looking north. To right are Walls 13098, 13103, and 1311, with Surface 13109; to left is courtyard Surface 13089/13095, with Jarstands 13115 and 13106; at upper left is Str. 7 Trench 13058 (pp. 26–28; Plan XII).

PL. 72B. Area 13, Str. 11–10, looking northwest. Str. 11 Ṭabûn 13118, Surface 13123, and Wall 13111, overlain by Str. 10B–A Wall 13098 (pp. 22–28; Plans XI, XII).

PLATE 73

Pl. 73A. Area 33, Str. 10B, looking west toward west balk. In center, Bin 33058 and Surface 33057; at left is Str. 9B–A Wall 33038 (pp. 29, 41: Plans XII, XIII).

Pl. 73B. Area 34, Str. 10B–A, looking east forward east balk. Cistern Shaft 34046 (partially sectioned), with stone-capped Drain 34095, Surface 34114, and Wall 34108 (pp. 29, 30; Plan XII).

PLATE 74

Pl. 74A. Area 34, Str. 10–6 Cistern 34110 (p. 30).

Pl. 74B. Area 14, Str. 10B–A, looking south. To left are Wall 14110 and Drain 14131, with 10A Surfaces 14129 and 14140; to right are Flag-stones 14146, Surface 14122, and Jarstand 14126, broken by Str. 7 Pit 14090 in center and Str. 7 Trench 14083 above and below (pp. 30, 31; Plan XII).

PLATE 75

Pl. 75A. Area 14, Str. 10B–A looking north. To left is Str. 10B–A Wall 14110; to right is Str. 10A Drain 14131, with capping stones removed to show construction (pp. 30, 31; Plan XII).

Pl. 75B. Area 23, Str. 10B–A, looking northeast. In center is Str. 10B–A Courtyard Surface 23095, with Str. 12 Rockfall protruding through surface at upper left, Jarstand 23081 at upper right, and Wall 23087 to right (broken by Str. 8 Pit 23049 and Str. 8 Trench 23060); at extreme right is Str. 10A Surface 23088, Wall 23069, and Cistern Shaft 23054 C (pp. 28, 29; Plan XII).

PLATE 76

Pl. 76A. Area 35, Str. 11–10, looking west toward west balk. Str. 11 Cobbled street 35093, overlain by Str. 10 Wall 35082; to left is Wall 34095, to right Wall 35088; in balk is Str. 7/6 Pit 35071 (pp. 24, 25, 32; Plans XI, XII).

Pl. 76B. Area 15, Str. 10B–A, looking south. Drain 15186, with Wall 15181 to left; below is Str. 7 Trench 5158 (p. 32; Plan XII).

PLATE 77

Pl. 77A. Area 5, Str. 10A, looking west toward west section. In center is corner Wall 5155/5116, with Surface 5118 to left and right; all across foreground is Str. 7 Trench 5095 (p. 32; Plan XII).

Pl. 77B. Area 13, Str. 9B–A, looking southeast. Plastered Drain 13085, with capstones partially removed to show "stepped" construction; to left is Wall 13080, to right Cobbles 13077, (pp. 36, 37; Plan XIII).

PLATE 78

Pl. 78A. Area 23, Str. 9B–A, looking west. At left are Cistern Shaft 23054B, Drain 23091, and Surface 23054B, Drain 23091, and Surface 23058 (the latter cut by Str. 6 retrenching of the cistern shaft); in center is Surface 23058, cut by Str. 8 Pit 23049 (pp. 40, 60; Plan XIII).

Pl. 78B. Area 23, Str. 9B–A, looking west. Drain 23071, with capstones removed, emptying into Cistern Shaft 23054B; to left is Surface 23058, to right courtyard Surface 23058, cut by Str. 8 Pit 23049 (pp. 37, 40; Plan XIII).

PLATE 79

Pl. 79A. Area 13, Str. 9B–A, looking north. To left, Wall 13074, cornering with Wall 13075, Surface 13073 and Wall 13075 broken by Str. 7 Trench 13057; to left is Str. 9A Surface 13072, broken by Str. 8 Trench 13060; at upper right is Wall 13080, at center Cobbles 13077, and upper right Str. 7 Trench 13058; Str. 8 plaster Surface 13055 shows in section at upper right (p. 37; Plans XII, XIV).

Pl. 79B. Area 14, Str. 10–8, looking east. Below is Str. 10B–A Wall 14110; at east balk is Str. 9B–A Surface 14125 (cut away), with Str. 8 Surface 14100 above (p. 38; Plans XII–XIV).

PLATE 80

Pl. 80A. Area 24, Str. 9B–A, looking east. Wall 24130 and Surface 24154A, broken to right by Str. 7 Trench 24098; in left background is Str. 10–9 Wall 24105; Str. 7 Trench 24127 shows in section (pp. 38–40; Plans XII, XIII).

Pl. 80B. Area 24, Str. 12–9, looking south. At left and upper center is Granary 24220 emerging, with corner Walls 24197/24195 and Silo 24181 to left, Jarstand 24198 and Silo 24174 to right; below is Str. 9 Corner Wall 24128/24130 and Threshold 241745 (below meter stick; pp. 11–16, 38–40; Plans X, XIII).

PLATE 81

Pl. 81A. Area 34, Str. 10–9 9B–A, looking north. In center is Str. 9. Exterior Surface 34098; above is Str. 10–9 Wall 34099; below is Cistern Shaft 34046 and Drain 34095, with Breakthrough to Macalister Tunnel 34084 at lower left (p. 41; Plans XII, XIII).

Pl. 81B. Area 34, looking northwest toward north balk. Breakthrough to Macalister Tunnel 34084 (tunnel behind ladder); to left is Str. 10. Bin 33058 and Surface 33057 (pp, 15, 23, 29, 41; Plan XII).

PLATE 82

Pl. 82A. Area 24, Str. 9A, looking southwest toward south balk. Marine pumice in L. 24144; to right is Wall 24130 (pp. 40, 42; Plan XIII).

Pl. 82B. Area 3, Str. 9–8, looking east. In center is Wall 3071, Surface 3074, and Jarstand 3073. Wall 3071 is broken by Str. 7 Trenches 3048 and 3055; Str. 8 Surface 3041 is seen above in section (pp. 37, 47; Plans XIII, XIV).

PLATE 83

Pl. 83A. Area 13, Str. 8B–A, looking north. Vat 13054B, with Surface 13055 and Jarstand 13053; at top left is Str. 7 trench 13058, below Str. 7 Trenches 13057 and 13040 (pp. 47–48; Plan XIV).

Pl. 83B. Area 13, Str. 8, looking north. In background is Vat 13043B; in foreground is Str. 8A Surface 13054; above, Str. 8B Surface 13055 in probe; at lower right is Str. 7 Trench 13040; at upper right is Str. 6B–A Wall 13022A–B (pp. 47–48; Plan XIV).

PLATE 84

Pl. 84A. Area 34, Str. 7, looking northwest. To upper right is Wall 34070, Bin 34069, and Surface 34072; below is Str. 10–6B Cistern Shaft 34046 at Str. 7 levels (p. 53; Fig. 9).

Pl. 84B. Area 34, Str. 6C–A, looking west. In center is Wall 34063A–B, cornering with Str. 6B–A Wall 34028A to right, where Str. 6B Cobbles 34043 are visible; to left are Str. 6B Cobbles 34044A and Str. 6B–A Wall 34027A–B, Cistern Shaft 34046 at Str. 6B level (pp. 60, 67, 68; Fig. 11, Plan XV).

PLATE 85

Pl. 85A. Field VI.NE, general view of Str. 6B–A Granary 24000 on the lower terrace, looking north; Str. 5C–B Northeast House partly visible on the upper terrace, beyond east–west control balk (pp. 63, 87, 88; Plans XV, XVII).

Pl. 85B. Area 3, Str. 6B–A, looking northwest. Str. 6B–A Wall 3008A–B, cornering with Wall 3006; at upper right are Str. 6B Wall 3017 and Surface 3031; at lower left are Str. 6B Wall 3030 and Surface 3029 (p. 63; Plan XV).

PLATE **86**

Pl. 86A. Area 4, Str. 6B–A in Room 1 of Granary 24000, looking east. At top is Str. 6B–A Wall 4078 (note two phases), cornering with Str. 6B Wall 4022B; to right is Str. 6B Surface 4041, to left Courtyard Surface 4025; to right is sub-6 probe (p. 63; Plan XV).

Pl. 86B. Area 4, Str. 6C–A, looking east. At left is Str. 6B–A Wall 4016, beyond that Str. 6C–B Wall 4026; at right is curving Str. 6B Drain 4015 and Surface 4025 (pp. 63–65; Plan XV).

PLATE 87

Pl. 87A. Areas 13, 14, Str. 6B–A in Room 2 of Granary 24000, looking north. At right is Str. 6B Wall 13022B, cornering with Str. 6B–A Wall 14011A–B (note two phases); in distant left background is Str. 6B–A Wall 14019A–B and Surface 14065 (pp. 65, 66; Plan XV).

Pl. 87B. Areas 13, 14, Str. 6B–A Room 3 in Granary 24000, looking southwest. At right is Str. 6B–A Wall 4078, at left Str. 6B–A Wall 13035; in foreground are Str. 6A Surface 14032 and rockfall from Column Base 13034 (pp. 65, 66; Plan XV).

PLATE 88

Pl. 88A. Area 14, Str. 6B–A, Room 3 in Granary 24000, looking northeast. At left is Str. 6B–A wall 14019A–B (note two phases), cornering with Str. 6A Wall 14011A (running well above 6B Wall 14011B and blocked Threshold 14070); at upper right is Bin 24062 in Area 24; above is Courtyard Surface 14035 with ash-layer accumulation of 6B–A visible in section; (pp. 65–67; Plan XV).

Pl. 88B. Area 14, Str. 6B–A, Room 4 in Granary 24000, looking west. Str. 6B Threshold 14070 in Wall 14011B, with Str. 6A blockage at time of construction of Wall 14011A; at right is Str. 6B–A Wall 14019A–B (pp. 65, 66; Plan XV).

PLATE 89

Pl. 89A. Area 23, Str. 6B, Room 5 in Granary 24000, looking east toward east balk. Wall 23035, showing Str. 6B doorway (6A blockage and wall 23011 mostly removed); in foreground is Str. 6B Surface 23030, partly broken by Str. 2 Trench 23005 (p. 66; Plan XV).

Pl. 89B. Area 24, Str. 6B–A, looking southeast. In foreground is Wall 24027 of Room 7 of Granary 24000; in background is corner Wall 24072/24033 of Room 6, with Surface 24049 and Cobbles 24069 (pp. 66, 67; Plan XV).

PLATE 90

Pl. 90A. Area 13, Str. 6B–A, Room 2 in Granary24000, looking west/northwest. At left are Bin 13037 and Wall 13032, with Str. 6B doorway (Str. 6B/A Blockage 13084 removed); at right is Str. 6B–A Wall 13035; on Str. 6A Surface 13038 are ash deposits and three *in situ* vessels from destruction debris L. 13030 and 13038P (pp. 65–68, 71, 72; Plan XV; Pl. 26:10).

Pl. 90B. Areas 23, 24, Str. 6B–A, Room 5 in Granary 24000, looking north. In center is Str. 6A Wall 23072A (with Str. 6B doorway blocked); at left are Str. 6A Wall 23007A and Bins 23021, 23033; at right is Str. 6A Wall 23011; in center is Str. 6A Surface 26014; in background is Room 6 in Area 24 (pp. 65, 66, 70; Plan XV).

PLATE 91

Pl. 91A. Area 34, Str. 6A, Rooms 11–12 in Granary 24000, looking west. To left in Room 11 are Str. 6A Cobbles 34017 and 34027A; to right in Room 12 are Str. 6A corner Walls 34011 and 34011A, with Surface 34020, Wall 34028, and Bin 34026; below at bottom can be seen Str. 6C–B Wall 34060, and below at right center can be seen Str. 6B Wall 34051/52 (p. 71; Plan XV, Fig. 11).

Pl. 91B. Area 13, Str. 6A, Room 2 in Granary 24000, looking west. To left are Wall 13032 and Bin 13037, with Blockage 13034 in part of doorway; to right is Wall 13035; on Surface 13038 and in Bin 13037 are several smashed storejars in Destruction Debris 13030 (Pl. 26:1, 3, 10; 27:1–3; pp. 68, 71, 72; Plan XV).

PLATE 92

Pl. 92A. Area 14, Str. 6A, Room 3 of Granary 24000 looking. Smashed vessels (Pl. 30:1, 4; 31:3) in Destruction Debris 14015, near corner of Walls 4078 and 13035 (p. 72; Plan XV).

Pl. 92B. Area 15, Str. 6C–B. Section showing Threshing Floors 15061 (p. 73; Fig. 12).

PLATE 93

Pl. 93A. Area 25, Str. 6C–B. Section through Threshing Floors 25063 (p. 76; Fig. 12).

Pl. 93B. Area 5, Str. 6B, looking south. Drain 5057, with Surface 5064 to left, Wall 5061 to right; below is Str. 6A./5C Trench 5072 (p. 74; Plan XVI).

PLATE 94

Pl. 94A. Area 16, Str. 6A, looking south. To left is Wall 16084B, in background cornering Wall 16114 (with stub of Cobbles 16115 visible); beneath meter stick is "Installation" 16989; at far right are Cobbles 16118 (pp. 74, 75; Plan XV).

Pl. 94B. Area 16, Sᵗr. 6A, looking north at north section. Winepress 16100 (p,75; Plan XVI).

PLATE 95

Pl. 95A. Area 25, Str. 6C–B, looking north. Str. 6B corner Wall 25084, built atop accumulation of Str. 6C–B Threshing Floors 25063 (partially sectioned through; p. 76; Plan XVI).

Pl. 95B. Area 25, Str. 6C/B, looking northwest. Lamp-and-bowl deposit L. 25091.1, nestled in corner of 6B Wall 25084, with Str. 6C Wall 25093 below (p. 76; Plan XVI; Pl. 22:18, 19).

PLATE 96

Pl. 96A. Area 25, Str. 6C–B, looking southwest. Lamp-and-bowl deposit L. 25063, of the west balk (p. 76; Plan XVI; Pl. 22:12, 13).

Pl. 96B. Area 26, Str. 6C–B, looking south. Tee-walls 26085/26097/26099, with Cobbles 26093 and 26102, Silo 26092; to right are Threshing Floors 26083 (p. 76; Plan XVI).

PLATE 97

Pl. 97A. Area 35, Str. 6C, looking northwest. Drain 35047 (partially uncapped) within Str. 6C–B Threshing Floor accumulation L. 35037 (p. 76; Plan XVI).

Pl. 97B. Upper terrace, Str. 5C–B. Northeast House, looking west (p. 88; Plan XVII); Northwest House in background; Muslim *wêli* at upper right.

PLATE 98

Pl. 98A. Areas 15, 16, Str. 5C–B, Rooms 2 and 2A in the Northeast House, looking north. Across center is Wall 15031, with sectioned Str. 6C–B Threshing Floors 15061 below exterior Str. 5C Courtyard Surface 15050. Extending north is Wall 15063/16053; to right is Room 2, to left Room 2A;' at upper left is Wall 16042, at upper right Wall 26062 and Threshold 16071; beyond that is the courtyard, Room 3 (pp. 88–90, 92; Plan XVII).

Pl. 98B. Area 25, Str. 5C–B, Doorway 25052 to Northeast House, looking northeast. Walls 25040 and 25050, cornering with Wall 35016; to left is Room 1 with Cobbles 26069 and Walls 26034, 26068; to right is Room 4; at lower right excavation is down into Str. 6C–B Threshing Floors 25063 (pp. 88–90; Plan XVII).

PLATE 99

Pl. 99A. Area 36, Str. 5C, looking west. Pottery Deposit 36018 lying against east face of Northeast House Wall 36009 (p. 10; Plan XVII; Pl. 38:9–13).

Pl. 99B. Areas 15, 16, Str. 5C–B, looking south. In back ground is Wall 15031, cut to right by Str. 5B/A Trench 15045; in center are corner Walls 16042 and 15063/16063; to lower left is Threshold 16071, to lower right Blockage 16061 (Str. 5B) and Wall 16068 (surfaces still being probed for at this stage; pp. 90, 92; Plan XVII).

PLATE 100

Pl. 100A. Area 26, Str. 6A/5C Flint Cache 26080, at north balk of the Courtyard, Room 3, of the Northeast House (p. 90; Plan XVII; Appendix C).

Pl. 100B. Areas 25, 26, Str. 5C–B, Rooms 1 and 4 of the Northeast House, looking south/southeast. In foreground is Room 3, the courtyard, with Wall 26062 to the right; in the background is Room 1, with Wall 26034/26068 and Cobbles 26069 to the left; at extreme left is Room 4, with Wall 36009 (pp. 88–90; Plan XVII).

PLATE 101

Pl. 101A. Areas 6, 16, Str. 5C–B, Corridor and Threshold 6085 of Rooms 5/6 of Northeast House, looking north. Room 5 in the foreground, Room 6 beyond Threshold 6085 in Walls 6044 and 16068; to right is Str. 5B Surface 16052 (sectioned through; p. 90; Plan XVII).

Pl. 101B. Area 5, Str. 5C–A, Lane 5048 between Northwest and Northeast Houses, looking north. To left is Wall 5004, with Str. 5A Surface 5030 cut away to show retrenching in Foundation Trench 5027; in center is Drain 5036; to right is Str. 5C–B Wall 5042 protruding through surface (p. 96; Plan XVII).

PLATE 102

Pl. 102A. Area 6, Str. 5C, Room 5 of Northeast House, looking east at east balk. Charred wooden beams in Destruction Debris 6050, above Str. 5C Surface 6053 (pp. 90–92; Plan XVII).

Pl. 102B. Area 16, Str. 5A, Northeast House, looking southeast. At center left are Terrace Wall 16027 and Vat 16031, with Wall 16040 at upper left; to right are Walls 16042 and 16043; in center is Surface 16039/16949 (p. 95; Plan XVIII).

PLATE 103

Pl. 103A. Area 5, Str. 5A, Northeast House, looking northeast. Wall 5031, Threshold 5031A; in center are Surface 5030 and Drain 5036, with robbed Str. 5C–B Wall 5042 protruding through the surface and 5A Wall 5039 built atop it; at lower left is corner of Str. 5C–B Northwest House, with 5A rebuilt Wall 5004 atop it (pp. 96, 103; Plan XVIII).

Pl. 103B. Area 18, Str. 5A, Vat 18049, looking northeast (p. 98; Fig. 17).

PLATE 104

Pl. 104A. Areas 5, 15, Str. 5C–B, general view of Northwest House, looking north/northwest. From right to left, at Str. 5B stage: Room 1, Room 2/2A, Room 3/3A; at far left is Room 4, cut by Str. 1 Pit 5022 (pp. 98, 101, 103; Plans XIX, XX).

Pl. 104B. Areas 5, 15, Str. 5C, general view of Northwest House, looking north. To right is Room 5 of Str. 5C; beyond Threshold 5038C in center (above meter stick) is Central Courtyard 6083; to left is Str. 5B addition which divides Room 5 into Room 1 and 2/2A (pp. 98, 101; Plans XIX, XX).

PLATE 105

Pl. 105A. Area 6, Str. 5C, Courtyard and Rooms 2–3 of Northwest House, looking east. At right is Courtyard 6083/Surface 6059, cut slightly by Str. 5B/A Pit 6051; in background, in Section, is Str. 4A Pit 6012; at upper left is Room 3, at lower left Room 2 and Surface 6064 (probed through; pp. 98, 100; Plan XIX).

Pl. 105B. Area 6, Str. 5, Room 2 of Northwest House, looking northeast. At right is Wall 6070; at left, cornering with it, Wall 6080; at upper left is Str. 2 Citadel Wall, emerging from under the Muslim *wêli* (pp. 100, 126; Plan XIX).

PLATE 106

Pl. 106A. Area 6, Str. 5C, Room 2 of Northwest House, looking south. Threshold in Wall 6062, from Room 2 into Courtyard 6083; in foreground is Surface 6064; in background are "Platform" 6060 and Str. 5B/A Pit 6051 (p. 100; Plan XIX).

Pl. 106B.. Area 5, Str. 5C–B, Northwest House, looking north. Str. 5C Wall 5027 and Wall 5040, at north of Room 5; in foreground is Str. 5C Pit 5073 (sectioned through); at upper center and right are Str. 5B additions (now "Room 1") of Wall 5025B, Pillar 5025C, and Threshold 5038B, above Str. 5C Destruction Debris 5043.1 (note more than meter-long burned beam at base of Wall 5025B; pp. 101, 106; Plans XIX, XX).

PLATE 107

Pl. 107A. Closeup of Str. 5C burned beam in Destruction Debris 5043.1 in Room 1 of Northwest House (Pl. 106B).

Pl. 107B. Area 15, Str. 5B-4, Room B/3A of Northwest House, looking south. To left is Wall 15026, to right Wall 15025; from top to bottom: Walls 15012B, 15027B, 15041; Cobbles 15054 above, 15052 below (pp. 101, 102, 103; Plan XX).

PLATE 108

Pl. 108A. Area 5, Str. 5B, looking west. Foundation Trench 5046, along south face of Str. 5B Wall 5010B; Str. 5C Wall 5047 visible below Wall 5010B (pp. 103, 106; Plans XIX, XX).

Pl. 108B. Area 15, 5B–3, Room 3/3A of Northwest House, looking south. To left is Wall 15026, to right Wall 15025; from top to bottom Walls 15012B, 15027B, 15041; Cobbles 15048 above, 15044 below (p. 103; Plan XX).

PLATE 109

Pl. 109A. Area 5, Str. 5B–3, Rooms 1, 2/2A of Northwest House, looking north. To left is Room 2/2A; to right is Room 1, with Wall 5025B, Pillar 5025C, and Threshold 5038A; Str. 5B–3 surface is L. 5041; note robbed out stretch of Str. 5C Wall 5047 at bottom, now used as House entrance (p. 106; Plans XIX, XX).

Pl. 109B. Area 5, Str. 5B, Northwest House, looking east. Lamp-and-bowl deposit L. 5052, against west face of Wall 5033 (p. 106; Plan XX).

PLATE 110

Pl. 110A. Area 6, Str. 5C, Northwest House. Stoneheap 6061, with smashed pottery vessels *in situ* (p. 107; Plan XX; Pl. 35:18).

Pl. 110B. Area 5, Str. 5A, Northwest House, looking north. To left are Walls 5010A, 5024, 5029, and 5027, with Bin 5031; to right are blocked Threshold 5038A, Pillar 5025C, and Wall 5025A (pp. 108, 109; Plan XXI).

PLATE 111

Pl. 111A. Area 6, Str. 5B/A, Northwest House, looking north. Wall 6018, with Surface 6035 in foreground, broken by Pit 6051 (p. 110; Plan XXI).

Pl. 111B. Area 6NW, see Str. 5A, looking east. Lime kiln 6076, with stone lining on either side (p. 110; Plan XXI).

PLATE 112

Pl. 112A. Area 15, Str. 4B, looking northwest. Silo 15010 (p. 117; Plan XXIII).

Pl. 112B. Area 6, Str. 4B–A, looking north. Walls 6007 and 6010, with Surfaces 6002 to left, 6011/6011A to the right; below is Str. 3 Trench 6012 (pp. 118, 124; Plan XXIII).

PLATE 113

Pl. 113A. Area 17, Str. 5A–4B, looking west/southwest. *Ṭabûn* 17026 to left, Wall 17033 to right; Str. 2 Citadel Wall 17066 to far right (p. 119; Fig. 20).

Pl. 113B. Area 17, Str. 3, looking east/northeast. Vat 17020, with Str. 2 Citadel Wall 17006 to the right (p. 124; Fig. 23; Plan XXIV).

PLATE 114

Pl. 114A. Areas 17, 27, looking east. STr. 2 Citadel Wall 17006/27--5; Str. 3 Vat 17020 to the left (pp. 124, 126, 127; Plan XXIV; Fig. 23).

Pl. 114B. Area 27, closeup of Str. 2 Citadel Wall 27005, looking east (pp. 126, 127; Plan XXIV).

PLATE 115

115B. Ceramic Chariot Wheel, No. 1392; from L. 24187, Area NE24, Str. 12 (p. 19; Plan X; see Pl. 49:8 for drawing). Scale = 1:1.

Pl. 115A. Chalk Funnel (or *Tuyère*?), No. 1394; from L. 14147, Area NE14, Str. 12 (p. 19; Plan X: see Pl. 49:3 for drawing). Scale = 1:1.

115C. Silver Earrings, No. 1381, from L. 24181, Area NE24, Str. 12 (p. 19; Plan X; see Pl. 49:6 for drawing). Scale = 1:1.

115D. Ceramic Crucible, No. 1371, from L. 24144, Area NE24, Str. 9 (p. 45; Plan XIII; cf. 116A, and see Pl. 51:1 for drawing). Scale = 1:1.

PLATE 116

Pl. 116A. Ceramic Crucible, No. 1371, from L. 24144,
Area NE24, Str. 9 (p. 45; Plan XIII; cf. Pl. 115D, and see
Pl. 51:1 for drawing). Scale = 1:1.

116B. Bronze Serpent, No. 1229, from L. 24144, Area NE24, Str. 9 (p. 45; Plan XIII; see Pl. 51:2 for drawing).

116C. Ceramic Stopper, No. 1216, from L. 14144, Area
NE14, Str. 9/8 (p. 49; Plan XIII, XIV; see Pl. 52:1 for
drawing). Scale = 1:1.

116D. Bronze Chisel, No. 1123, from L./
23056, Area NE23, Str. 9/8 (p. 50; Plans
XIII, IVI; see Pl. 52:5 for drawing).
Scale = 1:1.

PLATE 117

Pl. 117A. Ceramic Zoomorphic Figurine, No. 1108, from L. 3059, Area NE3, Str. 7 (p. 57; see Pl. 52:13 for drawing). Scale = 1:1.

117B. Bronze Needle, No. 1140, from L. 14083, Area NE14, Str. 7 (p. 59; see Pl. 53:1 for drawing). Scale = 1:1.

117D. Chalk Figurine, No. 1062, L. 6041.1, Area NE6, Str. 5C/B (p. 115; Plan XVII; see Pl. 60:5 for drawing). Scale = 1:1.

117C. Bronze Chisel, No. 954, from L. 50421, Area NW5, Str. 5C/B (p. 115; Plans XIX, XX; see Pl. 60:1 for drawing). Scale = 1:1.

PLATE 118

Pl. 118A. Bronze Cauldron Handle, No. 951, from L. 15039.1, Area NW15, Str. 5C/B (p. 115; Plans XIX, XX; see Pl. 60:8 for drawing). Scale = 1:1.

118B. Ceramic Zoomorphic Figure (or *Kernos* Head, No. 537, from L. 35010, Area NE35, Str. 5B (p. 115; Plan XVII; see Pl. 60:12 for drawing). Scale = 1:1.

118C. Ceramic Phallus, No. 459, from L. 5040.1, Area NW5, Str. 5B–4/3 (p. 115; Plan XX; see Pl. 60:11 for drawing). Scale = 1:1.

118D. Ivory Chariot Fitting, No. 1081, from L. 5027, Area NE5, Str. 5B/A (p. 115; Plans XVII, XVIII; see Pl. 61:1 Plan XXI; see Pl. 61:1 for drawing). Scale = 1:1.

PLATE 119

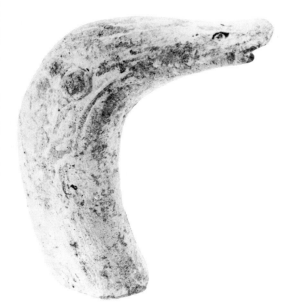

Pl. 119A. Ceramic Swan's Head, No. 417, from L. 5018, Area NW5, Str. 5A (p. 116; Plan XXI; see Pl. 61:10 for drawing). Scale = 1:1.

119B. Basalt Tournette Base, No. 423, from L. 5029, Area NW5, Str. 5A–4 (p. 115; Plan XXI; see Pl. 61:12 for drawing).

119C. Ivory Gaming Piece, No. 456, from L. 17032, Area NE17, Str. 3 (p. 126; see Pl. 62:12 for drawing). Scale = 1:1.

119D. Ceramic Swan's Head, No. 442, from L. 13000, NE13, surface find (pp. 126, 127; see Pl. 62:16 for drawing). Scale = 1:1.

PLATE 120

Pl. 120A. Scaraboid, No. 412, from L. 17000, Area NE17, surface find (p; 127; see Pl. 62:15 for drawing). Scale = 1:1.

120B. Stamp Seal, No. 482, from L. 25000, Area NE36, surface find (p. 127; see Pl. 62:17 for drawing). Scale = 1:1.

120C. Ceramic Cultic Couch Figurine, No. 533, from L. 15000, Area NW15, surface find (p. 127; see Pl. 62:18 for drawing). Scale = 1:1.